D0845744

THE
SEVENTIES

CHRISTOPHER BOOKER

THE SEVENTIES

THE DECADE THAT CHANGED THE FUTURE

Stein and Day/*Publishers*/New York

First published in the United States of America in 1981
Copyright © 1980 by Christopher Booker
All rights reserved
Designed by Louis A. Ditizio
Printed in the United States of America
Stein and Day/*Publishers*/Scarborough House
Briarcliff Manor, New York 10510

Library of Congress Cataloging in Publication Data

Booker, Christopher.
The seventies.

1. Civilization, Modern—1950-
2. Great Britain—Civilization—1945-
3. United States—Civilization—1970-   I.   Title.
CB428.B67   909.82'7   80-5389
ISBN 0-8128-2757-0

For Christine

CONTENTS

Part Four: Culture Heroes—Nostalgia and Self-deception

Part Five: Cultural Collapse

Part Six: Reappraisals

Part Seven: Epilogue—Act Five, Scene One

As long as one is within a certain phenomenology one is not astonished, and nobody wonders what it is all about. Such philosophical doubt only comes to the man who is outside the game.

—C. G. Jung, "Psychology and National Problems,"
Collected Works, Vol. XVIII, p. 509

ACKNOWLEDGMENTS

A substantial part of this book is made up from essays which I wrote during the seventies for a variety of British newspapers and magazines—notably the *Daily Telegraph,* to which I have contributed a monthly "Saturday Column" since 1973, and the *Spectator,* for which I have written regularly since 1976, during the welcome revival in its fortunes under the editorship of Alexander Chancellor. I am most grateful both to him and to Bill Deedes, Editor of the *Telegraph,* for permission to reprint so much that originally appeared in their pages.

I am also indebted to Donald Trelford, Editor of the *Observer,* both for permission to adapt the profile of David Frost which he originally published in 1977, and for serializing the opening chapters of this book at the turn of the decade; to Mel Lasky, Editor of *Encounter,* for permission to reprint the essay on Tom Wolfe; and to Kate Wharton, late Editor of *The Architect,* who originally commissioned the article "The Brave New World of Leisure."

More specific and personal thanks are due to all those who helped me in various ways to make the book possible: to Malcolm Muggeridge (father of all "decadologists"), Arianna Stassinopoulos, and Simon Jenkins, who all in different ways suggested I should write it; to Philippa Harrison, of Allen Lane/ Penguin, who gave the idea such a warm welcome; to Brigid Hardman-Mountford, Loraine Philip and Serena Booker, who helped to assemble the contents; to the staff of Stein and Day, who assisted so efficiently in its editing and production; and to my agent, Felicity Bryan.

Finally, my very particular thanks to Bennie Gray, for kindness and friendship throughout the decade, for helping to sharpen up so many ideas in conversation and for being London's most generous landlord; and to Shirley, Cassian, Lucan, Rosie, and Sebastian for providing such happy diversion while the book was being written.

Hampstead Hill Gardens, May, 1980

AUTHOR'S PREFACE

What is the true nature of the times we are living in?

Ten years ago I wrote a book called *The Neophiliacs,* a detailed, analytical account of the astonishing changes which had come over Britain and the Western world in the fifties and sixties. This is a very different kind of book about a very different decade. It does not set out to give a detailed history of the seventies. Anyone looking for such an overall picture would instantly notice a great many glaring omissions.

What I *have* tried to do, through a linked series of essays and profiles (many of which have already appeared elsewhere), is to penetrate rather more deeply to what the seventies were about; to pick out the underlying themes which shaped our thoughts and our lives in those years, and to show how an understanding of the seventies in this historical context may help us to see where we are going next.

The book begins with a specially written section, entitled "The Death of Progress," which attempts to give a brief overall framework to the decade and to show why I think that, far from being just the rather depressing, drifting interlude they often seemed at the time, the seventies were in their own way "the most important decade of the twentieth century."

I then go on to draw some "Global Perspectives," on some of the major issues which have affected mankind. This is followed by a section on Britain in the seventies, "The Politics of a Sad Little Island." The fourth section, "Culture Heroes—Nostalgia and Self-deception," looks at a number of significant figures—

Kenneth Clark, David Frost, Tom Wolfe, Arthur Koestler, Germaine Greer—whose writings or careers in the seventies seem to me to have shed particular light on the changing mood of the times.

The fifth section, "Cultural Collapse," looks in a less personal way at some broader aspects of what was undoubtedly one of the most revealing characteristics of the decade—the collapse of cultural self-confidence, the strange exhaustion of the Modern Movement in architecture and the arts, the general flight into nostalgia and love of the past, the great "natural craze." This leads into a section on "Reappraisals," touching on some of the ways in which I believe the seventies marked the beginning of one of the most profound shifts in psychological, intellectual, and spiritual perspective to have taken place in Western civilization for several hundred years. I conclude with a brief epilogue which, in an oblique way, may I hope be taken as a summing up of what the whole book has been about.

THE
SEVENTIES

Part One

THE DEATH OF PROGRESS

1

A MOST IMPORTANT DECADE

If it were not for our quasi-religious modern obsession with anniversaries, centenaries, decades, and other arbitrary spans of time, it might at first sight seem a crazy proposition to essay an account of the 1970s.

Of all the decades of the twentieth century, it would be hard to pick out one with a less distinctive, recognizable character.

We have no hesitation, for instance, in summoning up a mental image of the twenties—the Charleston, the wail of saxophones, Model T Fords, flappers in waistless dresses, silent films and Charlie Chaplin's "little man," the Wall Street boom.

Similarly, the thirties, the forties, the fifties, all carry with them their own, clearly-defined package of associations, while the decade immediately preceding the seventies, the "swinging sixties," instantly evokes perhaps the clearest set of images of all—Beatlemania and mini-skirts, Carnaby Street and "swinging London," Harold Wilson's "dynamic new Britain," the assassination of President Kennedy, the horrors of Vietnam, LSD, "flower power," and the rest.

But what in years to come will evoke the sober, gloomy seventies—which in so many ways seemed like little more than just a prolonged anticlimax to the manic excitements of the sixties? What was the seventies sound, the seventies look? What was the seventies "image"?

Of course memorable things happened. We shall remember the seventies as the years of Watergate and the first resignation in history of an American President. We shall remember the ending of the Vietnam War, the final, tragic ignominy of America's catastrophic bid to keep Southeast Asia from falling under Communist domination, the horrors of Cambodia and the mass-evictions of the boat people. We shall remember the onset of the worst and most intractable economic recession since the war, the first serious signs of the great gathering world energy crisis. We shall remember the toppling of the Shah and the rise of the Ayatollah Khomeini, the end of Franco's Spain and Salazar's Portugal, the countless wars, coups, rebellions, hijackings, acts of terrorism and other lesser disorders which daily filled the headlines from almost every corner of the globe. In Britain, we shall remember the end of the Wilson-Heath era in our politics, the steady rumble of trade union power continually threatening chaos in almost every area of national life, above all perhaps a decade of unending hard slog through the quicksands of inflation.

But altogether, if this constitutes an image, it is a pretty blurred, depressing one. The seventies were scarcely a decade to cheer about, to quicken the pulse, to remember with excitement—hardly a time which in years to come is likely to inspire us with an overpowering sense of nostalgia. Indeed this in itself is scarcely surprising, since such an enormous amount of our cultural energy in the seventies seemed devoted—on our television and cinema screens, in the booming antique shops and salesrooms, in the unprecedented fervor with which we sought to preserve and do up old buildings—to dwelling on the charms of almost every time except our own.

Against the steady background drizzle of grim global warnings from Solzhenitsyn, from the ecological "doom-watchers" and other pessimists about the future of mankind, we may in short remember the seventies primarily as a kind of long, rather dispiriting interlude: a time when, in politics, in the arts or in almost any other field one considers, the prevailing mood was one of a somewhat weary, increasingly conservative, increasingly apprehensive disenchantment.

Yet it is my firm belief—one which underlies almost every

essay in this book—that the seventies were in fact the most important decade of the twentieth century. Something has been beginning to happen to us all in the past ten years—even if most people are as yet only dimly aware of it—which marks out this decade as one of the most profound historical significance, not just in the context of the twentieth century, but over a perspective stretching back many hundreds of years. And the key to understanding just what it is that has been happening to us lies in appreciating the peculiar nature and depth of that disillusionment we have been heading into through the seventies.

The truth is that, in the past ten years, the old sources of optimism which have sustained the human race throughout the twentieth century (and which began to emerge a very long time before that) have begun to collapse on an unprecedented scale. Men have, individually, been questioning the belief in human progress for generations. But in our own time, as never before, we have actually begun to see the first real death throes of that belief—that underlying conviction that, whatever disasters and mistakes marked the way, the human race, through its own efforts, was climbing out of the darkness and ignorance of the past into some unimaginable future of light, knowledge, and material abundance. However dimly, we have in the past few years not only come to see that the future may not be all that light, may indeed hold out to us the greatest range of catastrophes the world has ever known; we have also just begun to see that possibly, in our dizzying, upward flight, we have lost something of inestimable importance to us, that thing whose image at least we seek in our desperate desire to recreate the simplicities of the past, to preserve threatened species, to contemplate the unconscious beauties and harmonies of nature, to visit the last, vanishing "unspoiled" human settlements and wildernesses of the earth. At the eleventh hour and fifty-ninth minute perhaps, we are willy-nilly being pushed and pulled into the most dramatic and fundamental change of perspective on where we have come from and who we are that the human race has ever experienced. Over the next 20 years, I suspect, that change of perspective will become one of the most obvious and crucial factors in all our lives. And as its importance becomes more and more evident, we shall look back on the late sixties and seventies as the time when, although only a few people may initially have been aware of it, the whole of this fundamental shift in the way we look on ourselves and the nature of our civilization really began.

Two unfailing barometers of cultural optimism in our century have been the height of buildings and the height of girls' hemlines. In times of high excitement, like the twenties and the sixties, when people looked forward to the future with hope, the skyscrapers and the skirts went up. At times when men became fearful of the future, or began to look back nostalgically to the past, as in the early thirties, the late forties and the seventies, they stopped building towers and the skirts came down again. Never, however, did skirts rise so high, nor was there such a universal frenzy for building skyscrapers as in the sixties: and never, in either case, was the reaction so complete as it has been in the seventies.

Perhaps the most obvious and immediate way to get the seventies into perspective is to see the extent to which they were a kind of prolonged morning after to the euphoria and excesses of the sixties. So many of the events and moods which marked out the seventies were simply a winding down or reaction to trends which had been set in motion by the sixties that it is really difficult to draw a firm dividing line between one decade and the other.

In my earlier book *The Neophiliacs,* subtitled "A Study of the Revolution in English Life in the Fifties and Sixties," I depicted the shape of postwar history as having been not unlike that of a gigantic wave. It was a wave which began to gather in the mid-fifties, as the world finally began to emerge from the shadows cast by World War II—a wave of expectation, of nervous excitement, born of the growing sense that somehow Britain, the West, and mankind were moving forward into a new era of a kind never known before.

This sense of anticipation was above all generated in the mid-fifties by the dawning realization that, thanks to the miraculous advances of technology, an entirely new kind of material prosperity was coming into being. Hundreds of millions of people, for the first time in their lives, were able to own cars, buy fridges and washing machines, shop at the new supermarkets for detergents and frozen foods. Television passed into the center of our homes and our lives. There was suddenly much more money around than would have seemed imaginable to any previous generation, and every year that passed seemed to bring yet more technical marvels, more change—transistor radios, jet airliners, computers, super highways, new kinds of architecture in steel, concrete and glass.

At the same time, in large part generated by this sense that we had all climbed onto an escalator moving ever more rapidly up into the future, sweeping away so many of the traditional landmarks and patterns of life, a new spirit emerged in Western society—a spirit of revolt against the "restrictive" conventions of the past, and in favor of some new "liberated" vision of the future. Nowhere did this show more obviously than in the remarkable new importance which in the late fifties came to be attached to youth—manifesting itself in the emergence of a whole new, rebellious youth culture, in the James Dean cult and the rock 'n'roll craze which swept the West in 1956-8, and Britain's "Angry Young" playwrights and novelists who shot to prominence at the same time.

On a wider stage, across the world, this anticipation of a new age of liberation, and the sweeping away of old restrictive structures, gave rise to that mass of nationalist movements which, in Africa, Asia, and the Caribbean, began to work as never before for emancipation from the centuries-old domination of European imperialism. In America, in the mid-fifties, the same mood gave rise to the civil rights movement. Yet despite this world-wide stirring of a new radicalism, in favor of the young, the blacks, the colonially oppressed, and any group which could see itself as an underdog, there still seemed little doubt at the end of the fifties that the future of mankind lay with the way of life of that country which stood unequaled in material abundance, in military and technological power, in self-confidence of all kinds—America. It was America which was pioneering the road toward a materialist Utopia that the rest of the world—including the countries under Communism—might eventually hope to follow.

In the sixties, the tidal wave of change and euphoria rolled ever higher. If there was one man above all who seemed to embody the radical youthful idealism and energy which was to carry mankind into a new age of boundless prosperity and peace, it was that inexpressibly glamorous figure who, in November 1960, was elected President of the United States, John F. Kennedy. In Britain, as the Conservative Macmillan government collapsed in a turmoil of TV satire, security and sex scandals, and general irreverent rage at a tired old "upper-class Establishment," Harold Wilson's promise of a "classless, dynamic New Britain," forged out of "the white heat of technology," seemed to offer our own prospect of a bright New Frontier future.

On all sides, standards, sensibilities—even the landscape—seemed to be changing faster than at any time in history. The cities of the world in the sixties, from London to Liverpool, from Melbourne to Moscow, from Paris to Peking, were going through the most dramatic transformation they had ever known, as the bulldozers moved in, as the high-rise buildings and new housing projects rose in their tens of thousands, and the Brave New World visions of the Modern Movement-inspired planners and architects finally came into their own. In the heyday of Beatlemania, the Rolling Stones, and all that was implied by "swinging London," the heroes and values of the new youth culture came to exercise glamorous sway over half the globe. Before the triumphant onward march of "permissiveness," age-old conventions of dress, language, and behavior seemed to be dissolving like snow as the Western world plunged ever more obsessively after a vision of complete sexual freedom—while, in books and magazines, on the cinema screen and the stage, the image of sex (and of sexual perversity) emerged into the open as never before.

The sixties were certainly a time when it was still possible for most people to look forward in hope to an as yet unrealized future. But as that frenetic decade wore on, it became increasingly apparent that not all was well with the dream. After the world-wide shock of President Kennedy's assassination in 1963, America in particular seemed to be floundering deeper and deeper into trouble. Year by year, as civil rights aspirations turned into the horrific series of race riots, as the growing shadow of the escalating war in Vietnam lengthened across the world, the dream became more of a nightmare. President Nixon's election in 1968 represented at least in part a desperate yearning by "the silent majority" for a return to quieter, more peaceful, more orderly times—and when America finally managed to land two men on the moon in the summer of 1969, this astonishing technological triumph was already not without undertones of deepest irony, as the world viewed the impotence of American technological power elsewhere.

In Britain, the bright hopes held out by Harold Wilson's promises of "dynamism" had swiftly faded, as it became clear that Britain's long industrial and economic decline was not to be halted by mere bureaucratic tinkerings—nor by a Prime Minister who, more than any of his predecessors, seemed to be acting out a mere fantasy version of his role, concerned primarily with the kind of image he would create in the receding-mirror world of the media.

As the youth culture ran through an ever more bizarre series of permutations—Flower Power and hippiedom, LSD and hard drugs, the wave of student protest and pseudo-Marxism of 1968—it increasingly lost its glamour and became shadowed by violence (e.g. the Manson murders) and by the strains which led to the arrests, suicides, or simply the fading away of many of its leading figures.

In the Third World, the dreams of the liberation which would follow independence increasingly gave way to disillusionment, as one newly-independent state after another fell foul of military coups and tyrants, civil war, or just the intractable problems of poverty and even mass starvation which the coming of independence alone had failed to solve.

Above all in the West in the late sixties there were abundant signs of a new countervailing spirit to that great tidal wave which had swept up mankind since the fifties in its onward rush. There were the first signs of a conservative reaction, of a growing weariness with the relentless battering of change. Around 1967, we suddenly began to hear a new set of words— "conservation," "the environment," "pollution," "ecology"— expressing a growing sense of horror at what our wonderful, runaway technology was doing to our cities, to our countryside and rivers and seas, to other species, to the whole balance of nature on the planet. Somehow, the feeling ran, things seemed to have got out of hand. The paradise we had all been moving toward so rapidly in the late fifties and early sixties seemed to be proving curiously elusive. And so, on a deep note of questioning, did the sixties come to an end.

It has been a fairly general rule in this century that each decade in turn has turned out very differently from what was generally predicted at its outset. At the end of the forties the outlook for mankind was taken to be very gloomy indeed. Ten years later, at the end of the fifties, *The Economist* caught the almost universal mood of optimism when it declared, "At the gates of the new decade, the main peril, blinding our eyes to what we could achieve, seems almost to be smugness."

At the beginning of the seventies, few people could imagine that the new decade would be all that different from the sixties. *Time* magazine, for instance, predicted that young people would continue to rebel, that Women's Lib would get more strident, that gays, old age pensioners, and other groups would climb on the protest bandwagon, that stage nudity would get more daring, that the Western world would continue to enjoy an economic boom, that technology would continue to produce new triumphs—in other words, that the mixture would be much as before, only more so.

Indeed, for the first year or two of the seventies, this was pretty well how things turned out—even though the difficulties of sustaining the onward rush became more and more apparent.

The world economy did continue to boom, partly as a result of the way America was choosing to finance her war in Southeast Asia. Increasingly desperate about her impotence in Vietnam, the United States made a last attempt to bludgeon her way to victory, as in 1970 President Nixon ordered the invasion of Cambodia and stepped up still further the blasting of those unhappy lands with high-explosive, napalm, chemical defoliants, and every kind of sophisticated technological horror. At the same time, as if foreshadowing her eventual weakening of will, America pursued *détente* with the rest of the Communist world more fervently than at any time since World War II, leading to the SALT disarmament talks, Helsinki, the Nixon-Brezhnev summit, and, most surprising of all, Nixon's visit to Mao's China in 1972.

In Britain likewise in the early seventies, the new Conservative government under Edward Heath (elected in 1970), far from reflecting that desire for quieter, more conservative times which had already begun to show in English life, made a last effort to bludgeon Britain into a bigger, brighter, more "efficient" future, by a series of grandiose bureaucratic and technological gestures only too typical of the wishful thinking of the sixties. For a time the economy boomed in all sorts of rather sick and unreal ways. The property boom unleashed on Britain's cities the greatest concentration of redevelopment they had ever known. Inflation rose alarmingly. The trade unions, already at odds with the Heath government over its maladroit Industrial Relations Act, became more and more aggressive.

The world in general, as an explosion in commodity prices pushed up inflation across the globe, was passing into a strangely jumpy state. And so, in 1973, began that period of general disorder which, in many ways, we can look back on as having been a kind of grand climacteric to the whole of the vision of a new age opened up 20 years before, and the attempt to achieve which had already, since the mid-sixties, begun to produce such signs of strain.

The most obvious place where the climacteric showed was, of course, America. As Dr. Kissinger prepared at the beginning of 1973 for the United States' final, ignominious scuttle from Vietnam, the country was suddenly plunged into the shadow of that miasma known generically as "Watergate" which in just over 18 months was to lead to the resignations of Vice-President Agnew and of President Nixon himself.

Just as significant, however, were the consequences of the Yom Kippur war between Israel and her Arab neighbors, which broke out in October 1973. It was almost eerie how the ripples from that event were to spread out across the rest of the seventies. The immediate reason for the Arab world's quadrupling of oil prices over the succeeding 12 months was simply to show disapproval for the West's support of Israel. But at the same time, it seemed like the most dramatic example yet of the non-industrialized world's growing desire to protest at the reckless exploitation by only a fraction of mankind of the earth's finite and rapidly diminishing natural resources. Indeed it was the first really serious, practical symptom of that approaching crisis for mankind of which the environmentalists had been warning for six or seven years. And the most immediate and obvious consequence was that the world's economy was plunged into its deepest recession since 1945.

As on all sides we began to hear talk of "zero growth" and "diminishing expectations," country after country took drastic steps to contain the new threat to their economies. Almost the only exception was Britain which, thanks to peculiar political circumstances, was over the next 18 months to drift into an unreal little climacteric of her own.

Initially, in his typically rather wooden way, Prime Minister Edward Heath attempted to follow other countries in taking steps to meet the crisis. But as his government's authority dissolved in the early months of 1974, amid industrial chaos, power cuts, food shortages, and the "Three Day Week," events could scarcely have conspired more effectively to complete the work of financial chaos which the Heath government had already begun.

For 18 months, Harold Wilson's new Labour government in effect gave way to the unions in everything they asked for. Wage demands and government spending went through the roof—as did inflation, public borrowing, and the huge balance of payments deficit that were their inevitable price. By the summer of 1975, with an inflation rate of 27 per cent, higher than any other country in the industrialized world, Britain stood on the edge of what eventually even Mr. Wilson himself, though lost to the last in his own imperturbably self-regarding fantasy world, warned could become "a catastrophe of unimaginable proportions." The unions, led by the man now widely described as "the second most powerful figure in the country," Jack Jones, at last agreed to moderate their wage demands. But it was not until after a further autumn of crisis in 1976, when the IMF stepped in and some attempt was made to cut government spending, that the threat of the unimaginable catastrophe finally, for the time being, receded.

The rest of the world, during these watershed years of the mid-seventies, had not been without rather more serious troubles of its own. While America, the leading champion of capitalist democracy, had been introspectively locked in the gloomy toils of Watergate, the other great ideology holding sway over mankind, Communism, had enjoyed its greatest series of advances since the late forties. Most spectacular, of course, was the collapse into Communist hands in just a few weeks of the spring of 1975 of the whole of Indochina. Over countries which for years had been bathed in the glare of the world's publicity, there suddenly fell a black wall of censorship—through which percolated rumors, from Cambodia in particular, of the most frightful aftermath to the Communist victory, with perhaps anything up to *two or three million* of Cambodia's population of seven million being effectually put to death in 1975-6.

Two countries which for 40 years had embodied for the world the other extreme of the ideological spectrum, Spain and Portugal, briefly seemed likely so to overreact to the end of their right-wing dictatorships that they too might teeter over into Communism, although both eventually pulled back. But certainly Portugal's two largest and richest African colonies, Angola and Mozambique, both fell quickly after independence under semi-Marxist, totalitarian regimes, as did other parts of Africa, including Ethiopia and Somalia. It was perhaps hardly surprising that, emboldened by their burgeoning military and political strength, while America flagged, the leaders of the Soviet Union should finally in 1974 have begun to seize the nettle of that internal dissent which had grown up since the early sixties by expelling the most powerful of all Russian dissidents, Alexander Solzhenitsyn, who came to the West as a prophet of terrible doom.

Certainly as the world emerged from those turmoils of the mid-seventies, and as America emerged from the long dark night of Watergate, electing as President the almost unknown Georgia evangelist Jimmy Carter in token of the general desire for a "fresh start," the global landscape began to seem very different from the way it had looked only a few, brief years before. Gone were the expectations that mankind was heading up into an ever more glorious, prosperous future, on an ever-rising curve of production and consumption. Gone was the old unchallenged standing and pre-eminence of America, whose self-confidence indeed was to diminish even further as the somewhat ghostly, milk-and-water nature of the Carter presidency emerged.

Almost without it being noticed, a tremendous change had

come over the world's mood. Already so many of the more garish and strident phenomena which had marked out the sixties and the early seventies seemed to have faded away so far that they belonged almost to another era. The great heyday of youthful protest was now so much a historical memory that occasional nostalgic television programs would appear, showing how the hippies and flower children and Marxists of the late sixties had become transmogrified into short-haired computer programmers or prosperous antique dealers or even, as in the cases of the Black Power leader Eldridge Cleaver, singer Bob Dylan and others, committed Christians. If Gay Lib continued to flourish, as *Time* had predicted in 1970, certainly Women's Lib had lost much of its initial dark energy, and the great wave of protest and demands for rights which had once seemed likely to engulf the whole of Western society had markedly lost momentum.

Of all the cultural symptoms of the late seventies, few were more revealing than the spectacular collapse of that ideology which, for 20 years, had sought to bulldoze our cities into a Brave New World. Certainly the economic recession following the 1973 oil crisis had played its part in bringing rebuilding to a sudden standstill. In Britain, for instance, the years 1974-6 had seen a wave of bankruptcies of unprecedented size, affecting a whole series of major property companies, fringe banks, and other institutions which had gambled recklessly on the property bubble of the early seventies. But running much deeper than these mere financial factors, the same years had seen a quite astonishing reaction to the Modern Movement dream, that vast areas of the older parts of the world's cities should be swept away, to be replaced by mighty towers, concrete housing projects, highways, multi-story car parks, and all the other outward expressions of the age of Technology Triumphant. Although the ideas derived from the Modern Movement might still be a long time in dying among the architects and planners primarily responsible, the reaction to the more inhuman excesses and horrors of the years of the great "concrete explosion" was an almost world-wide phenomenon.* The desire to preserve old buildings, or at least only to build in future on a smaller, more "human" scale, had suddenly become one of the great driving forces of the age. And nowhere did this loss of confidence in the Modern Movement go further than in the country which, in some ways, had embraced its ideas for comprehensive redevelopment more wholeheartedly than any, Britain.

In all sorts of ways, in fact, Britain reflected the new mood of the late seventies more obviously than many countries. This was not least made apparent in the fact that, within little over a year in 1975-6, both Britain's major political parties had chosen new leaders. Those two typical fantasy figures of the sixties, Heath and Wilson, had departed (as at much the same time, though for rather different reasons, had the leader of Britain's third largest party, Jeremy Thorpe). And in many ways, the two figures who succeeded Wilson and Heath could not have provided a greater contrast.

However much his detractors claimed that the bluff, avuncular style of Jim Callaghan, who succeeded Harold Wilson as Prime Minister in April 1976, was just a façade, in reality hiding a weak man, prone to panic, the fact remains that the atmosphere of British political life did change markedly after Wilson's departure. Seeing himself initially as "Moses," come down from the mountain top to utter stern truths to his people,

---

*When Britain's Environment Secretary Peter Shore formally proclaimed to the 1976 Habitat Conference in Vancouver that "Britain has pensioned off the bulldozer," he was applauded by delegates from many countries. In France an edict in 1977 prohibited future building above seven stories, except in special circumstances. In America the disillusionment with the Modern Movement expressed itself in such books as *Form Follows Fiasco* by Peter Blake, once one of its most fervent champions. Even in East Germany the only form of social criticism occasionally permitted on television was that relating to the difficulties of living in high-rise buildings and the social problems caused by vast new housing projects (cf. "A Tale of Three Cities," BBC-TV documentary, 1978).

Callaghan did run a tighter, more orthodox monetary policy,* and unlike his predecessor was not afraid on occasion to spell out to the unions the economic facts of life. Inflation did come down a long way from its traumatic peak in 1975 (in fact to 9 per cent by 1979) and, assisted by that greatest unlooked-for bonanza of the seventies, North Sea oil, which only four years after it began to flow in 1974 was already meeting four-fifths of Britain's needs, the country's financial picture by the late sev enties looked, at least outwardly, rather more rosy.

Even more interesting, in terms of the changing mood of the times, was the emergence of Mrs. Margaret Thatcher, symboliz-ing a very different kind of conservatism from that which Mr. Heath had stood for. By the late seventies, indeed, it was widely accepted that the revival of conservative attitudes which had begun to show as early as ten years before had at last reached the point where it was the most powerful, even intellectually vigorous force in English life. Certainly it seemed a long way from the days of that triumphant onward march of "permis-sive" morality, "progressive" attitudes in education, and gen-eral neophilia which in the sixties had dominated English life in all directions.† Similarly there was a widespread and deep-seated reaction to those heady days of the Wilson government in the mid-seventies, when it had seemed that the trade unions and an ever-expanding bureaucracy were carrying all before

---

*One of the success stories of the seventies was the influence of the monetary theories of Milton Friedman, which by 1977 were even carrying weight with the British Labour government. In the inflation of the early seventies, almost every country in the Western world had seen an unprecedented expansion of its money supply. The later success of "Friedmanism" could be seen as a reaction to that, and as one of the many symptoms of the end of the Keynesian era whose orthodoxy had been that governments could and should "spend their way out of trouble."

†Another reflection of Britain's more conservative mood in the late seventies was the extraordinary nationwide rejoicing which surrounded the Queen's Silver Jubilee in 1977. It is hard to imagine that such an occasion would have been celebrated in quite this way in, say, the mid-sixties. The mood of nostalgia was quite explicit. The *Times* report of one East End street party quoted a participant as saying, "It's like the old days—before the planners came."

them. Various former left-wing writers, such as Paul Johnson, and politicians, like the one-time Labour Foreign Secretary Lord George-Brown, were now in the forefront of those warning that the power of the unions and the overmighty spread of government (which by 1975 had come to represent or control 60 per cent of the entire British economy) might be just the fore-runners of Britain's possible eventual collapse into the kind of Marxist, totalitarian state which many of the more extreme members of the Labour Party, such as Mr. Anthony Wedgwood Benn (who had changed his name during the seventies to plain Tony Benn), seemed to see as increasingly desirable.

By the last two years of the seventies, the thought that at least one more last-ditch attempt should be made to save Britain from such a fate, by giving a try to Mrs. Thatcher's new Conservatism, had for many clearly become irresistible. If there were any doubts that she might be pre-empted by the success of Mr. Callaghan's Moses act in talking tough to the newly-quiescent unions, they were rudely dispelled in Britain's "winter of discontent" in 1978-9, when the lower-paid unions in particular plunged the country into the kind of social chaos it had never known before. Amid three months of the worst winter weather of the decade, and a flood of newspaper headlines and television interviews reflecting a mood of surly, inhuman aggression among the strikers and their leaders that was almost entirely unprecedented in English life (e.g. the ambulance drivers' spokesman who said, "If it means lives lost, that is how it must be ... we are fed up of being Cinderellas, this time we are going to the ball"), hospitals were closed, ambulance services withdrawn, water supplies and sewage shut off, even bodies remained unburied; while a combination of strikes by truck drivers and gasoline tanker drivers seemed for a while to threaten that the country's entire economic activity might be brought to a standstill.

In May 1979, Mrs. Thatcher's election victory seemed to mark an appropriate break with much of the kind of thinking which had dominated English life for 25 years. As for whether it might be a real turning point, or just a short-lived interlude, only the events of a new decade, the eighties, could tell.

2

THE END OF THE TWENTIETH-CENTURY DREAM

The crisis which may develop as early as 1988 will be of such magnitude as to make the current situation appear like a mere passing event of trivial consequence.

—Sheikh Yamani, June 19, 1979

It is time to look a little more deeply at what had really been happening to Britain, the West, and mankind in the seventies.

As we have seen, the late fifties and sixties, with their tidal wave of change and euphoria—the coming of affluence and television, the Kennedy era, the youth and pop revolutions, permissiveness in social mores and the arts, the rebuilding of our cities according to the ideology of the Modern Movement— were the last great moment when it was possible for most people in our culture to look forward in hope to an as yet unrealized future. But if we look more closely at the nature of that optimism, that wave of expectation which so markedly died away in the seventies, we may see that in essence it was rooted in precisely those same sources of hope that have sustained the human race throughout the twentieth century.

The Twentieth-century Dream has had three central, interwoven strands:

1. the belief that, through science and technology, we should be able to unlock all the "secrets of the universe," we should be able to "master" nature, and thus create a materially secure and comfortable life for the majority of mankind;

21

2. the Utopian belief that, through drastic social and political reorganization, aided by the greater use of state planning, we should be able to create an entirely new kind of just, fair, and equal society;

3. the belief that, through the dismantling of all the old repressive taboos and conventions of the past—whether in social attitudes or the arts—individuals would be able to enjoy a much greater degree of freedom and self-realization.

The importance of the seventies was that, in each of these great avenues of human exploration, they had marked a moment of truth, a point at which, more obviously and inescapably than ever before, the dream ran out. As a friend put it to me recently, "The seventies were the time when our bluff was called"—not least in the extent to which, in being actually realized, the dream had turned out (like the "Brave New World" visions of high-rise buildings) to produce such a very different kind of reality to that originally promised.

Let us consider each of these strands in turn.

1. The Technological, Scientific Dream

Some time in the seventies a profoundly significant moment was passed in the history of mankind—the moment when it became apparent that, even on their own terms, science and technology were no longer necessarily making life better, easier, more efficient for us all. Of course there continued to be technological advances—from the availability of cheap electronic calculators to the world's first test tube baby. But for the first time in centuries, if not in millennia, it became apparent in the seventies that the whole advance of human technology was beginning to operate on the law of diminishing returns.

On the one hand, there was nothing new which could really startle us any longer. A deeply symbolic moment, casting its shadow over the seventies, was that which occurred just before the decade began, when men first landed on the Moon. For the first time (as I analyze in a later essay) technology had literally carried men so far outside their frame of reference that they no longer knew how to relate to it. Never again in human experience could there be such a moment. And even on a more mundane level, the seventies could offer nothing like a continuation of that avalanche of change which had transformed our lives out of recognition in the fifties and sixties. We had shot Niagara—it was impossible that our lives could ever be so deeply, radically changed again.

On the other hand, it became evident that, after all the advances of the previous 20 years, our societies were actually, in countless ways, becoming less efficient; we were actually, for all our computers, labor-saving devices, and electronic gadgets, beginning in many ways to get less service, less benefit. If you had asked the average Westerner whether, taking all things into account, the quality and ease of life had improved in those ten years, the chances are that for the first time since the fifties, he might well have replied "no." And not the least ingredient in making life seem more difficult, more unreal, more strained, was inflation.

No account of the seventies would be complete without some attempt to analyze this extraordinary world-wide phenomenon which has come so much to dominate our lives, our news, our politics, our conversation that we are scarcely any longer aware of just how strange it is. Why is it that, just as we appeared to be standing on the edge of the ultimate consumer Utopia, that world of universal abundance dreamed of by mankind for thousands of years, we should have become bedeviled by this extraordinary joke we have played on ourselves, that has made the quiet enjoyment of our materialist paradise like one of those mirage oases which constantly recede before the traveler in the desert?

If we look at the history of inflation, one of the most remarkable things is how comparatively stable over long periods in the past the value of money remained. The value of a pound sterling in 1910, for instance was very similar, in terms of what it could buy, to what it had been two and a half centuries before, in 1660. Almost the only times when its value had declined were during wars, when governments inflated the currency by massive borrowing, or printing paper money (a disguised form of credit)—and in fact more people had lived in periods when prices were falling than the reverse. The two world wars of this century pushed up prices considerably so that by 1956 the 1910 figure of 100 had risen to 301. But from that moment on, as the Western world climbed onto the escalator of the fifties consumer boom, prices began to shoot up in a way they had never done in peacetime before. By 1970, in Britain, they had reached 500, by the end of the seventies they had easily topped 1000—an increase bringing in its wake such a state of social neurosis and instability that it was not unusual to hear sage commentators like Mr. Peter Jay warning that inflation had become a threat to our civilization potentially as great as overpopulation or the H-bomb.

Yet the economists, for all their talk of "Phillips Curves," "cost-push," and "demand-pull," were ultimately quite baffled by this new problem—in a sense not surprisingly. For its real causes ran much deeper in Western civilization than anything which could be explained by mere economics. At root the great inflation was a psychological phenomenon—an inevitable consequence of that great unleashing of material expectations that had taken place since the fifties, which had led people more and more to lose touch with the inexorable fact that you cannot spend what you have not got. Not only had the great consumer boom (like the near-tenfold increase in house prices between 1970 and 1979) been fueled by an unprecedented expansion of credit—the "fantasy money" that is spent today and earned tomorrow—the trade unions (not to mention almost everyone else) had come to expect more money as a matter of course, regardless of whether the goods or the production were there to justify it. The whole spiral of financial unreality, increasingly separating money from any true criterion of value (a process assisted on its way in Britain by the introduction of decimal coinage in 1971) had become self-perpetuating, the symptom of a gigantic act of collective make-believe. Inflation thus became one of the most obvious measures of the way our material expectations had begun to outrun our capacity to justify them.

An even more fundamental danger sign in the seventies that mankind could no longer hope to look for an unlimited upward spiral of economic growth was the abundant host of early warnings that for the first time in history the earth's supplies of energy and natural resources were coming under severe and genuine strain. One of the most significant statistical land- marks of the seventies (apart from the fact that the world's population for the first time reached four billion—it had reached three billion only as recently as 1950) was that for the first time since our civilization began to develop its astonishing dependence on oil a mere 80 years ago, the rate at which new oil reserves were being discovered was overtaken by the rate at which we were consuming oil. By the end of the decade that world energy crisis (which at the end of the sixties had still seemed little more than an environmentalists' scare story) had already begun to become a reality. With that, and sober fore- casts of the exhaustion of other resources, such as a number of metals, within 30, 40, or 50 years, it began to become apparent that the whole technological explosion of the twentieth century, far from preparing the way for some Utopian future, might well turn out before long to have been just a very short-lived phase in the story of mankind.

At a deeper level still there was growing evidence in the seventies of a new kind of questioning and reappraisal of the whole role played by technology and science in Western culture since the Renaissance. This was not just a matter of the wide- spread revulsion against the deadening, destructive character of technology itself, its power to inflict untold harm on nature, the increasing noise, ugliness, and pollution it had brought into the world. Such feelings were largely neurotic since there were few signs that those who experienced them were actually prepared to deny themselves the benefits of technology. What was more interesting was the growing recognition by a good many scientists and others (cf. the essay later in this book on Professor Ehrenfeld's *The Arrogance of Humanism*) that the scientific and technological modes of relating man to nature and to the universe *might in themselves have severe and potentially catastrophic limitations;* that the whole tradition of rationality which had dominated Western thought since Descartes, Galileo, and Bacon had, even by its own methods, begun to reveal disastrous shortcomings when measured against the boundless and delicate complexities of nature. This was indeed a sign that some absolutely fundamental shift of opinion was taking place, even within the citadels of science itself—and that one of the most substantial underpinnings of twentieth-century thought might be dissolving toward an entirely new way of looking at the world.

2. Political Utopianism

If one Utopian dream, that of the material paradise to be brought about by technology, began to turn as never before into a mirage in the seventies, another aspect of the twentieth-century dream which took an unprecedented beating was that of the social and political Utopia—that vision of a just, equal, and compassionate society associated above all with all the countless variants of Socialism.

Although the late sixties had seen a last infantile flicker of the tradition of Socialist idealism—in the wave of student protest and pseudo-Marxism that ran around the world in 1968, associated with such idols as Marcuse, Guevara, Trotsky, and Ho Chi-Minh—the decade which followed could scarcely have exposed the dark underside of Socialism more starkly. More than ever before in the seventies was it borne in on us all just how cruelly the Socialist dream could betray the originally proclaimed humanitarian ideals of its leaders and their hundreds of millions of not always willing followers.

Solzhenitsyn's *The Gulag Archipelago,* published between 1974 and 1978, revealed to the world in an entirely new way just how horrific had been the experience of Russia under Socialist totalitarianism—not only at the height of Stalin's purges in the thirties, but from the earliest days of the Bolshevik Revolution: how the systematic policies of enslavement, extermination, and genocide carried out against the peoples of the largest country on earth for 50 years had amounted to the greatest crime in the history of humanity, dwarfing even the more familiar atrocities committed by Hitler.

As if to demonstrate that such savagery was by no means a matter of history, the aftermath of the Communist takeover in Indochina in 1975 (cheered on by many young Western sympathizers) led to the almost unbelievable nightmare of Cambodia, where even on Communist figures, over a third of the population were in effect put to death by the new Pol Pot-Ieng Sary regime in just two or three years. By the end of the seventies, the spectacle of the boat people fleeing in their hundreds of thousands from Vietnam gave the world at least some tiny glimmering of the sufferings inflicted on that country by its new "Socialist" masters. In Mozambique, Angola, Ethiopia—wherever Marxist regimes had taken over during the seventies—reports of slave camps and massacres trickled out.

Such distant horrors across the world may have seemed a far cry from Britain's rather cosier politics. But even there, one of the most conspicuous developments of the seventies was the way that Socialism showed a little more of its ugly underside. The trade union movement became more and more of a dark presence in national life, showing itself more than ever before concerned with little other than money, power, and the winning of privilege above the law, capable on occasion of exercising brute force to achieve its ends quite as ruthlessly as the stereotyped capitalist villains of old. Many trade union leaders, such as Jack Jones, Clive Jenkins, and Arthur Scargill, now displayed quite open sympathy with the Soviet Union and the Communist world—as when, in 1976, the TUC received a fraternal visit from Shelepin, the head of the KGB. At the end of a decade in which the Labour Party had become increasingly synonymous with trade union power, the dead hand of bureaucracy, and Trotskyite infiltration, it was harder than ever to recall how deeply it had once been associated with the humanitarian ideals of liberty and compassion.

In fact one of the most graphic illustrations of the evaporation of that twentieth-century dream of a fairer, juster society, planned to give a better life for all its citizens, lay in the astonishing disillusionment which now surrounded the attempt in the fifties and sixties to rebuild our cities. Inspired like Le Corbusier and others in the early decades of the twentieth century by the vision that we could sweep away the old cities of the past and replace them with an entirely new kind of city, planned down to the last detail to give a better, healthier, fuller life for all its inhabitants, the politicians, architects, and planners of Britain had produced little more than a series of bleak, grimly regimented wastelands. Vast areas of cities such as London, Liverpool, Glasgow, and Newcastle had been transformed into inhuman moonscapes of high-rise buildings, set in a sea of dereliction. The millions of (mostly poorer) people who had been herded into the concrete Gulags of the new housing projects were victims of one of the most dramatic of all attempts to realize the twentieth-century dream of Utopia. In the seventies it became clear how profoundly this version of the dream, like others, had failed.

3. The Dream of "Individual Self-realization"

Alongside the dream of salvation through technology and of a collective Utopia, the twentieth century has been haunted by a third—although it was closely linked with the others and, like them, its roots in fact went back much further in history than just the twentieth century, at least to the time of the Industrial and French Revolutions at the end of the eighteenth century. This was the dream that if only we could throw off the repressive shackles of convention, and "bourgeois," socially imposed morality, we should arrive at a wonderful new age of "liberation," in which human beings would at last be free to "be themselves."

In essence this mighty impulse, first appearing in the form of the Romantic Movement, was a revolt against structure, order, discipline—a reaction in the name of "life" against the dehumanization of an increasingly machine-dominated, money-conscious, bureaucratic civilization. And it showed itself nowhere more than in the arts and in the realm of sexual morality.

In the nineteenth century the Romantic revolt against bourgeois respectability took the form of wave after wave of Bohemianism, Estheticism and the self-conscious pursuit of Decadence. At the beginning of the twentieth century it made a further huge leap forward, particularly in that *avant-garde* explosion which convulsed the arts, that whole reaction against Victorian academicism which marked the birth of the Modern Movement in music, painting, literature, and architecture. Amid the frenzied *avant-garde* experiments and sexual liberation of the twenties, it reached still further heights—but even these were to pale into insignificance when set against what was to follow in the late fifties and sixties.

In the youth revolution, the permissiveness, the general world-wide hysteria of the "swinging sixties," the collective impulse that had begun with the rebellion of the early Romantics reached its peak. In the flashing lights and blaring cacophony of the discotheques, in the four-letter words and displays of nudity, in the drug obsessions, the "love festivals," the cults, the crazes, the dazzling patterns of Op Art and the infantile playthings of Pop, the children of the sixties sought to shake, deafen, blind, and drug themselves into the "ultimate experience" on a scale never before seen—until there was almost nowhere further to go. To put it at its simplest, the mini-skirts could go no higher, the pop music could get no louder, even the available permutations on sexual normality must eventually be exhausted. One of the main reasons why the seventies had such an air of hangover, of aftermath, was that a psychological climax had been passed which could never be worked up to with the same frenzied excitement again, simply because so many of the "kicks" had come from the very act of pushing back frontiers, dismantling taboos, and flouting conventions which could never again, in the same way, be re-erected.*

At the same time in the seventies a strange exhaustion settled over the Modern Movement in all the arts. As I point out in a later essay, it is remarkable how many of the giants of the Modern Movement died in the ten years between 1965 and 1975—from Le Corbusier to Picasso, from Eliot to Stravinsky—leaving very few major figures left on the world arts scene. The truth was that the Modern Movement had exhausted itself for precisely the same reasons as the other manifestations of our modern neo-Romanticism. For decades it had gone on pushing back frontiers of form, structure, and tonality, until there was no structure left to topple. The concert halls were still full, the theaters busy, the queues outside the art galleries longer than ever—not so much in honor of the masterpieces of our own time as because the appetite for the music, the plays, and art works of the past had never been greater. After tens of thousands of years of seemingly endless fertility, the artistic imagination of humanity had at last reached, for the time being at least, a more or less gaping void. It was perhaps the most profound reflection of all of the strange plight of late-twentieth-century man.

---

*One of the more pitiful shadows of all this in the seventies were the so-called Punk Rockers who, with their safety pins stuck through noses, their circus-clown make-up, their abysmal music, showed how virtually impossible it was any longer to exceed the "bounds of convention" in order to excite some last vestige of sensation.

3

ON DOVER BEACH

... the world, which seems
To lie before us like a land of dreams,
So various, so beautiful, so new,
Hath really neither joy, nor love, nor light,
Nor certitude, nor peace, nor help for pain;
And we are here as on a darkling plain
Swept with confused alarms of struggle and flight,
Where ignorant armies clash by night.

—Matthew Arnold, "Dover Beach," 1867

Just before the seventies began, one of the more interesting symptoms of that groundswell of reaction which was already beginning to form against the frenzied contemporaneity and rude disorder of the sixties was the astonishing popularity of Kenneth Clark's *Civilisation,* the most successful series television has ever produced.

A powerful ingredient in the immediate impact of *Civilisation,* particularly in America, was the contrast it struck with the strange times in which it first appeared. There, on television screens which had been purveying nightly images of Vietnam, race riots, protest demonstrations, and pop festivals, was this urbane figure, in his beautifully cut suits, taking us back into a different world—a realm of exquisite paintings, tapestries, cathedrals, palaces, the rich, ordered harvest of a thousand years of European culture. Amid the chaotic nightmare of the present, Clark seemed a symbol of all that sense of permanence and stability we thought we had lost and were beginning again to yearn for.

Indeed as he magisterially surveyed the whole sweep of Western civilization since the Middle Ages, not the least appealing thing for many viewers was the way Clark did not conceal his distaste for the way the story had ended up. Apart from stray asides directed throughout the series at modern architects, playwrights, psychiatrists, "hellish traffic," and "all those forces which threaten to impair our humanity—lies, tanks, tear gas, ideologies, opinion polls, mechanization, planners, computers," Clark's fear that we were no longer civilized, his suspicion that we were sinking into a new barbarism, constantly intruded on his survey of the glories of the past like a specter at the feast. In Chartres Cathedral, he could not help remarking, "Even the tourists have not spoiled its atmosphere, as they have in so many temples of the human spirit." From the octagon room at the top of Greenwich Observatory, surrounded by all the noble impedimenta of seventeenth-century science, his gaze strayed out across the trees and the elegant buildings of Wren's Royal Hospital below, to a distant skyline of smoking factories and high-rise buildings, "the squalid disorder of industrial society."

Why should we have come to such a pass? This might well have been one of the major underlying themes of such a series; indeed, up to a point, Lord Clark seemed to be giving his answer. The trouble with our present civilization, he implied, was that we have lost touch with our spiritual roots, our sense of human scale, our sense of man's proper place in the frame of nature. We have become, in short, materialists on a heroic scale, defying the universe, but at the same time losing that sense of proportion in all things which has been the secret of all those societies along the way which may be held to have been truly civilized.

So where did it all start to go wrong? If we are to see the past thousand years of our civilization as an evolutionary development and not just as a set of disconnected episodes, there must have been certain points along the way where those disruptive tendencies now bearing such unwelcome fruit began to show themselves. But here Lord Clark showed himself strangely reluctant to accept the full implications of his own evidence.

He began his story with a somewhat melodramatic account of how civilization was brought through the Dark Ages following the fall of Rome, "by the skin of its teeth." He made no bones about what constituted this holy relic, being carted about on the extreme Western shores of Europe by a handful of barbarian monks. It certainly had little to do with Christianity, the latest of those "mystery religions," full of "meaningless rituals," that had "destroyed the self-confidence" of the antique world. It was the humanist tradition of Greco-Roman culture.

Around A.D. 1000 this frail flame was fanned back into life. "Civilization" was reborn. And the moment Clark chose to illustrate this was particularly significant—the reemergence in Christian art of a "recognizably human" figure. From then on, despite his previous lukewarm sympathy for Christianity, the Church passed into favor as the chief pillar of Western civilization, and over the next two episodes, describing the Middle Ages, it could do little wrong. But even here, despite his passing insistence on the "civilizing" importance of the Christian view that the spiritual world was ultimately more real than the material, it was again revealing what incidents and people Lord Clark chose to illustrate this. He homed in with particular delight, for instance, on the figure of the Abbé Suger of St. Denis (whom he compared to "Van Horne, the builder of the Canadian Pacific railways"), the man who had consciously revived the Greek belief that men's minds could only come to appreciate the spiritual world through material beauty. Even the sculptors of Chartres must have drawn their original inspiration from Greek models.

In short, for all his apparent sympathy for the world view of medieval Christendom, Clark's real admiration for the Middle Ages was centered on the way they marked the beginning of a revival of the humanistic values of the classical world. All of which might lead one to suppose that, as the Middle Ages drew toward their close, and as civilization reached that mighty turning point where men reached out to find still greater significance in the material world (and in themselves) without necessarily retaining the all-embracing framework of religion, Lord Clark would have found himself increasingly at home; indeed that, in the Renaissance, that time when the old Greco-Roman culture was revived more fervently and consciously than ever before, and when (as he borrowed from Protagoras for the title of one of his programs) man might again become "the measure of all things," Clark would find his true center of gravity.

Yet here was a curious thing. Of the Middle Ages themselves, Clark had spoken with almost unreserved enthusiasm. They had almost everything he regarded as a necessary condition of "civilization"—"a sense of permanence," of "eternity," of man's place in nature and so forth. But in each of the three programs covering the Renaissance and the Reformation, in which he represented man bursting forth from the constrictions of the medieval frame, he so chose to arrange his evidence that, after an initial wave of optimism, liberation and creativity, they ended in blackest pessimism. From the order and light of Urbino and Alberti's Florence to the romantic, almost nihilistic gloom of Giorgione's *Tempestà*, from the glories of the High Renaissance to Leonardo's world-destroying deluges, from the sunlit humanism of Erasmus to what Clark rather curiously took to be Shakespeare's conviction that life is ultimately meaningless, each time the great leap forward and upward of these two centuries in which our modern world came to birth was represented as ending in doubt, if not total despair.

Why should Clark have portrayed that very moment which saw the triumphant re-emergence of his own highest values, the leap of the Renaissance into a newly liberated, man-centered world view, in this way? Was it that he unconsciously sensed this to be the crucial moment of the birth of that restlessness, that refusal to accept the restraints of a universal order, that insatiable curiosity about and desire to "master" the external, material world, which had finally led to his nightmarish vision of the present?

Certainly in the next episode, on the Counter Reformation, Clark seemed to take unusual delight in running counter to the modern grain as he extolled the partial re-establishment of authority and religious certainty in the Tridentine Church. But even here, as he surveyed the attempts of Bernini and Co. to give their spiritual visions material expression, he was driven to end his story unhappily on the dissipation of the ceilings and paintings of the late Baroque into swirling clouds of illusion.

From there on, as the modern world grew closer, Clark found it ever harder to keep a secure foothold. He rejoiced briefly in the reordered universe of Newton and Descartes, of Vermeer's prosperous Holland—but even this was an order based ulti- mately (except for Rembrandt) on the materialism of emergent capitalism and scientific observation, and as he gazed out from Greenwich, he was only too gloomily reminded of what that love of wealth and scientific knowledge was to lead to. He found universal truth in the masters of eighteenth-century music, Bach, Handel, Haydn, Mozart, but saw them leading inexora- bly to *Don Giovanni:* "the pursuit of happiness and the pursuit of love, which had once seemed so simple and life-giving, had become complex and destructive, and [Don Giovanni's] refusal to repent, which makes him heroic, belongs to another phase of civilization."

Loth to plunge on such a perfect cue into the whirlpool of nineteenth-century Romanticism, Clark returned to the Age of Reason—but again the smile of Voltaire faded into the self- destructive make-believe and irrationality of the French Revo- lution. He tried the revolutionary ideals of brotherhood and liberty themselves but found them fading faster than ever into the "Fallacies of Hope" and totalitarian violence.

Increasingly, in his final episodes, Clark was forced to clutch at straws for anything he could really call "civilization"— Balzac's defiance of "fashionable opinion" (really?—was that why Balzac so liked living in a large house and being invited to smart dinner parties?), the technological Romanticism of Brunel, the "heroic materialism" of the Manhattan skyline (as long as you don't look at it too closely), the "love of nature" which he traced from Rousseau and Wordsworth to the cloud studies of Constable, the gaseous canvases of Turner, and Monet's lily pools, where the figurative image finally and delicately hovers on the edge of complete abstractionism. All this was pretty thin stuff when measured against that confident universality which Clark had found in the past, above all in the Middle Ages; only by shutting the best part of both eyes was it possible to see in those closing episodes anything more than the faintest vestiges of those ideals of "harmony," "proportion," "a sense of permanence," and "eternity" which in earlier programs he had claimed were essential to any definition of "civilization." And so, with this increasing sense of dissipation, of a reluctance to lift his head, we reached Lord Clark's melancholy peroration on the whole series, his quotation from Yeats:

> Things fall apart; the centre cannot hold;
> Mere anarchy is loosed upon the world,
> The blood-dimmed tide is loosed, and everywhere
> The ceremony of innocence is drowned . . .

As if finally reluctant to end his story on quite so bleak and despairing a note, he showed some "idealistic" students at Essex University (vintage 1968), and then, as he later put it in his autobiography, "I walked into my library, patted a wooden figure by Henry Moore, as if to imply that there was still hope, and it was all over."

Perhaps the most apposite comment on this superbly polished performance, which was greeted in 1969-70 with near-universal rapture (but noticeably by almost no attempt to discuss what Clark was actually saying), might have been some lines from the dialogue of Plato named after that same Protagoras who had once pronounced that "man is the measure of all things."

"Do you think it a beautiful and well-written poem?"

"Yes, both beautiful and well-written."

"And do you think a poem beautifully written if the poet contradicts himself?"

"No."

"Then look at it more closely."

Almost everyone at the beginning of the seventies took the view that *Civilisation* was a "beautiful and well-written poem" —indeed it remained throughout the decade the *beau idéal* of the "intellectually prestigious" (and money-spinning) series which all good little TV chiefs were constantly seeking to repeat. But at the heart of the series was a contradiction so glaring that it might be thought astonishing it was not picked up more widely at the time. On the one hand, Lord Clark was arguing that the rise of Western civilization in the Middle Ages had rested on the revival of the humanist ideals of Greece and Rome. On the other, he could not conceal his intuition that somehow the "drowning of our innocence' may have begun at precisely the moment when those values again became uppermost; when to the heroes of the Renaissance it seemed possible that man and his works, to a degree which not even the ancient world could have imagined, might become truly "the measure of all things." Clark hated much of the way the story had ended up. Yet somehow he seemed unable to draw the connection between all these things.

Of course one reason why Lord Clark was not picked up on such a fundamental hiatus in his argument was that his position is one almost universally shared. As they consider the contemporary plight of mankind, it is not uncommon these days for people to opine that the modern world appears to be going to hell in a handcart. They believe that civilization is in decay. Certainly the state of our arts shows that we have culturally lost confidence on a scale which is quite unprecedented (imagine a world in which we were condemned only to listen to the music, look at the pictures and live in the buildings of the last 20 years—a definition of hell?). Yet the last thing which most people are prepared to accept is that possibly such an outcome might have been absolutely inevitable from the whole course Western civilization has taken over the past 500 years. Of course we revere the past, as an escapist refuge from the spiritual dissonance of the present, as a source of reassuring images to shore us up against our present ruin. We admire Chartres Cathedral more than the New York World Trade Center, Rembrandt more than Mark Rothko, *War and Peace* more than *Last Exit to Brooklyn*. Yet we refuse to put the whole picture together with a proper sense of intellectual consistency, to admit that the ugliness, noise, pollution, triviality, totalitarian horrors, and threatened catastrophes of our world may spring just as surely from our view of man and his relations with the universe as did the Gothic cathedrals from the medieval view of those things. And the chief reason why we do this is our last-ditch reluctance to abandon our one-sided belief in the religion of Progress—that belief that somehow our mighty voyage out of the past has only been a journey out of darkness up into light, out of ignorance into knowledge, out of helpless dependence on nature toward some fondly imagined state of omnipotence. We cannot imagine that we may have got it, at least half, very seriously wrong.

It took a very long time for that gigantic shift of psychological perspective that was implicit in the ending of the Middle Ages and the coming of the Renaissance really to work through in our culture. In a sense it did not fully work through until the middle of the nineteenth century, when the religion of human Progress finally emerged in all its self-congratulatory splendor. The triumphant advance of nineteenth-century industrialism, bringing unimaginable material comfort to millions, the Macaulayan "Whig" view of history, which saw the past as a gradual winning of individual liberty from ancient tyrannies, the Darwinian theory of evolution, which saw the whole history of creation as an impersonal, ineluctable process whereby lower beings evolved into higher (culminating of course in the final glory of mid-nineteenth-century *Homo sapiens* himself), were all the underpinnings of that world view whereby mankind seemed to be being carried up into an ever more delightful, comfortable, omniscient future.

Yet even at that very moment when the doctrine of Progress was finally burgeoning forth, there were a few who recognized that something very fundamental was going astray, that something very important to humanity was being lost. In 1867, the year Karl Marx published the first volume of *Das Kapital* (which he originally wanted to dedicate to his fellow "progressive," Darwin), Matthew Arnold wrote "Dover Beach." This remarkable poem, as poignant as anything in Victorian literature, was an elegy for the lost certainties of those past ages when men still felt themselves to be a part of nature, and religious faith was an expression of that fact:

> The Sea of Faith
> Was once, too, at the full, and round earth's shore
> Lay like the folds of a bright girdle furl'd.

Now, in the high noon of Victorian industrialism, as the human race was being carried forward by the irresistible advance of new technology, new knowledge, that old simple, largely unconscious faith was, scarcely surprisingly, vanishing like a fast-ebbing tide:

> ... I only hear
> Its melancholy, long, withdrawing roar,
> Retreating, to the breath
> Of the night-wind, down the vast edges drear
> And naked shingles of the world.

A new faith had arisen, a faith in man himself—the religion shared by Macaulay, Darwin, Marx, and almost all the leading prophets of that age. Yet, as Arnold sharp-sightedly perceived, the vision of a future world which that religion held out to its devotees, though it

> ... seems
> To lie before us like a land of dreams,
> So various, so beautiful, so new,

would ultimately bring to mankind

> ... neither joy, nor love, nor light,
> Nor certitude, nor peace, nor help for pain.

Exactly a hundred years after Arnold wrote those words, in 1967, Kenneth Clark began writing his *Civilisation*—taking a very much less one-sidedly rosy view of where Progress had led us all to than would have been fashionable in the mid-nineteenth century. Today, a mere 13 years or so after that, we are in an even better position to appreciate Arnold's scepticism, just as, when we look around our contemporary world (or even just switch on the TV news) we can only too easily recognize what he meant by the poem's closing lines, when he said:

> ... we are here as on a darkling plain
> Swept with confused alarms of struggle and flight,
> Where ignorant armies clash by night.

Today we are all on Dover Beach, with a vengeance.

Of course we can all see the benefits which Progress has brought us—hot baths, color television, jet air travel, kidney transplants, frozen food and all the rest—largely those material advances which have cocooned a minority of mankind from the vicissitudes of nature and made their lives more comfortable on a scale which even the most fervent of those Victorian preachers of the Progressive religion would have found unimaginable.

On the other hand, we can also see more clearly than ever before just where that short-lived religion has been taking us, how astonishingly limited it was in its view of the totality of human nature. Even if we do not consciously accept these things, we have begun to express our implicit sense of loss in all those countless hankerings which were perhaps the supreme characteristic of the seventies, hankerings after a lost wholeness, a lost simplicity, a lost innocence—whether they took the form of passions for "whole food" or "nature," for the preservation of old buildings, the following of "new religions," or just those innumerable television serials set amid the cosy reassurance of past ages, from *Upstairs Downstairs* to dramatizations in period costumes of Hardy, Dickens, and Tolstoy. However superficially, every one of these things was in its own way a symptom of that overwhelming desire to take refuge from the dreadful spiritual oppression and vacuity of the world technology and Progress had led us to. Never before in history had there been an age so distrustful of the present, so fearful of the future, so enamored of the past. Therein lay the true significance of the seventies.

But however unconsciously or semiconsciously we betray our feelings, our intuitions about these things, we still have not consciously worked out, any more than Kenneth Clark, just why we should have come to this pass. To do that will require as gigantic and profound a shift in our psychological perspective as that which marked the four centuries after the ending of the Middle Ages and the coming of the Renaissance. It cannot be a shift back to what has gone, it can only be a shift forward to an entirely new view of human nature. To find that new center of perspective is the most urgent challenge confronting mankind today. I hope the rest of this view of the seventies may be seen as making some tiny contribution to that immense task.

Part Two

GLOBAL PERSPECTIVES

INTRODUCTION

As we watched the story of mankind unfolding through the seventies, four great themes consistently overshadowed almost everything else that was happening in the world.

The first, at times obscured by the deceptive pleasantries of *détente,* was the relentless advance in the power and influence of Communism—the greatest such advance since the years after World War II.

The second was the quite startling decline in the power, self-confidence and world standing of the United States— battered by virtual defeat in Southeast Asia, the Watergate scandal, and then the years of well-meaning but confused non-leadership under President Carter.

The third was the steadily looming prospect, not just of the exhaustion of the earth's natural resources, particularly, of course, oil, but of the potentially catastrophic tensions which might be unleashed as the nations of the earth fell to squabbling and warring among themselves over how those diminishing resources might be divided up.

The fourth was the shadow cast over the individual spirit by the advance of a kind of pathological urge to collectivism— urging men to take refuge from the increasing complexities and instabilities of contemporary existence by submerging themselves in every kind of "group think," from the neurotic clamor for "rights" to openly violent terrorism.

As the decade neared its end indeed, with the growing crisis over Iran, Afghanistan, and the future of the Middle East in general, it seemed ominously as though all these stresses and strains were converging as never before—to produce a scenario in which the power drive of Soviet Russia, the newfound weakness of America, the competitive rush to secure dwindling supplies of oil, and that supreme manifestation of pathological "collectivism," the new militant mood of Islam, were combining to demonstrate just what a dangerously unstable mixture they added up to.

This section is made up of a series of reflections on these themes as they emerged to command our attention in the seventies—and I have no hesitation in placing an essay on Alexander Solzhenitsyn at the head of the section because on all these themes he spoke with unrivaled eloquence.

Not only was Solzhenitsyn, for obvious reasons, in a position to warn of the terrible dangers implicit in the growing weakness of the West and the advancing influence of the totalitarian East. He took a lofty enough perspective to perceive that, at root, the two great ideologies which have come to divide our modern world—the "Consumer Capitalism" of the West, the "State Socialism" of the East—have a great deal more in common than we usually suppose. They are both expressions of that humanistic materialism which marks the final phase of mankind's great post-Renaissance adventure; both are ultimately committed to the same fundamental view of man and the purpose of his existence on earth; both are equally inimical to the flowering of man in his individual fullness and spiritual maturity; and both are trying to do something which, in terms of human nature and of the earth's resources, cannot be done. If there is any way forward for mankind, Solzhenitsyn was saying, it cannot lie with *either* of these ideologies: a third, quite different way must be found, transmuting the deadly self-deceptions implicit in both—or our future will be short.

Almost all the remaining essays in this section bear the mark of Solzhenitsyn's preoccupations. After the opening chapter, devoted to some of his various utterances on both the Eastern and Western way of life, I have included a rather more personal and I hope affectionate elegy of my own on the melancholy change which came over our European view of America during the seventies: "Dear America: Meditation on a Lost Dream." I then return to the Socialist East for two essays on our Western attitudes to totalitarianism in China. The essay on that conspicuously world-wide psychopolitical phenomenon of the seventies, terrorism, is chiefly concerned with the West German Baader-Meinhof gang, but the same points could equally have been made about the Palestinian Liberation Front, the IRA in Northern Ireland or any other of those symptoms of "collectivist" thinking at its most brutally anarchic which checkered the history of the decade.

It might seem impossible to say anything new on that internal drama which overshadowed American political life in the seventies—but the essay "Nixon and the Darkness of Watergate" is a reflection on the personal failure which lay at the heart of that black episode. The following brief essay on the moral ambivalence of the Vietnam War was written just before the fall of Saigon in 1975, although its conclusions have only been underlined by events in Southeast Asia since, including of course the world-wide horror evoked by the plight of the escaping boat people in 1979. There is then a philosophical and psychological reflection on that mania, so characteristic of our time, for insistence on "rights"—a notion which, as I try to show, rarely stands up to examination as having any validity other than as a symptom of a psychological condition.

"Ex Africa Semper Id" is a survey of Western attitudes to Africa, where the decade ended with the overthrow of three of the most horrendous tyrants which even that unhappy continent had thrown up in the years following emancipation from "imperialist oppression"—President Amin of Uganda, President Ngueme of Equatorial Africa and the self-styled "Emperor" Bokassa of the Central African Republic; while the same year 1979 also, of course, saw the beginnings of black rule in

Zimbabwe-Rhodesia, a story whose outcome remained as uncertain when the decade ended as the future of the rest of Southern Africa.

The section ends with a brief meditation, written in 1979, on that theme which was likely to dominate the world's politics even more in the eighties than it had done in the seventies—the gathering global energy crisis.

4

THE REAL MESSAGE OF SOLZHENITSYN

Some time in the mid-seventies, I recall a year-end television discussion in Britain in which various commentators were asked which of the events and personalities of the previous 12 months they thought would still be remembered in a century's time. One of the contributors was Malcolm Muggeridge who, in his customarily sweeping way, said that the only figure of our time who would have the remotest claim on the interest of our descendants was Alexander Solzhenitsyn.

Even at the time, I remember, this seemed a rather startling example of Muggeridge overstatement—while today such a claim would probably seem to most people incomprehensible. After he first soared like a skyrocket into the Western heavens in the late sixties and early seventies, as the most glamorous dissident of them all, there is no doubt that Solzhenitsyn's reputation has for some time been on a sharply downward curve. He is still, of course, the most famous writer in the world. But since the zenith between 1970, the year of his Nobel Prize for Literature, and 1974, the year of his expulsion from Russia, when he was besieged by the engines of Western publicity as though he were a Jackie Kennedy or Marilyn Monroe, he has unmistakably begun a slip back into eclipse. On all sides there has been a rising chorus of puzzlement and impatience at some of his more extreme utterances, even of downright hostility. He is dismissed as a "mystic," as a "self-righteous prophet," a "cold warrior." People have long since begun to say that he was overrated as a novelist, that his books are turgid and unreadable. Now that he is holed up in Vermont, behind that security screen, earning all that money, he has lost both roots and role. We need be bothered with him no longer.

In fact, I believe, Solzhenitsyn's writings and pronouncements since he came to the West in the mid-seventies have done more to command our attention than anything he said and wrote (or at least published) before that time. Five years later I have come around entirely to the Muggeridge view—Solzhenitsyn *has* towered over the past decade like no one else. And that is why I have chosen to preface these global reflections on the seventies with a prolonged meditation on various aspects of what Solzhenitsyn has been trying to say to us all—not because we should agree with every word he has uttered, but because, I believe, he has, more powerfully and searchingly than anyone else, managed to draw a perspective on the real nature of the crisis which confronts us.

The first and most obvious reason why Solzhenitsyn laid such particular claim on our attention in the seventies was that these years saw the publication of that somber and majestic work which few who have grasped its message can doubt is the crown of his literary work, *The Gulag Archipelago*.

I remember first becoming aware of the existence of this book, appropriately enough, when driving along a remote road in Czechoslovakia in 1973. A newscast, crackling over the car radio from Austria, announced that in the course of a raid on an apartment in Leningrad the KGB had seized the manuscript of an enormous and hitherto secret book by Solzhenitsyn on the history of the Soviet slave-camp system. The woman who had the illegal manuscript in her possession had committed suicide —but the fact that it was at last in the hands of the Soviet authorities persuaded Solzhenitsyn that it should be published (he had finished it five years before). Within a year the first volume had come out in the West (and Solzhenitsyn himself had been forced into exile). The second volume appeared in 1975, the third in 1978.

The Gulag Archipelago has an unrivaled claim to be called the most important book of the seventies simply because, like no other published during the decade, it has substantially changed the whole way we look at our century. This may seem an odd thing to say. Of course we had "known" almost since the start that the Russian revolution of 1917 was a very two-edged affair: that beneath the surface propaganda that the Bolsheviks were creating a "Brave New World" they were in fact committing the most appalling crimes against the Russian peoples. From Bertrand Russell's *The Practice and Theory of Bolshevism* in 1920, through Muggeridge's *Winter in Moscow* (1934) right up to Robert Conquest's *The Great Terror* in the late sixties, the line of eyewitnesses and historians to tell us that all was not well had been long.

What we had not really hoisted aboard until *Gulag,* however, was the sheer scale of the catastrophe which fell upon the largest country in the world 60 years ago. For decades we were able to think that the Third Reich was the supreme manifestation of evil in our century, simply because we had no real point of reference for the shadowy horrors that had been taking place over a much longer period in Russia. We could at least relate in some small way to Auschwitz and Belsen because we had seen film of them, because they had been documented, described by eyewitnesses, endlessly written about.

It was the first measure of Solzhenitsyn's achievement in *Gulag* that he did at last give us such a frame of reference for what had happened to Russia in the years after 1917. And as a result we began dimly to perceive that the Soviet regime's record of mass-brutality, mass-enslavement, mass-extermination, and genocide had been such as to make the achievements of Hitler and the Nazis seen almost pale by comparison.

Solzhenitsyn brought this home to us in two ways. Firstly he succeeded in providing us for the first time (heaven knows how, for such information can scarcely be freely available in the Soviet Union) with at least the semblance of an overall *history* of the Soviet prison camp system and its associated reign of terror. He was able to take the story right back to the year 1918 when the "organs," that dark, mysterious power which has lain at the heart of Soviet life ever since (the Cheka, the NKVD, the KGB, call it what you will—only the name has been changed) first began to fasten their deadly grip on the Russian people. He was able to chart, step by step, the assembling of that "sewage disposal system" through which wave after wave, millions upon millions of people, were eventually to pass to slavery and death. To produce anything resembling such a documented history was remarkable enough. But Solzhenitsyn's additional master stroke was the way he managed to keep the horror of his story continually alive and in human focus, by counterpointing it with personal detail, vivid snapshots of both his own experiences and those of innumerable others.

No one who has read all the way through *Gulag* can ever forget the nightmarish vision which Solzhenitsyn gradually unfolds, right from the opening section where he simply describes the experience of "Arrest": what it was like for him and for millions of other normal, reasonably happy, innocent Russian citizens to find themselves suddenly one day, without warning, snatched down through the trapdoor into the Kafkaesque underworld, that vast, black cellar which stretched underneath the entire Soviet Union. There are times, as during the description in Volume Two of how hundreds of thousands of prisoners died building the useless White Sea canal in the north of Russia, when one almost thinks one can take no more. As the corpses pile up ever higher in those subzero Arctic wastes, the narrative simply passes beyond our comprehension, made only worse by the sense that for every recognizable face we see, as it were, briefly illuminated by the campfire, there were millions of others suffering in the darkness beyond, of whom we shall never know anything—as in that still almost entirely undocumented episode when, during the collectivization of Russian agriculture in the early thirties, up to 15 million peasants, men, women, and children, were driven out into the wilderness, without food or any means of support, never to be heard of again.

In addition to painting this mighty descriptive canvas, as a memorial to the millions who died (20? 30? 40? 50?), Solzhenitsyn was also anxious throughout the book to make a number of more general points. One was his determination to dispel the view that the Gulag system was just an aberration brought about by the peculiar personality of Stalin. He was at pains to document just how soon after the Revolution the Terror began—how in a sense the Terror was the Revolution, how implicit it was in Lenin's own psychopathic fantasies long before 1917 (as Solzhenitsyn underlined in his novel *Lenin in Zurich,* published between volumes two and three of *Gulag*).

Similarly Solzhenitsyn was at pains to dispel the misconception that somehow the Bolsheviks were only "carrying on" what the old Tsarist regime had begun. Of course the regime under which Tolstoy and Dostoevski had written and published their novels had been authoritarian. It censored books, sent people into exile, deprived them of communion with the Orthodox Church. It even—from time to time—practiced capital punishment against those who sought to overthrow it by force, such as those who assassinated Czar Alexander in 1881, or those who, like Lenin's brother, attempted the same against his successor in 1887. But some of the finest passages of that searing, half-humorous irony in which so much of *Gulag* is written are devoted to recalling the true nature of those horrendous "sufferings" experienced by the pre-1917 revolutionaries in prison or in Siberian exile—where Lenin, for instance, was provided by the authorities with a sheep a week to feed his household, not to mention the services of a housemaid whom the champion of the proletariat did not, of course, disdain to employ.

The fact is that what Solzhenitsyn described in *Gulag* is something that has never happened before in the history of the world. It is something which cannot be explained away as peculiarly Russian, or as just the creation of a lone psychopathic dictator. The catastrophe which has fallen on Russia in the past 60 years must be looked on, in Solzhenitsyn's view, as something absolutely implicit in the strange, deceptive, and self-deceptive nature of that ideology which began to emerge in the Western world a century ago, and which today has more than a third of mankind in its grip. Again and again, in *Gulag* and his other writings, he seeks to emphasize that the "dark underside" of Soviet society cannot be looked on as just some inexplicable, local aberration of the Socialist ideology. The slave camps of the Gulag archipelago were the place where Socialism showed its true face, its true values, more clearly and completely than anywhere else. Forget all the slogans about "the brotherhood of man" and "compassion for the underdog" Solzhenitsyn is saying—they are not just brave ideals which unfortunately have not been realized, they are simply empty noises to conceal the Socialist's true, unconscious intention which is to achieve the maximum power over his fellow human beings and to crush them into submission. Of course, even the Socialist himself may be taken in by his own slogans before he attains complete power: he may genuinely believe, in his conscious mind, that he is doing something fine for mankind, working for a better world. But unconsciously what he is really after all along is to reduce the whole of society to an antheap— an antheap of victims under his control, which may—if "historical necessity" dictates—have to end up as an antheap of corpses.

The real greatness of *The Gulag Archipelago,* like that of any great book, lies in what it can tell us about human nature. And one of the things which *Gulag* tells us, more vividly than any other book ever written, is just how far it is possible for human beings to travel en masse from the human ideal; how it is possible for a human society to fall so far into the shadow of its own consciously-proclaimed intentions that every human value becomes inverted, so that there seems to be no truth, no love, not a shred of kindness any longer, where violence, lies, depravity and cruelty are all that exist. Under its hideous pall of bureaucracy and jargon, Solzhenitsyn describes a world in which human values can be so stood on their head that, as Shakespeare put it, "goodness and wisdom to the vile seem vile, filths savour but themselves"—as we see, for instance, in the official Soviet description of genuinely depraved criminals, thieves, and murderers, as "the socially friendly," "class allies" in the war against the only enemy who matters, the political prisoner, whose only mistake may have been to suggest by a raised eyebrow that the society he is living in is not in every respect perfect. It is a world in which human life can be reduced to such a surreal inversion of "normality" as to become totally meaningless. Yet these things not only can happen and have happened, Solzhenitsyn is saying, they could only have happened in our own time.

Why have I chosen to preface a look at the state of the world in the seventies by discussing a book which is entirely taken up with recording the events of earlier decades of this century?

Partly, of course, because the story Solzhenitsyn had to tell had so many echoes in our world of the 1970s. The dark empire which fathered all these unimaginable horrors might seem to have developed a more human face since the days when Stalin's terror was at its height. But it was still the same empire. It had not, like Hitler's Reich, overreached itself in a meteoric blaze of self-aggrandizement, and then burned out. It had simply continued growing—to the point where, in the seventies, in terms of global influence and military and naval might it finally became the greatest power in the world.

In the 20 years between 1950 and 1970, only two nations in the world indisputably "went Communist," North Vietnam and Cuba (possibly three if you include the Chinese annexation of Tibet). In the 1970s an average of one nation a year toppled over from some kind of neutral or "West-leaning" regime into some kind of Marxism, including South Vietnam, Laos, Cambodia, Angola, Mozambique, South Yemen, Ethiopia, and Afghanistan. From every one of them garbled reports sooner or later emerged of massacres, the setting up of slave camps (or "re-education centers") and all that familiar apparatus of mass terror which Solzhenitsyn had described. From Cambodia indeed, in 1975-6, came a story so chilling and beyond our capacity to imagine that, in cold statistical terms alone (taking into account the proportion of the population that died), it must rank as the worst example of man's inhumanity to man in all history.

It is very hard for us, living amid the cushioned comfort of the West, really to recognize the extent to which our century—which we think of as the highest point yet reached by human civilization—has also created an ever-growing shadow which marks the lowest point ever reached by human civilization. No amount of televised pictures of the fleeing Vietnamese boat people or the empty streets of Pnom-Penh, not even the grim eloquence of Solzhenitsyn himself, can really bring home to us the true horror of what has been, and still is happening "over there" on the other side of the great psychic gulf which divides mankind. But not only do we have an almost inexhaustible capacity (perhaps it is just as well) to cocoon ourselves against a full realization of what is going on in the Communist third of the world. We have an equal capacity to persuade ourselves that our own societies, our own ways of life, are morally and in every other conceivable respect better—and this, of course, is one reason why Solzhenitsyn's reputation has taken such a nosedive since his expulsion from Russia in the mid-seventies.

When Solzhenitsyn came to the West, he not only published *The Gulag Archipelago*. He also, after a decent pause, had the audacity to deliver himself of his thoughts on what he found when he arrived, for the first time in his life, on our side of the fence. And at this point, for all the plaudits and best-seller awards which had been won by his previous onslaughts on the Soviet way of life, the cheering became somewhat thin.

Not to put too fine a point on it, the general reaction to the speech which Solzhenitsyn gave at Harvard in June 1978—when he gave his first extended verdict on the West—was one of incomprehension mingled with outrage. In Britain, the speech—at least initially—was scarcely noticed at all (much more coverage was given to Mrs. Rosalynn Carter's "reply" to

Solzhenitsyn than to his own remarks). While in the United States itself the comments of Harvey Johnson in the *Washington Post* were far from untypical, when he lashed back at Solzhenitsyn for being "arrogant," "infuriating," "annoying," humorless, and generally tiresome.

What on earth did Solzhenitsyn say to arouse such ire? I believe that his Harvard speech was so much the most interesting and important public utterance of the seventies that it is worth dwelling upon in some detail.

Solzhenitsyn devoted the first two-thirds of what he had to say (to a crowd of some 5,000 huddled beneath umbrellas in the pouring rain) to a description of those things which had most forcibly struck him about the state of the West and the Western way of life when, after 60 years living under Communism, he had finally been able to look at them face to face. He did not mince his words. He was profoundly shocked by what he found.

One thing which had struck him was "the decline in courage." The Western world, it seemed to him, betrayed a loss of "civil courage" which had apparently seeped through every level of life. Political, academic, intellectual, and social leaders of all kinds no longer spoke with real inner conviction and authority: they had fallen into a kind of universal weak geniality, a desire to placate, to say what people wanted to hear rather than what they ought to hear.

A second thing which startled Solzhenitsyn, as he came from the backward Soviet Union into a society which had managed to give its citizens a degree of material comfort which even 30 years ago would have seemed inconceivable, was how strained and unhappy so many people look. "The constant desire to have still more things and a still better life, and the struggle to obtain them, imprints many Western faces with worry and depression, though it is customary to conceal such feelings."

A third thing he could not help noticing was the quite extraordinary degree to which our societies have come to place importance on "rights" rather than "obligations" (forgetting that one cannot exist without the other). The speed and regularity with which we were prepared to see any social relationship in terms of the "rights" of one side rather than the "obligations" of both clearly struck him as the manifestation of some profound collective neurosis which had run so deep in our societies that we no longer noticed how strange it was.

A fourth shock which Solzhenitsyn had on coming to the West was to look at our newspapers and television. Only someone who is familiar with the Communist press, with its heavy diet of enormously lengthy speeches, no gossip, no crime and an almost eerie lack of hard facts, can perhaps imagine the eagerness with which Solzhenitsyn looked forward to reading for the first time in his life a press that was truly "free." But two things soon depressed him beyond measure. The first was the relentless triviality of so much of what is still laughably known as the "serious" press. The second was how astonishingly conformist it is, in terms of what it thinks important and in terms of those ideas, acceptable to the conventional wisdom, which it allows through. "Without any censorship, in the West fashionable trends of thought are carefully separated from those which are not fashionable: nothing is forbidden, but what is not fashionable will hardly ever find its way into periodicals or books or be heard in colleges."

So far it might have been possible to see in Solzhenitsyn's picture of the West as a society full of weak, unhappy, squabbling, self-righteous children, obsessed with comformity and trivia, little more than a grotesque caricature, a string of overstated cliches—though even here some Westerners might have caught in Solzhenitsyn's words an echo of that profound spiritual sickness which they themselves sense has come over Western civilization in recent decades, and which has given the whole flavor of our public and private life a sickly, strained, superficial quality, as if something terrible has been happening to us all, without our really daring to admit it.

But then Solzhenitsyn went on to draw a conclusion to the first two-thirds of his speech in which he really came out of his corner—and it is not exactly difficult to see why his American hosts took it so hard. Not only, he said, could he no longer recommend Western society as an ideal to which the Communist world should aspire. He would now, as a result of his direct experience of life in the West, have to go much further. "Through intense suffering, our country has now achieved a spiritual development of such intensity that the Western system in its present state of spiritual exhaustion" looks singularly unattractive. "A fact which cannot be disputed is the weakening of human beings in the West, while in the East they are becoming firmer and stronger." In the six decades since the Revolution, "we have been through a spiritual training far in advance of Western experience. Life's complexity and moral weight have produced stronger, deeper, more interesting characters than those generated by standardized Western well-being."

It is scarcely surprising that the plastic battalions rose up behind Rosalynn Carter when she howled in outrage at this suggestion that, morally and spiritually, free Americans might actually score less points than Soviet slaves (she pointed out that, in the previous year, Americans had given more than 35 billion dollars in philanthropic contributions). But Solzhenitsyn was still not finished in his almost desperate attempt to find some chink in that bland complacency. "There are meaningful warnings which history gives to a threatened or perishing society. Such as, for instance, the decadence of art or the lack of great statesmen. There are evident and open warnings too. The center of your democracy and your culture is left without electric power for a few hours only, and all of a sudden, American citizens start looting and creating havoc. . . . The fight for our planet, physical and spiritual, a fight of cosmic proportions, is not a vague matter of the future. It has already started. The forces of evil have begun their decisive offensive, you can feel their pressure, and yet your screens and publications are full of prescribed smiles and raised glasses. What is the joy about?" Thus saying, Solzhenitsyn switched for the last third of his speech onto a new, rather more startling tack.

* * *

How was it, he asked, after centuries of apparently triumphant advance as the spearhead of man's progress, that our Western civilization should quite suddenly have been reduced to this appalling state of spiritual debilitation? How is it that, since World War II, the West has become so placatory, so impotent, so lacking in moral fiber? He saw us as a weak man who simply wants to cling onto his easy life, and to hide from reality, desperately hoping that the status quo will somehow be preserved—while year by year, the great shadow of Soviet power lengthens ever further over the future of mankind, and one "faraway little country" after another slips into the totalitarian darkness. He saw us even pathetically hoping that China, a worse totalitarian power than the Soviet Union, might prove to be an ally in preserving our fragile freedom and our material comforts. Again and again, the force of his argument here was reminiscent of those words of Yeats which, with only a shift in tense, could still become the epitaph for our twentieth-century civilization: "Things fell apart, the centre could not hold . . . the best lacked all conviction, while the worst were full of passionate intensity."

What Solzhenitsyn was working up to was his belief that, to an extent which few have accepted, mankind in the last 20 years of the twentieth century is approaching a real moment of crisis; not just a hiccup like the two world wars, but a watershed in man's development more important than any since the end of the Middle Ages and the dawn of the Renaissance. No longer was it just a matter of blithely hoping, as did he and his friends during the darkest night of Stalinism, that somehow the superior moral values of the West would one day prevail and that the Communist system would eventually become gentler, more liberal, and more humane. The day when any of us could take refuge in such foolish hopes is past. We had to take a much deeper, more honest, and more painful look at the reality of what has been happening—which must involve a drastic shift in our perspective, not just on the past 20 years, but over a period going back very much further into our past. "The West," as Solzhenitsyn put it, "kept advancing socially in accordance with its proclaimed intentions, with the help of brilliant technological progress. And all of a sudden it found itself in this present state of weakness. This means that the mistake must be at the root, at the very basis of human thinking in the past few centuries."

What Solzhenitsyn was referring to was nothing less than that entire shift in Western consciousness which had begun to take place during the Renaissance and which began to find "its political expression from the period of the Enlightenment"; that world view which gradually came to underlie the whole political, social, and scientific advance of the West and which may be defined as "rationalistic humanism" or "humanistic autonomy." Solzhenitsyn was not, of course, suggesting that European civilization could or should have remained stuck in the Middle Ages. The culture of the Middle Ages had so one-sidedly exalted man's spiritual nature above his physical nature that some kind of pendulum-swing in the opposite direction was "historically inevitable." But he then asked us to consider what had been the real consequence of that fundamental shift in man's view of himself which took place after the Renaissance (a view incidentally which has so come to dominate the outlook of our civilization that most people are no longer aware there could be any other). What eventually emerged was a view of man such as had never been held before in the history of the world. And here, expressing more forcefully than ever before a conviction which had clearly been growing on him for some time, Solzhenitsyn came to the real crux of his speech.

Seen in this light, he argued, the light of man's development over the past five centuries, the two great ideological poles which now divide the earth look nothing like so far apart as we have been accustomed to think them. Both the Eastern and the Western ideologies are fundamentally materialist and humanist in their view of man. For a long time our Christian heritage, with its "great reserves of mercy and sacrifice," appeared to give a spiritual underpinning to the whole forward thrust of Western civilization. But increasingly those reserves have been exhausted, to the point where we are being finally forced face to face with the fact that the real driving force behind both the Socialism of the East and the "despiritualized humanism" of the West is precisely the same: it is nothing more elevated than the desire that as many citizens as possible should be enabled to live as long as possible in the greatest degree of material comfort.

Now most people's reactions to such an argument are probably that it begs so many questions as to be meaningless. For a start, it simply ignores the colossal differences between the two kinds of society—let us say American and Russian—which nobody can deny. On the one hand, we have a society which is more free than any in history; on the other, we have a society which has oppressed, imprisoned, and murdered its citizens on a scale never known before. How can Solzhenitsyn possibly be making any equation between such polar opposites? Well, we may remind ourselves who, more than anyone else, has been able to tell us about the unprecedented iniquities of the Soviet system. It is scarcely likely that the author of *The Gulag Archipelago* would have overlooked such a simple point. In other words, he must be meaning something, in his view, even more important.

What Solzhenitsyn was in fact addressing himself to was the curious way in which there appears to have been built into this "current of materialism" which has run ever more strongly through Western civilization in the past few centuries, a fundamental drive to the Left. The "logic of materialist development" seems to have dictated that the Left will always end up "stronger, more attractive and victorious, because it is more consistent. Humanism without its Christian heritage cannot resist such competition. We watch this process in the past centuries, and especially in the past decades, as on a world scale the situation has become increasingly dramatic. Liberalism was inevitably displaced by Radicalism. Radicalism had to surrender to Socialism, and Socialism could never resist Communism."

Certainly from a British point of view it cannot be denied that such a "leftward drift" has made the overall running in our political development for a very long time, even if it has not yet ended in a victory for Communism. Ever since the heyday of *laisser-faire* liberalism in the mid-nineteenth century, the on-ward march of state control, bureaucracy, welfarism, and social engineering ("egalitarianism") has been pretty well unchecked; and despite occasional flurries of "reaction," such as Mrs. Thatcher's present attempts to "reverse the tide" in the name of her "new Conservatism," the underlying process has continued in recent years with remarkable speed. In view of the dramatic move to the left of the British Labour Party during the seventies (e.g. the now open sympathy of many trade union leaders with the regimes of Eastern Europe) it seems quite extraordinary to contemplate that, in 1959, less than 20 years ago, influential Labour leaders like Hugh Gaitskell were con-templating the abandonment of plans for further state owner-ship as "no longer relevant." In those days most people in Britain looked on America as the most likely model for our future social development; whereas, a year or two back, when I was watching a fairly glowing account on British TV of life in East Germany, showing a society with full employment, no inflation, no taxes, and cheap subsidised housing for all, I could not help reflecting how the picture it presented would now strike many people in Britain as rather enviable.

Much more importantly, however, the same general pattern Solzhenitsyn is talking about (with such comparatively trivial exceptions as Greece after World War II, or more recently Chile and Portugal) has been observable all over the world. The overriding political tendency of mankind in the twentieth cen-tury has not been to move in the direction of Western-style democracy, but toward the totalitarian left, with the proportion of the earth's nations living under such regimes rising by a seemingly inexorable momentum. The chief international odium of our century has been reserved for those countries and governments which, in attempting to stand out against this tide, have lurched to the other end of the political spectrum— above all, of course, Hitler's Germany, but also South Africa and the juntas of South America. One must also include, among such attempts to stem the tide, America's intervention in Vietnam. Indeed the most dramatic development of all on the world political scene in the past decade has perhaps been the extent to which the United States itself, the chief flagship of Western democracy, which 20 years ago was the undisputed "superpower" of the world, both in terms of its military might and political authority, now seems to have faltered and fallen away—to the point where it seems little more than *primus inter pares* among that small group of Western nations most of whom, to a greater or lesser extent, have been afflicted by a not dissimilar crisis of confidence.

Are we then to assume that somehow it is built into the whole underlying tendency of our post-Renaissance, materialist civilization that sooner or later the superior confidence and single mindedness of the totalitarian left will conquer everywhere; that all attempts to stem the tide will look as absurd and short-lived as America's adventure in Indochina, or Ian Smith's stand against black nationalism in Southern Africa; and that ultimately the whole globe will languish under the same totalitarian night as do Russia, China, and some 30 or 40 other countries today?

Obviously it is not as simple as that. It seems inconceivable that the "leftward tide" will simply roll on until it has swallowed up not just Western Europe, but Australia, Canada, and even the United States itself. The West may in recent years have shown unprecedented weakness and uncertainty. Indeed the curious difficulty the West appears to have in standing up effectively and with conviction for its own values, may mean that yet more "faraway little nations" (Iran? Turkey? Zimbabwe? Nicaragua? Saudi Arabia?) will slip away onto the other side of the ideological fence. But sooner or later, as the pressure of the great leftward impetus is maintained, a line, however messily or irrationally, will have to be drawn. Some kind of final confrontation between the two great world systems—one retreating, the other advancing—is inevitable. And after that, who knows?

The essence of what Solzhenitsyn was saying at Harvard is that ultimately the great humanist, materialist adventure on which man has embarked in the past 500 years is not going to work. Even at this late stage, we desperately try to convince ourselves by every conceivable means that it *has* worked. It has so transformed man's relationship with nature that we have for some time now seen dancing tantalizingly in front of us the possibility of achieving the final materialist Utopia, in which everyone on earth is fed, clothed, and surrounded with every good thing he could wish.

But somehow, all along, this wonderful advance has been dogged by an equally-advancing shadow—a shadow which has already produced a series of catastrophes unprecedented in mankind's experience and which threatens even worse to come. In particular there seems to be built into the whole pattern of man's advance down this road the tendency to a fundamental state of conflict which it is inconceivable can ever be peacefully resolved. Even the Communist world itself is far from being a monolith and is riven by every kind of nationalistic discord (Russia v. China, China v. Vietnam, Vietnam v. Cambodia) which could sooner or later break out into wars just as terrible and destructive as any between East and West. And the likelihood is that all these existing strains will finally be exacerbated to breaking point, if they have not reached it before, by the struggle to lay hands on that ever-dwindling supply of natural resources on which the whole materialist adventure depends.

Ultimately, of course, Solzhenitsyn does not derive his certainty that the materialist view of man's destiny cannot work from his appraisal of geopolitics, but from something much deeper and more personal. It cannot work, he believes, simply because it is based on a total misreading of man's fundamental nature and of his relations with the universe. If the Soviet experiment of the past 60 years has demonstrated one thing above all else it is that, if you subject men to the very extremes of material and spiritual deprivation, if you force lies into their ears and surround them from birth to death with nothing but the materialist, humanist view of man in its most grandiloquent, exalted form, you will find that in the end many of them discover an entirely new, spiritual center to their existence *within themselves,* because it is imprinted within us to an extent which it is beyond the power of any earthly force or ideology to eradicate.

When I said earlier that the greatness of *The Gulag Archipelago,* like that of any great book, lies in what it has to tell us about human nature, I mentioned only what it reveals about the darker side of human nature. But in the second volume of *Gulag,* as Solzhenitsyn relentlessly heaps up his ever more horrific mass of evidence about the nature of that dark, frozen kingdom of death to the point where one thinks one can take no more—suddenly, just as the darkness is blackest, there is an amazing shaft of light. In the chapter called "The Ascent," Solzhenitsyn speaks for the first time of the extraordinary way in which, in the very depths and extremes of misery, deprivation, and suffering, it proved possible for human beings to find in some inmost recess of themselves a quite unexpected source of spiritual light and strength, making it impossible for them ever to look upon human existence in quite the same way again. This was the turning point in the story Solzhenitsyn had to tell in *Gulag,* not unreminiscent of that moment in the *Divine Comedy* when Dante reaches the very bottom of the *Inferno,* thinking he can take no more, and then suddenly, in the freezing, suffocating darkness, discovers that he is no longer traveling downward but up. Such an experience was obviously the turning point in Solzhenitsyn's own story, suffusing his own life with undreamed of new meaning, gradually transforming the whole way in which he came to look at the collective experience of mankind in the twentieth century. And that was why, nearly 30 years later, he was able to end his Harvard speech on such a note of unshakable confidence in saying:

"If the world has not come to its end, it has approached a major turn in history, equal in importance to the turn from the Middle Ages to the Renaissance. It will exact from us a spiritual upsurge, we shall have to rise to a new height of vision, a new level of life, where our physical nature will not be cursed, as in the Middle Ages, but even more importantly, our spiritual being will not be trampled on as in the Modern Era. This ascension will be similar to climbing onto the next anthropological stage. No one on earth has any way left but—upward."

One reason perhaps why few people in the West were able to grasp what Solzhenitsyn was trying to tell us all that day in 1978 was simply that so few of us have even remotely shared the kind of experience and the kind of suffering that had led him to such convictions. Yet I believe that nothing he has said should give us more pause for thought than his shocked realization, when he came to the West, that in some fundamental way we had lost our spiritual and moral bearings even more completely than the enslaved peoples of the East he had left behind: his conviction that it has not been in the free, affluent, complacent West in recent decades that individuals have most obviously developed inner strength and stature by rediscovering the core of their identity as human beings, but in the Soviet empire itself, at the heart of the most appalling crime against humanity ever recorded, where for untold millions life has often been reduced to its very barest material essentials, where the outer world has been transformed into meaningless nightmare, where all external grounds for hope have been removed. At least in the Communist world, Solzhenitsyn is saying, the materialist-humanist philosophy has reached the end of the road; it has revealed its true nature, its moral, spiritual, intellectual, and esthetic bankruptcy, so starkly that it has been possible for men to see it clearly for what it is. In the West, we have not yet seen these things. We have been lulled by our material abundance into a state of weak, infantile, wishful thinking, where we have forgotten what it is to be fully human in a rather different way—and the worst thing of all is that we are not even aware of the true nature of our disease. It is for this above all, I believe, that we should honor Solzhenitsyn—as the towering figure who, more than any other in our time, has been trying to recall us to ourselves.

5

DEAR AMERICA: MEDITATION ON A LOST DREAM

In the late autumn of 1979, shortly before the end of the decade, there arrived in London a film called *Yanks*. Its intention I gather (I'm afraid that, like most other people, I did not actually go to see it) was to exploit that cosy nostalgia on both sides of the Atlantic for those brave days 40 years ago when, amid the darkness of World War II, the towns and villages of England were suddenly filled with warmhearted, glamorous, gum-chewing GI's, come to help us deal the final blows against Hitler's Europe.

As I read the accounts of *Yanks,* I found myself reflecting on just what an extraordinary change had come over our image of America since that time 40 years ago. As fate would have it, the film came to Britain at just about the time of the seizure of the U.S. Embassy in Teheran—precipitating that crisis which, more than anything else, brought to a head our realization of just how weak, or impotent, the United States seemed to have become on the world stage. And for anyone of my age, the psychological impact of what has happened to America in the past decade or so has been arguably the single most disturbing thing to have happened to the world in our lifetime.

As was true of millions of other Britons, my inward image of America was first formed during World War II at the very time the film *Yanks* was describing. I lived as a child in the remote county of Devonshire, in southwest England. As I came to consciousness of the outer world, around 1940 and 1941, I became aware that my country was beleaguered in a battle to the death with some enormous, terrifying, seemingly all-powerful monster called Hitler, who was "over there" across the sea which lay only a few miles from where we lived. With fearful excitement, we used to watch his planes flying in low across our hills to bomb cities such as Exeter, Cardiff, and Bristol. On one occasion, the planes even flew with seemingly total impunity up our own valley, machine-gunning the main street of our little market town of Honiton.

Then slowly, around 1943, the mood changed. We began to think we might actually be going to win the war. And the most important reason why we felt this growing sense of confidence was the increasingly obvious presence all around us of a huge American war machine. To put it like this makes the American presence in Devon in 1943 and 1944 seem something grim and impersonal—but, of course, it was not like that at all. Despite the fact that our country lanes were now filled by a mass of unfamiliar vehicles, jeeps and trucks and DUKW amphibious landing craft, and our skies with Liberators and Flying Fortresses from nearby airfields, the main thing any of us knew about the Yanks was how likable, friendly and informal they were.

We even used to make jokes about this lack of formality—how these GI's lacked real discipline, they couldn't march in step properly (like our British soldiers), how they wore their uniforms and caps in a sloppy way. And some of our jokes betrayed something deeper.

After the North African campaign, for instance, I remember how we six-year-olds used to tell the story of how there was some hill, strongly held by the Germans, which the Americans, for all their expensive equipment, had been unable to take. The British Guards Division had been called in, drove the Germans out, and handed the hill over to their U.S. colleagues. But the Yanks had taken so long in moving up their refrigerators, Coca-Cola, and other comforts, that the Germans had taken the hill back—so the Guards had to be called in to do their stuff all over again.

Or, around the time of D-Day, there was the story of how the U.S. 8th Air Force had been given the task of "taking out" a crucial bridge over the Seine at Rouen. Hundreds of B-24's and B-17's had gone over at 20,000 feet and showered the ancient city of Rouen with high explosive. When the smoke cleared, the cathedral and much of the old city lay in ruins—but the vital bridge still stood, undamaged. The R.A.F. were called in, sent in two Mosquito precision bombers at 30 feet, and they neatly demolished the bridge on their first run.

Looking back, I suppose that we used to tell these stories at least partly just as a salve to our national pride, to console ourselves for the way we had come to look on the Americans—these hugely rich and powerful cousins from across the Atlantic—as our protecters. We relied on them completely. If they were casual, it was only the casualness born of total confidence and unlimited material resources. But for the people of a country who had been through the Battle of Britain, which was still in theory the center of a worldwide empire, covering a quarter of mankind, it was quite a blow to find just how much we had suddenly become the weak, dependent junior partner.

From 1945 onward, of course, with the dawn of the atomic era, it became second nature for us to look on the Americans not just as by far the most powerful nation in the world—but as our ultimate psychological guarantee that all was going to be well, that our future peace and security were assured. There were sticky moments, Korea, Suez. But through the 15 years after the war, through the Truman and Eisenhower eras, we never really had to worry very deeply about the future because America would always be there to look after us.

In the late fifties, indeed, there was another way in which we came to look on America as a symbol that our future was bright. In the years after 1950, as Britain and other Western European countries began to recover (not least thanks to Marshall Aid) from the devastation of the war, we slowly realized that the kind of prosperity we were emerging into was not just a return to the better times many older people remembered from "prewar." We were heading forward and upward into something quite new. As television and car ownership, washing machines and refrigerators spread down through the whole of society, as supermarkets and office blocks in the "modern" style began to proliferate through the streets of our towns and cities, we found we were heading for that paradise which we learned from Professor Galbraith to call "affluence"—and of course the country which, way ahead of us, already represented that paradise was America.

The cultural influence of America had been fairly strong in Britain for decades, thanks to Hollywood, popular songs, musicals, and all those other expressions of the way America had in the twentieth century pioneered the techniques of a mass consumer society. But all this was as nothing compared to the tidal wave of American influence which hit Britain in the fifties (symbolized as much as anything by the arrival of "commercial television," with its advertisements and jingles, such a shattering contrast to the staid and deferential BBC). At all levels of society, the image of the United States and "the American way" became unimaginably glamorous. At a typically traditional English boarding school in the mid-fifties, I remember how, as an almost holy ritual, we would creep down at dead-of-night to listen to Willis Conover on "The Voice of America Jazz Hour," how I risked expulsion one day by running away to London to hear the first postwar concert given in Britain by Louis Armstrong. Up at Cambridge University in the late fifties, where the old "class barriers" seemed suddenly embarrassing, we took refuge more than ever in Americanism as the way forward to a liberated future—as we read *The Catcher in the Rye* and *Lolita,* wore jeans and dark glasses, listened to Miles Davis and Buck Clayton, flipped our fingers, described everything as "cool," and addressed each other as "man." Here was the "classless" middle ground on which, for the younger generation at least, all the taboos and class-oriented conventions which had bedeviled English life for so long could and would be finally dissolved.

For me, as I suppose for many, the high point of this love affair with everything American was the election of John F. Kennedy as President in 1960. I recall listening to Kennedy's inauguration speech on that freezing Washington day in January 1961, sitting in the basement cinema of the U.S. Embassy in London, along with several hundred members of the Embassy staff and not a few Britons. For us it was a religious ceremonial—and I do not use the metaphor lightly. Our faith and belief in America and all she stood for provided so many of the props which a religious faith can give that it was, if truth be told, the most profound source of reassurance which many of us at that time knew.

Then came that day which I suppose must be looked back on as the central moment of the whole post World War II era— November 22, 1963, and the assassination in Dallas. As an American friend put it to me, years later, "The world went a little crazy at that moment, and it has never really recovered."

I made my first visit to America only a few weeks after the assassination (in fact I was over there with the British TW3 team to re-enact our "Tribute to JFK" in Madison Square Garden—I had written a certain amount of the script). New York was everything I had dreamed of—a spectacular, exhilarating city, of which I spent most of my time taking moving pictures. But people were still stunned by the Dallas tragedy, there was a kind of muffled air to conversation. A few weeks later, after a trip to the West Indies, I returned to New York to find that the whole atmosphere had changed. Obviously as an Englishman I noticed it more than some, but as I realized from my first conversation with the proverbial cab driver (and from the store windows of Fifth Avenue full of cardboard cutouts of Big Ben and pictures of London "bobbies") the city had gone Britain-crazy—or, to be more precise, "Beatle-crazy." There was a kind of surreal infantilism about the way everyone was obsessively talking about these four English adolescents (who had just arrived in the city) that was like a premonition of what was to come.

A few months later, in the summer of 1964, I made a second return to New York. I was given a memorable tour of every corner of the city by the film maker Emile di Antonio. As we came down through Harlem and saw the sullen faces watching us from the sidewalk, he said, "There's going to be trouble here soon. Harlem is like a great black bird sitting on New York's shoulder, and soon it is going to pounce." Within weeks that trouble had erupted—and over the next three or four years our image of America underwent a transformation. First there were the race riots, then the years of the great escalation in Vietnam. In Europe we began to look in amazement at what was happening to this country which for so long had been the almost unconscious cornerstone of our sense of security.

Of course America's own view of herself changed just as radically during these years. In 1968 I recall spending an evening in a cottage deep in the tranquil Sussex countryside with the editor of *Esquire,* Harold Hayes. As we talked into the night he was gloomy about the world in general and the state of America in particular in a way I had never known an American to be before. It was not just Vietnam, race riots, assassinations, and violence, but that whole wave of change, insecurity, and doubt that seemed suddenly to be roaring unleashed through American life—permissiveness, hippies, drug addiction, fears over pollution and the poisoning of lakes and rivers, runaway technology—what *was* this nightmare which seemed to be engulfing America?

Despite a brief flicker of hope on the accession of President Nixon, things continued to get worse—My Lai, the Manson killings, the bombing of Cambodia, Kent State. But at least during those first years of the Nixon Administration, with Kissinger's shuttle diplomacy and the opening up of relations with Mao's China—and for all her continuing difficulties in Southeast Asia—the United States still seemed very much a superpower, even if one which had got slightly and temporarily out of control.

Then, however, came Watergate, the resignations of Agnew

and Nixon, the "scuttle from Southeast Asia," the great mid-seventies advance of Communist power and influence almost all over the world—and we began to look on America in an even more alarming light. As we watched the unfolding presidencies of Gerald Ford and his successor, the unknown from Georgia, we began to wake up to the unnerving fact that we no longer felt that America was a great, confident presence towering benignly over the world scene. The old rock had become as shaky as the once almighty dollar itself. As the world entered the early stages of the "energy crisis," doubts began to multiply even over that picture of mankind's forward march toward an American-style future, based as it was on the premise of unlimited economic growth. America no longer seemed able to throw up strong, mature, responsible politicians—she seemed to have become soft, bewildered. As we looked at the beginnings of the 1980 Presidential election campaign and the array of rather weak, mediocre men vying for the leadership of America, as we sat through the beginnings of the Teheran hostage crisis, the invasion of Afghanistan, and the confused Olympic boycott campaign, we became very worried indeed. What had happened to this great, rich, powerful transatlantic cousin on whom we so deeply depended? There seemed finally no bucking the admission that she had lost her way. And in the cloud of doubt and anxiety which gathered through the seventies over our image of America were written question marks which overshadowed our whole view of the future of the human race.

To get some deeper perspective on the real significance of the change that has come over our European view of America in the past ten or 15 years, I think one has to consider the enormous psychological importance of America to Europe not just since World War II, but over a period going very much further back into history—right back indeed to the time when the Western Europeans first discovered America in the late fifteenth century. Europe in the late Middle Ages was in a state of deep, inner unease. The great medieval construct of a world view based on the identification of God, Papacy, and Empire and a universal framework of religious and feudal obligation binding together the whole of European Christendom, had been one of the greatest achievements in building an effective "social myth" in the history of mankind. But beneath this mighty cathedral-like structure, the foundations were shifting.

Men were beginning to look outward into the world in a new way. They were turning their attention from that spiritual, inner dimension which held the whole structure together, out into the external, natural, physical world—as was shown nowhere more subtly than in the change which came over painting as early as 1300, when artists like Giotto ceased to be content with painting timeless, placeless icons, and began with increasing confidence to reflect the "real" outward world, the way things "actually looked."

In fact few things more obviously burst a hole in the tight frame of the medieval world view than the voyages of the fifteenth century, and in particular the discovery of the New World. Over the next century, the Europeans began that massive series of projections onto the New World which have comforted them ever since. The Americas were Eldorado, the land of gold and fabulous riches. They were the land of freedom, where men could escape from the restrictions of closed societies at home to live in a new, unfettered way. They were the land where, confronted by the vastness of the wilderness, with fierce tribes to be subdued, men could be men.

From 1500 to 1900, these projections grew and grew. For millions it was only the dream of America which made life in Europe supportable: she was the ultimate refuge for the oppressed, the only way out from the suffocating weight of the past, the very symbol of hope and of "new life." Then, in the early twentieth century, we began to look on America in a new way—not just as a free, boundless extension of the European way of life, a way of renewal for millions who had found life in Europe too much for them—but as a country which was now in many respects overtaking the civilization which had given it birth. As America grew ever richer, producing a wealth of inventions from the elevator to the airplane, from refrigeration to barbed wire, she was actually beginning to pioneer the way forward for our whole civilization.

It was not long before we also began to rely on America for the first time in a still more unexpected way—when those first, fresh American divisions poured out onto the soil of France in 1917 to push the balance of the war fatally against Germany, and in favor of "democracy" and "freedom." America had become the backstop to our highest values. She had entered on that role which reached its zenith in the minds of Englishmen on the day in 1941 when, in his famous speech to Congress, Winston Churchill proclaimed the words of the hymn, "... but Westward, look, the land is bright!"; that role which continued to underpin our confidence in the future right through to Kennedy's proclamation in 1963, "Ich bin ein Berliner"—and which has so catastrophically begun to crumble in the seventies.

What is it that has so fatally begun to undermine our almost unconscious faith in America in the last ten years, an event which, as I am suggesting, has significance not just on the time scale of these past few decades but going back almost 500 years?

It cannot be explained merely by the fact that America has had the misfortune to go through an unprecedented political crisis, or lost the war in Southeast Asia, or has produced a series of weak, unimpressive leaders. After all, the United States has had her major internal crises, like McCarthyism, before; she has had unimpressive Presidents before, such as Harding or Hoover; these things did not detract from our view of her as a mighty, if occasionally slumbering giant.

What I think has really worried us is that, for the first time, we have come to have real doubts about the whole process of mankind's evolution which America has increasingly in the past century come to symbolize. America has become the supreme symbol of the belief that mankind's future lay in becoming ever richer, ever more the master of nature, ever more capable of arranging the world to our material comfort and convenience. The whole history of America from Columbus on has been the story of "manifest destiny," of European man's ability to make a break with the past, to smash out into virgin lands, to subdue the wilderness and the barbarous, uncivilized people who lived there—and to build a new society, freer and richer than any the world had seen. It was entirely appropriate that, from the mid-nineteenth century on, America should increasingly have been the pioneer of new technologies—because it was above all through inventions and machines that this Utopia was to be ushered in.

Yet in the past ten years, more than ever before, doubts have crept over the very basis of the belief that this is the way mankind should or can go. We have seen the beginnings of the world energy crisis, we have seen mounting worries over pollution and the whole balance between man and nature. We have seen the dottiness and superficiality which can come over societies as they embrace the values of materialism and surrender to the omnipresent invasion of television—bringing a wholesale regression into infantilism, a subtle undermining of the sense of reality. In all these respects, America has become the symbol not of a strong, assured, confident giant, striding into the future—but of a society which now stands more than ever as a warning of where such a self-deceptive process can lead to, the country which more than any has fallen under the spell of television, with all the trivilization of life which that induces, not to mention the possibly fatal effect on the grasp of reality of its leaders. We see a country trying to do something which it is becoming obvious simply cannot be done—which is to exploit and to defy nature merely to become richer and richer without limit, and without wreaking a mortal blow to the psyche of all those involved.

What is most worrying of all is that we are still all dependent on America. We see the dark shadow of Communism spreading like a malignant growth across the globe. We still love and put our trust in America, as a country which is exhilarating to visit, whose people are still full of energy, boundlessly generous. But we wonder whether the whole course of America has not been based on a false premise. Can she change that course—or is she inevitably heading for some ultimate disaster, the seeds of which were sown right back at that time when the Europeans first began to dream that they had discovered a kingdom of heaven on earth, their "New World?"

6

THE DESTRUCTION OF CHINA

July 28, 1978
You are all old enough to remember our old towns—towns
made for people, horses, dogs—and the trams too; towns
which were humane, friendly, cosy places, where... there was
a garden to almost every house and hardly a house more than
two stories high.
—Alexander Solzhenitsyn, *Letter to Soviet Leaders,* 1974

According to the late-lamented Marshall McLuhan, we live in
the age of the "global village." It might be more apt to say that
we live in the century of the "Potemkin village." Grigory
Potemkin, it will be recalled, was the favorite of Catherine the
Great who, in 1787, when his sovereign was about to make a
tour of the newly annexed Crimea, arranged for a number of
large, prosperous-looking fake villages to be erected along the
line of her route so that Catherine would believe her new domin-
ions to be much richer and more populous than they in fact
were.

Anything Potemkin could do, his twentieth-century succes-
sors have done far more effectively and on an infinitely grander
scale. We are all now familiar with the success in the 1930s of
the Soviet propaganda campaign to convince gullible Westerners that starving, oppressed Russia was a land flowing
with *crèches,* power stations, and happy and contented citizens; or with the famous occasion in particular when, in 1944,
Henry Wallace and Owen Lattimore were taken around the
slave camps of the Kolyma and Magadan and shown NKVD

office staff dressed up as swineherds on a model farm, and healthy, smiling "prisoners" working in a gold mine.

The most eerie thing about the flood of reports which have come out of China in recent years, whether from distinguished Western journalists trotting around with Nixon, Heath, or Thatcher, bringing us first-hand reports on the menu at banquets in the Great Hall of the Peoples, or BBC-2 films showing the smiling peasants of the Kwang-ho commune indulging in "healthy self-criticism," has been how astonishingly reminiscent they have been of the general image that so many Western visitors gave of Soviet Russia 30 or 40 years ago.

It is obviously true that considerable changes have overtaken China in recent years—if only as reflected in the fact that Western visitors have once again been allowed into the country which, for the five or six years of the Cultural Revolution at least, remained almost wholly closed off to the outside world. The ending of that vast internal upheaval, the deaths of Chou-en-Lai and Chairman Mao, the emergence of a new leadership, even the pitiful and soon stifled flickerings of a desire for free speech—all these things mean that we came to look on China in a rather different way as the decade unfolded. But how much has the most populous totalitarian state in the world really changed its character? How much do we really know about what has been going on there over the past ten or 20 years? How much have we simply read into the enigma of modern China what we wanted to see, or more important still, what the Chinese themselves wanted us to see?

One of the most remarkable accounts of life in modern China to have been published in recent years is the book *Chinese Shadows* by Simon Leys. For almost the first time it gives us some glimmering of what has really been going on in China in recent decades, or at least a picture of how things looked to a relative insider who, although he was last there in 1972, is an art historian who is soaked in Chinese culture, is married to a Chinese wife, loves the country "more than my own" (he is Belgian), and certainly was able to observe what happened to

China in the crucial period between 1955 and the end of the Cultural Revolution more intimately than anyone else who has so far been able to give us an account of it.

Not the least telling thing about Leys's book is the way he prefaces it with a delightfully scornful account of just how the Potemkin village trick was worked on Western visitors by the Chinese—and no doubt to a great extent still is. The visitor's trail lay along the same tiny handful of well-trodden paths— the same three or four cities, the same half-dozen "model" communes, hospitals, factories—meeting only specially selected and groomed "workers" and "representatives of the people." He stays in hotels which are completely insulated from the rest of Chinese life. He is taken to the same carefully preserved "monuments of the past," proudly shown the same archeological relics dug up during the Cultural Revolution as evidence of respect for China's artistic heritage. If he was a Roman Catholic, he may even, as proof of the survival of religious freedom, have been taken to a celebration of the Tridentine Mass by a Chinese priest, nostalgically surrounded by all the trappings of Catholic ceremonial such as one would scarcely find surviving in the West. And it was all, of course, a carefully staged sequence of charades, a series of Potemkin villages, giving absolutely no indication of the terrifying cultural and spiritual desert to which modern China has been reduced.

In fact the real theme of Simon Leys's book is the story of the destruction in less than 20 years of what, even as late as the 1950s, was probably the richest and most deep-rooted popular culture in the world. Consider, for instance, the old Chinese passion for opera which, in city and country, at all levels of society, played a part in everyday life as nowhere else on earth ("no ceremony, no celebration, no solemn or joyful or exceptional circumstance in life was complete without some piece of opera"). By the end of the Cultural Revolution, the whole of that vast repertoire of traditional opera had simply been abolished. By 1972, the only operas being performed in China, endlessly and identically repeated from one end of the country to the other, down to the tiniest production detail, were six "feeble Punch and Judy shows, whose only "revolutionary" daring is to maneuver on stage, to languorous, Khatchaturian-like music, platoons of the People's Liberation Army complete with banners and wooden rifles." If you went to the cinema, apart from the occasional documentary, the only feature films you could see were of those same six "revolutionary model operas." If you were unfortunate enough to study Chinese literature at Peking University, the only texts you would have had to study (apart from the works of Mao) were the "childish" librettos of those same six "operas."

When those noted pianists Mr. Nixon and Mr. Edward Heath admired the "mediocre Rachmaninoff *pastiche*" piano concerto known as "The Yellow River," they were probably not aware that this (in fact prerevolutionary) work may well have been the *only* piece of music in the pianist's repertoire. And have you ever wondered at the apparent irony that so destructive an upheaval as the Cultural Revolution should also have allowed people the time off to engage in such a harmless and admirable pursuit as archeology—to produce all those wonderful old Chinese art objects which are now hawked about the world as publicity for the regime (vide the famous "Jade Princess" exhibition sent abroad in 1973)? The explanation of course is simple. "The Chinese soil is an inexhaustible mine of archeological treasures, whose sites are very well and precisely known." When in the late sixties the vandals set about destroying tens of thousands of temples, looting hundreds of once venerated tombs, it is hardly surprising that the regime was shrewd enough to save a few gems from the sack, to be later used as evidence for the "vitality" of revolutionary culture.

But the most haunting image of all is Simon Leys's picture of what has happened to the old city of Peking. When he first knew Peking in 1955, it was architecturally one of the most beautiful cities in the world, "a cultural legacy of all mankind." Its ancient walls, its great gates, its delicately-roofed *pailous* (or street arches), enclosed vistas and arrangements of temples and palaces were one of the most breathtaking and harmonious examples of Chinese art. The streets themselves were humming with life, "jugglers, booksellers, storytellers, puppeteers, the thousands of craftsmen, the inns, the little shops, the antique dealers and calligraphy shops," giving "Peking its lovely, diverse and wonderful face, all that made it into an incredibly civilized city."

Twenty years later, with a few carefully preserved exceptions (including the Forbidden City itself), it is all gone. *Pailous,* gates, walls have simply disappeared (Leys movingly describes his disbelief when, in 1972, he went to look for the ancient gates, as famous throughout the Chinese world as the Great Wall, and found just the "obscene stump" of the last of them being demolished). "Whole blocks were razed to assuage the hunger of socialist town planners for immense avenues, boulevards and squares ... intended for parades, mass meetings, pageants and rallies." Endless acres of empty asphalt lead past serried rows of tatty new concrete slums. The street life has been reduced to glum-looking, identically-garbed gray crowds moving to and from work, like the shuffling toilers in Lang's *Metropolis.*

Now, when I read this description of a city which 23 years ago seemed "full of youth and life," but where everything today seems "old, run-down and ramshackle," this account of the transformation of the rich, organic past of humanity into a grim, concrete wilderness, dominated by bureaucracy, technology, and stupefying boredom, I was reminded of a number of things. I was reminded of a passage in Solzhenitsyn's *Letter to Soviet Leaders* in which he talked about the reconstruction of Moscow in the fifties and sixties: "We have dirtied and defiled the wide Russian spaces, and disfigured the heart of Russia, our beloved Moscow.... The irreplaceable face of the city and all the ancient city plan have been obliterated, and imitations of the West are being slung up, like the New Arbat; the city has been so squeezed, stretched and pushed upward that life has become intolerable." I was reminded of one of the most remarkable images I have ever seen on television, in a recent documentary—mile upon mile of vast gray concrete slabs of new workers' housing in East Berlin, stretching in seemingly endless, inhuman ranks to the horizon. But I was also reminded of a good many parts of London, Liverpool, Glasgow, Paris, Barcelona, Copenhagen, Melbourne, Rio de Janeiro, and a great many other cities of the West.

We all these days have a certain image fixed somewhere in our minds of the incredible transformation which has come over the life of mankind in the past 30 years—and of which the fate of so many cities of the world has seemed to be only one of the more dramatic outward reflections. The destruction of Peking and the destruction of Birmingham have only differed in degree. Who, 30 years ago, would have thought it conceivable that the Manchester of *Coronation Street* back-to-backs or even the Glasgow of the old Gorbals slums would one day be looked back on as "human," "colorful," "alive," almost as objects of nostalgia?

Quite regardless of political ideology, or cultural tradition, it seems as though what has happened has been somehow implicit in the very nature of what mankind as a whole has been doing to itself in the late twentieth century. As Solzhenitsyn was recently saying at Harvard, "The split in the world is less terrible than the similarity of the disease plaguing its main sections." And the most remarkable thing of all is the extent to which this tremendous cultural catastrophe has almost universally been carried out, I do not say necessarily always with the best intentions, but certainly in the name of "humanity," and the "People." The most eloquently deceptive Potemkin village of them all has proved to be that vision—whether it took the form of a revolutionary manifesto or an architect's drawing for a new public housing project—which promised in advance a truly "brave new world," in which human beings could live purer, fuller, richer, happier lives. Just why that vision should so universally have proved such a tragic lie is one of the most profound and important questions we can ask about the time in which we live.

7

BIG BROTHER HATES EVERYONE

October 12, 1976

The city's loudspeaker system took up the refrain, "Down with Chiang Ching, Wang Hung-Wen, Chang Chun-Chiao and Yao Wen-Yuan"—the four chief targets. Fireworks went off as tens of thousands of people raised their voices in a deafening chorus of slogans above the sound of the horns and drums.
                    —News report from Peking, 1976

The horrible thing about the Two Minutes Hate was not that one was obliged to act a part, but on the contrary that it was impossible to avoid joining in. Within thirty seconds any pretence was always unnecessary. A hideous ecstasy of fear and vindictiveness, a desire to kill . . . seemed to flow through the whole group . . . and yet the rage that one felt was an abstract, undirected emotion which could be switched from one object to another like the flame of a blowlamp.
                    —George Orwell, 1984

In recent years the image of Chinese life most frequently presented in the West, particularly on television, has been that of a teeming anthill, of 700 million industrious citizens, all toiling happily under the inspiration of Big Brother Mao to build a new nation, after centuries of oppression, division and misery.

Many Westerners, as with Russia in the 1930s, have been disposed to take China at this face valuation, as a society showing an almost miraculous degree of unity and harmony.

There has, however, been one gigantic contradiction in the picture: namely, the enormous part obviously played in everyday Chinese life (which not even the most sycophantic admirers of Mao's China could disguise) by public expressions of aggression and hostility.

Not only have we been aware in the past decade of the remarkable persistence in such a "happy and harmonious" society of an apparently endless succession of subversives, "capitalist roaders," and "Confucian deviationists," from the enemies of the Cultural Revolution, through Liu Shao-chi and Lin Piao, to the presently hated "Gang of Four," but few things have been so conspicuous in the television films as the degree to which China's social unity seemed to be expressed not in smiling harmony but in expressions of hatred—even on the faces of the little children in the schools, acting out their playlets against American imperialist aggression and "goulash deviationism."

Rarely has the world seen a more vivid example of that phenomenon of mass psychology which, although it was brilliantly portrayed by Orwell in *1984,* has astonishingly never received proper analysis—viz. the absolutely unchanging requirement of Utopian, totalitarian movements for a constant supply of enemies, however imaginary, upon whom they can lavish a continual stream of aggression.

Whether we think of Hitler's Germany, Mao's China, or Stalin's Russia, we are aware that any such great collective movement requires three things.

The first is a Utopian vision or fantasy of the idealized future (however vaguely drawn) to which the whole forward thrust of the society can be directed—whether it be the perfect Communist state, or the thousand-year Reich.

The second is the semideification of the superhuman leaders, or "dream heroes," who will lead and inspire the struggle—the Fuehrer under the searchlights of Nuremburg, the icons of Lenin, Stalin, Marx, or Mao.

The third, to provide psychic personification of something to struggle against, is the constant invocation of enemies, both external and internal, whose very existence gives both justification to the battle, and a ready explanation for everything that goes wrong in pursuit of the dream—Jews, capitalist roaders, Wall Street imperialists, or whatever.

But even though all extremist political movements, whether of the Left or the Right, conform to this psychological pattern, we should not of course only be ready to perceive it in its extreme forms.

It is in fact one of the most basic psychic patterns in the political and social life of any society, particularly ones which are threatened by any degree of violent change or disintegration, which inevitably leads to the desire by various groups in that society for simple, instantly compelling and largely fantasy-based solutions.

We see it, for instance, wherever a conflict arises which tempts each side to exaggerate the other into a monstrous caricature. In British politics, we saw a particularly striking example in 1963/4 in the considerable psychic energy which was generated around Harold Wilson's vision of a "New Britain," which would somehow be dynamic, classless, efficient and forged in "the white heat of the technological revolution"— as opposed to the bumbling stagnant, "old-school tie" and "grouse moor" complacency of "thirteen years of Tory rule."

We saw it in the late 1950s and 1960s in the great imaginary struggle of those who wanted to be thought "young" and "swinging" and "with it" (with their "dream heroes" from the world of pop culture), against the "squares" and "blue meanies," later translated only too readily by some into "Fascists."

In the end, however, all these expressions of the same psychic phenomenon are perversions of the same, fundamentally religious archetype. The promised land to which we aspire (like the lost Eden of the past) are symbols of a sense of wholeness and unity from which we obscurely feel that we have been exiled.

To admit that any of those detestable qualities which are standing between us and the perfect world might actually lie in ourselves is obviously impossible. It is so much more comforting to project them on to other people, and other groups, because it makes our view of the world so much simpler. All that is wrong is the fault of "the others"—the Fascists, the Jews, the "squares," the "reds under the bed." If only these villains can somehow be got out of the way, the paradise we deserve will be ours.

The great religions (in their highest expressions) tell us that these things can only be achieved by each individual, in his struggle to recognize his own "darker" side and thus to work toward a "whole" view.

But as soon as the battle for salvation becomes collective rather than individual (whether it takes on religious, political or social expression) then the enemies are always outside us. Thus, in the comfort of knowing that we are the elect, do we launch on the world persecution, war, collective hatred, and all the other hideous consequences of our own psychic disintegration.

8

DESCENT INTO THE MAELSTROM

June 7, 1975

From California to the Middle East, from Italy to Japan, from Northern Ireland to northern Spain, there are few more obvious symptoms of the strange psychic instability which is today sweeping the world than the almost world-wide wave of terrorism.

What, in human terms, is the real nature of this disease? It cannot just be equated with such traditional, age-old forms of criminality as brigandage—because our late twentieth-century terrorists are often highly intelligent, come from prosperous or well-educated backgrounds, and because, above all, they are invariably acting, not to further their own personal ends, but in the name of some great political "cause."

In their own eyes, like Dostoevski's murderer Raskolnikov (or even more like his revolutionary gang in *The Possessed*), they have been freed from normal, mundane moral constraints because they are acting in the name of some "higher morality" which can justify any atrocity, any crime.

One of the most horrific examples of this collective psycho-pathology at work has been the trail of havoc wreaked by the Baader-Meinhof gang, now on trial in West Germany. It may seem a far cry from this gang of cornered desperadoes to Shakespeare. But in recent days my thoughts have been running on these apparently ingruous rails—partly because I have been reading Mel Lasky's fascinating study of the Baader-Meinhof gang in the June issue of *Encounter* and partly because I have been rereading what I believe to be the best book about Shakespeare ever written.

The most haunting ingredient in Lasky's article is his account of the "downward descent" of Ulrike Meinhof, the beautiful, highly intelligent daughter of two art historians, from fervent young Christian pacifist, through increasing radical chic sympathy with the underdog (expressed in a highly-paid magazine column) to infatuation with the terrorism of Andreas Baader. The devoted mother, who once burst into tears when her brother-in-law fired off a pistol in a wood, ends up as a ruthless terrorist herself, flinging around "Mollies" (Molotov cocktails) with gay abandon and prepared to commit almost any murder for the sake of her gang.

The book I have been reading about Shakespeare was published in 1959, never sold more than a few thousand copies, is out of print, and its author, John Vyvyan, died in February this year almost without remark.

In recent times it has been fashionable to see Shakespeare as a man without a moral point of view, and without any profound convictions. According to the Jan Kott school, he was so convinced of a random, meaningless universe that he was virtually the founder of the Theatre of the Absurd. Even Kenneth Clark in *Civilisation* described Shakespeare as "the first and maybe the last supremely great poet to have been without a religious belief, even without the humanist's belief in man."

"Who else," asks Clark, "has felt so strongly the absolute meaninglessness of human life?"

But Vyvyan says rubbish to all this. Shakespeare, he claims, had a completely clear and consistent moral view of "the meaning of human life." His plays are not just "magical poetry" and "excellent theatre" but "ethical theorems of Euclidean logicality," and in *The Shakespearian Ethic*, Vyvyan demonstrates with unanswerable lucidity just what that moral view was.

Each of the seven plays he analyzes in detail—four tragedies and three late comedies—shows the spiritual progress of a hero who is put to the test.

In the tragedies—*Macbeth, Othello, Hamlet, Julius Caesar*—the hero succumbs to the temptation. The play shows a battle taking place in a noble soul. Gradually light fades, hatred replaces love, all moral and spiritual values are inverted, and finally comes a physical death which only underlines a spiritual suicide which has already been committed.

The comedies on the other hand, *Measure for Measure, A Winter's Tale, The Tempest,* show a similar process of testing, through which the hero eventually takes not the downward but the upward path, through love, mercy, and self-understanding, toward realization of his "proper self," that "own self" to which a man must be true.

I cannot even begin here to summarize the rigorous detail with which Vyvyan traces a parallel nine-stage pattern through both the tragedies and the comedies or the skill with which he shows, for instance, how Desdemona and Ophelia are not just characters but also allegorical figures representing love, so that as both Othello and Hamlet turn on them, rejecting love, we can see a meticulous reflection of their downward spiritual progress.

Vyvyan's explanation of the underlying theme of Hamlet is particularly powerful—that it is the tragedy of a man who succumbs to the temptation of the Ghost, representing the Old Testament morality of an eye for an eye, a death for a death, and losing knowledge of his true self in the process, goes to pieces.

The very next play, *Measure for Measure,* shows us precisely the opposite—the triumph of the New Testament, as the pure moralistic Angelo tries to impose on Vienna the Old Testament "law that killeth," is exposed as a vicious hypocrite, and is only released at the end by repentance and the "creative mercy" of the wise old Duke of Vienna.

What has all this to do with Ulrike Meinhof? Simply of course that Shakespeare's "ethical theorems" are not just the stuff of academic study, but are acted out every day, in ways large and small, all around us. His plays are great art precisely because they are based on a profound perception of those archetypal patterns which govern both art and life—they are psychoanalytical case-studies of the utmost accuracy.

In talking of the downward descent of Ulrike Meinhof, Lasky says that the process whereby she became a terrorist "defied analysis by police psychologists and political pundits."

But it would scarcely have puzzled Shakespeare. In the Meinhof story, like that of the PLO, the IRA, or indeed any of the terrorists of our time (right back to Trotsky, Lenin and their bomb-throwing anarchist predecessors), we see what happens whenever human beings set off, individually or collectively, in the name of whatever noble-seeming, Brutus-like cause, to turn against love and self-awareness, to project all capacity for evil outward onto "the others," and to succumb to the temptation to become harsh and hard.

Gradually, we see light extinguished, fair become foul, and all that spiritual inversion which Shakespeare described so vividly and so often—concluding in the ultimate madness of total consumption by hatred (one of the Baader-Meinhof slogans was "24 hours of HATE each day"). "Untune that string," drive out love—and the only ending can be death.

Great art is so precisely because it shows us how life actually works—and what makes great criticism is that it tells us so.

9

NIXON AND THE DARKNESS OF WATERGATE

Based on articles originally published in 1973 and 1974

Looking back over our view of America in the seventies, we can see how it was overshadowed by one thing above all else—the almost incredible events of those two years, 1973 and 1974, which are summed up by the word "Watergate."

More than ever, as we look back a few years later, can we see how the great black cloud of Watergate seemed to settle over America like a kind of grand judgment, not just on Nixon himself, but on the whole of postwar America. For 20 years after World War II, the United States had seemed to tower over the rest of the world like a rock of prosperity, stability, unequaled political and military power. But the hubristic Kennedy years of the early sixties seemed to lead inexorably to the growing nightmare of Vietnam, racial violence, youthful protest, and all those symptoms which, in the late sixties and early seventies, betrayed a condition of terrible sickness. In clinical terms, Watergate was the "crisis"—since when the rest of the world has never been able to look on America in quite the same way again, anymore than the Americans have been able to recapture the same confidence in themselves.

In a previous chapter, I have already touched on some of the wider aspects of this collapse in America's self-assurance which the Watergate crisis did so much to precipitate and to symbolize. But no meditation on the seventies would be complete without some more specific reflections on the man who stood at the center of Watergate and whose personality had dominated American life during the five dark, unhappy years which preceded it.

It was of course something of an irony that Richard Nixon should have been cast as the ultimate "tragic scapegoat" for this period in American life—the President whose election in 1968 had itself been widely regarded as symbolizing an end to the corruption and sickness which had crept up on America in the mid-sixties. Pledged to bring an honorable end to the war in Vietnam, he had ended up by extending it even more devastatingly than before and then finally scuttling off to leave Southeast Asia to precisely that fate the whole war had been fought to avert. Pledged in the name of his "silent majority" to restore law and order, he ended up showing more contempt for legality than any President before him. Supported in 1972 by the largest democratic vote in American history, he ended up a bare 20 months later as the first American President in history to be forced out of office in disgrace.

Certainly the dark years of Watergate presented the world with one of the most amazing public dramas of the seventies— and "drama" is the exact word, for one of the more haunting aspects of the Watergate affair was the way literary parallels kept on intruding.

On the most superficial level, as the drama began unfolding in the summer of 1973 with the televised Senate Committee hearings under Senator Sam Ervin, was simply the eerie sense that we were seeing a "real life replay" of one of those *Advise and Consent*-type Washington political thrillers with which Hollywood had so often entertained us during the years of America's unquestioned self-confidence—with Charles Laughton playing the wily old Southern Senator, and all the other parts—the jowly heavies, Haldeman and Ehrlichman, the betrayed idealist John Dean, the comic relief of the Brooklyn cop Ulascewicz, almost too neatly cast.

But as the true gravity of what was at stake began to sink in, with the gradually emerging picture of just how deeply rotten the state of the whole Nixon administration had become, it was clear that Watergate was one of those moments in history when we see how great drama and life ultimately spring from the same profound mysterious source.

An obvious parallel was *Hamlet*. Certainly in many ways the picture of life at Nixon's court which emerged during Watergate was remarkably reminiscent of that other more ancient court at Elsinore. One of the most conspicuous features of *Hamlet* is the way everyone is engaged in plotting. The play is full of "plots"—Polonius commissioning Reynaldo, like some Howard Hunt-type C.I.A. agent, to spy on Laertes in Paris; Polonius twice trying to "bug" Hamlet's conversation behind the arras; Rosencrantz and Guildenstern, the "two Germans," being ordered by the king to compile a secret "psychological profile" of Hamlet. While over the whole play hang the two ultimate plots—that of Claudius to usurp and hold on to supreme political power and that of Hamlet to avenge his father—which between them lead to the grand tragic nemesis in which they are all brought down.

In fact the point about the intrigues in *Hamlet* (there are nearly a dozen of them in all) is the way every single one of them is shown rebounding on the plotters' heads. This is one of the central themes of the play, which Shakespeare constantly underlines, that of "purposes mistook fall'n on their inventor's heads," "the enginer hoist with his own petar," the schemer caught "like a woodcock" to his own "springe."

And this of course was the central theme of the unfolding drama of Watergate, just as it is the essential theme of all classic tragedy—that in life, just as on the stage, purposes mistook *do* fall on their inventors' heads, that *hubris* of any kind *does* lead in the end, by an almost mathematical pattern, to nemesis, just as we saw, by such a pattern, the "law and order" President being eventually caught up in the toils of his own proudest boast. Never before in history had there been quite such a devastating and public contemporary exposure of the life of a court, reeking with plots, paranoia and intrigue—all rebounding on their perpetrators. And just as *Hamlet* is shot through with famous lines underlining the moral, we even had Senator Ervin on hand in that Senate caucus room to provide appropriate choric comment—"as a man sows, so shall he reap," "God is not mocked." Perhaps the only biblical quotation lacking, at the moment of the revelation that Nixon had been "bugging" the White House with the very tape recorders that were to provide the evidence for his own downfall, was the observation of the psalmist, "In the same net which he hid privily is his foot taken."

But as the mighty drama of Watergate wound remorselessly through 1973 and 1974 to its conclusion, a still deeper parallel to some of the great tragedies of the world began to present itself.

It was the late John Vyvyan, in his excellent little book *The Shakespearian Ethic,* who first pointed out one of the most uncannily perceptive ingredients in some of Shakespeare's plays. The unfolding of tragedy does not always just consist of the hero committing a simple act of *hubris,* followed by nemesis. When the first "act of darkness" has been committed—as when Macbeth kills Duncan—it may well be followed by a second "act of darkness"—as when Macbeth kills Banquo—in a desperate bid to shore up his false position. And it may well be this second act—the attempt to "cover up"—which actually triggers off the coming together of those forces which ultimately bring the hero down, dealing him the final, catastrophic blow.

This is something we have seen so often acted out in real life in our times that we must accept it as a crucial ingredient in those secret patterns which shape the individual and collective behavior of men. It was not John Profumo's venial and remarkably short-lived affair with Christine Keeler which brought about the greatest political scandal in postwar Britain (even if, at the same time, she was friendly with the Soviet naval *attaché*); it was his attempt to cover up what he had done before the House of Commons. Similarly it was not the pitiful little break-in at the Watergate which brought down President

Nixon; it was the attempt to cover up which drew him ever further into that hideous, nightmarish web of self-deception that eventually made his fall inevitable.

There is no question that it is one of the hardest things in the world for any of us to face up to the consequences of our own past acts of moral weakness: to attempt to brazen it out is one of the subtlest and most powerful of all temptations (particularly if one's whole career seems to be at stake—it is so easy to forget the ancient truth that if we set out to deceive others, we end up only by deceiving ourselves).

One of the greatest tragedies in the world is the story of Oedipus, who sets out, promising to leave no stone unturned, to unearth the true cause of the terrible plague that has fallen on his kingdom of Thebes. President Nixon, of course, made precisely the same public boast in 1973 about the Watergate affair—he was prepared to go to any lengths, even, in the immortal words of Jeremy Thorpe, to the point of being prepared to "lay down his friends for his life," in order to drive away the plague that had fallen on his administration. But of course the psychological greatness of Sophocles' play hangs on the fact that, when Oedipus set out to find the cause of the plague, he really meant it. There was to be no cover up in Thebes, even though all the evidence Oedipus uncovered increasingly pointed to himself as the chief suspect.

That is why Oedipus is ultimately, in the purest sense, not a tragedy. It does not end in the destruction of the hero, simply because the very reason for his gouging out his eyes is that he has seen the light. Sophocles was himself to underline this point many years later in the sequel, *Oedipus at Colonus,* which showed us a man who, having plumbed the very depths of self-examination and made a full admission of his own guilt, has been thus illumined and made wise, eventually finding reconciliation and wholeness.

In a brilliant essay published some years ago, A. E. Dyson reinterpreted Kafka's *The Trial* not as the surrealistic story of an innocent man who finds himself quite unjustifiably on trial and cannot make sense of what is happening to him—but, in some mysterious way, as that of a man who has found himself in a nightmarish, inexplicable world precisely because the one thing he cannot admit to is his own guilt.

In 1973 and 1974 President Nixon presented such a tortured face to the world for precisely the same reason. Imbued to the end with a fatal sense of his own righteousness, he was Joseph K., not Oedipus. He was simply not prepared to face up to something which had ultimately become inevitable: the conflict between his fondly-imagined *persona* and his dark underside was something he just could not accept; and the main reason why he has remained such a shallow and uninteresting human being ever since (*vide* the pitiful interviews with David Frost) is that, even despite his fall, he appears to have learned nothing, is still at heart totally self-justifying, and still seeking the explanation for all the ills that befell him in the acts and moral weaknesses of others. The unseeing ego has become just a dried-up husk, and its owner nothing more than a lifeless self-parody—for reasons which the great playwrights of the world would scarcely have found difficult to understand.

10

Vietnam—A Black Fairy Tale

April 16, 1975

Some years ago I recall seeing a film of the Viet Minh preparations for the siege of Dien Bien Phu in 1954. It was an awe-inspiring sight—the tens of thousands of Vietnamese peasants toiling through jungles and across mountains, like an army of ants, carrying shells, parts of enormous guns, supplies of all kinds.

As I watched, I found myself being more and more reminded of something. This spectacle of tens of thousands of human beings all working selflessly on one enormous common enterprise was reminiscent of nothing so much as that extraordinary episode in twelfth-century France when from every corner of the country tens of thousands of peasants, monks and aristocrats came together to devote years to the building of Chartres Cathedral.

Corruptio optimi pessima. In one instance, of course, the end was to build a great cathedral to the Virgin which seven centuries later would still remain the most miraculously beautiful expression of the "age of Faith." In the other, it was to assemble a huge engine of destruction, whose only memorial was a pile of corpses.

But it was a parallel which has often recurred for me since—because it was for me a clue as to just why, over the past 30 years, we have followed the unfolding tragedy of Vietnam with such a peculiar sense of horror.

It has been because, in a particularly horrible way, Vietnam has been a kind of looking-glass war, or rather looking-glass morality play, upsetting all our deepest-rooted moral assumptions and expectations.

World War II has sown in all of us the pattern of war as a battle between undisputed good and absolute evil, in which eventually, after all sorts of trials and tribulations, good triumphs.

Similarly, in the fairy tale, which embodies our earliest notions of how the moral structure of the world works, we are accustomed to seeing the hero ultimately triumphing over all his adversaries. "The good ended happily, the bad unhappily. That is what fiction means."

But the war in Vietnam has been a kind of perverted fairy tale, in which the "hero," against terrifying odds, has continued to win through to the point where he now seems in sight of final victory—and yet in which all the moral values have been completely upside down.

All attempts by the "good" have ended up either in the good losing, or being corrupted, or, as it now seems, both at once—the most horrific example of all, of course, being the utterly impotent intervention of the Americans.

Riding in like Sir Galahad to save the beautiful maiden of South Vietnam from the clutches of the dragon, it is undeniable that the Americans gave to the world one of the most frightening spectacles of the twentieth century. Like the fairy-tale character who gets caught in one of those magic traps, which snare first one limb and then, with every attempt to get free, each of the rest in turn, the Americans became enmeshed in a mess that was uniquely horrible—above all because it was like an allegory of all that is most destructive in man's attempts to cocoon himself in technological power and insulate himself in jargon.

Has anything in our time, even the concentration camps, been more terrible than the spectacle of fresh-faced young Americans flying off from "Coca Cola, Color TV" comfort of their carriers to blast at random a few distant dots—Vietnamese peasants—into eternity? Was anything more chilling than Lieutenant Calley's dismissal of his victims as merely "oriental human beings?" Was anything more horrible than the debauching of that beautiful country and that ancient, delicate culture with all the detritus of American affluence, the drugs, the defoliation, the bar girls, the black market, the deliberate creation of tens of thousands of refugees as a propaganda weapon?

All this has been truly a paradigm of hell. But does one then turn with relief and gratitude (as one should in the fairy tale) to the gallant spectacle of the Viet Cong fighting heroically for the liberation of their country? Unless one is some dotty student or dim-witted actress, of course not.

For of course the spectacle of that fanatical, ascetic force, seeking remorselessly since 1946 to impose its will on Vietnam, regardless of any moral consideration whatever—spreading tyranny like a cancer along an unbroken trail of torn-up agreements, massacres and lies—has, in human terms, been just as terrible as anything the Americans have presented and, in the possibility that it may be ultimately successful, much worse.

What is it about Communism which in all its aspects makes it such a uniquely horrible thing? It is precisely its power to turn all normal human values upside down—to corrupt what is best in the human spirit for the worst ends—its capacity with all the force of a perverted evangelical religion to weld men together into an inhuman mass, based always on hatred and enmity, and subordinating every traditional human virtue—truth, loyalty, justice, love, to that end.

The reason why we look on the agony of Vietnam today with such horror—why, quite apart from the sufferings of the refugees and the continuing killing, we look forward to the end of a war for the first time in our lives without any sense of relief or rejoicing—is because, in a way that is somehow far more shocking than the mere brutal power politics of Hungary in 1956 or

Czechoslovakia in 1968, our comfortable fairy-tale world has been turned inside out. We are appalled, not because "the West" has suffered some "political defeat," but because the moral foundations of our universe have been disturbed. Not unnaturally, it is hard to take.

11

THE AGE OF SELF-RIGHTEOUSNESS

Written on July 13, 1978, during the "dissident trials" in the Soviet Union involving Anatoli Scharanksy, Alexander Ginsburg, and others.

As the fury of rage ("appalling gaffe," "worst blunder so far," "gravely embarrassing") continues to echo around the Western world over Mr. Andrew Young's remark that "there are hundreds, perhaps thousands of people whom I could describe as political prisoners" in American jails, we may perhaps pause to reflect whether, in a curious way, we should not be grateful to Mr. Carter's UN Ambassador for having performed a very useful service.

What his comment has demonstrated more clearly than anything, in this week of fevered international obsession over the plight of Alexander Ginsburg and Anatoli Scharansky, is a most dangerous confusion at present plaguing the West. In the past two decades, all over the world, there has arisen a mighty hubbub, in a hundred different languages—but all centered on that one wonderful, evocative word "rights." This week the word "rights" has most obviously been associated with the two trials in the Soviet Union which appear to us, in the West, to be such mockeries of justice.

But beyond the front-page headlines there has been little diminution in that other confused and noisy chorus which is such a perpetual background to our lives, using the word "rights" in all sorts of other contexts. With the fiftieth anniver-

103

sary in Britain of women's suffrage, there has been a renewed clamor over "women's rights." On the radio a day or two ago, I heard some "spokesperson" banging on about "the rights of school students." Almost every day we hear about the "rights" of workers, or homosexuals, or the IRA suspects who are no doubt on occasion rather roughly treated by the security forces in Northern Ireland.

Amid all this deafening cacophony of insistence on holy "rights," there appears to be only one powerful voice raised in interrogation, to ask what all this talk of "rights" is really about. "The defense of individual rights has reached such extremes," thunders this reactionary voice, "as to make society as a whole defenseless against certain individuals." "It is time in the West," this deplorably uncompassionate and unfashionable fellow continues, "to defend not so much human rights as human obligations."

The lone voice expressing deep alarm at what the universal obsession with "rights" reveals about the state of our society is that of Alexander Solzhenitsyn, in the speech he gave last month at Harvard—and the very fact that such a former dissident, representing the sort of group in the world about whose "rights" we all wax most eloquent, should be asking us to question our glib parrot-cries in this matter may give us pause to reflect precisely what it is we are on about.

What do we mean when we talk of "rights?" In a strictly legal sense, the idea of rights has invariably been associated with some kind of legal contract, under which, in any particular society, it is agreed that certain people shall have certain rights as part of their membership of that society. In Britain and America, for instance, it has long been agreed that we all have the right to a trial by jury and to be considered innocent under the law until we are found guilty. But there is nothing absolute about such a right. Other societies are perfectly entitled to arrange things differently.

All this goes back at least to the Middle Ages, before anyone had heard of such a term as a "social contract," but when society was generally considered to be a great organic whole under God, a hierarchy in which everyone, at every level, was bound together by an infinite network both of rights and duties. In the seventeenth and eighteenth centuries, as the mystical bonds holding society together began to lose their force, men more and more came to see their relationship with "over powerful" governments in terms of "rights" alone. Even so, these rights (such as those guaranteed by the American Bill of Rights in 1789) were still seen fundamentally as attaching just to individual citizens, by virtue of their membership of society as a whole, to which they also owed certain obligations—and it was equally accepted that such rights could only have any meaning where there was a formal contract to recognize them.

It was only in the late eighteenth century that men first began to talk of "rights" in a more abstract way as something absolute and preordained, something which existed without any need for a contract—as when Jefferson wrote, "Nothing is unchangeable but the inherent and inalienable rights of man." The shift of emphasis was profound—now every man had "rights," simply by virtue of his being a member of the human race. But who was to define such rights? Who was to guarantee them? Who, if everyone had rights, now had the obligations to fulfill them? These aspects of the equation began to slip conveniently from sight—yet without them (as his friends the Red Indians could have told him), such fine phrases as Jefferson's would, and usually did remain nothing but pious slogans.

What in fact, since the time of Jefferson, Rousseau, and Paine, has become even more obvious than talk of the "rights of man" in general is the tendency to see rights as attaching to lesser collectivities of people within society, simply by virtue of their membership of this or that particular group. As the deeper bonds holding society together have disintegrated still further, we have seen the emergence of that phenomenon whereby almost any group down the hierarchy of society may learn to see itself as separate from the rest, and its members as possessing "rights" collectively. In the past 20 years this process has galloped away. Workers, blacks, women, homosexuals, criminals, students, schoolchildren, every group that can conceivably see itself as some kind of underdog has begun to demand "rights" simply as a badge of recognition of its own separate existence in a hostile, exploiting world. Gone (or vastly diminished) is the old sense of a social whole, in which each individual, each group must play their part. What is conveyed instead is an impression of society under continual, disintegrative strain, as each part vies in isolation to assert its own identity against the rest. And of course the point is that there is no end to such a process, for once human beings begin to define their identity primarily in terms of their membership of some minority group, and come, like Lenin, to see society in terms of "who? whom?," there is literally no group of people who cannot somehow arrange to see the rest of society as exploiting them, until finally everyone is set self-righteously clamoring against everyone else.

Of course far behind all this talk of "rights" there does lurk a dim and shining vision of what human relations *should* be—and that is of a world in which people treat each other in the way they themselves would like to be treated, as full, sovereign individuals. But this is precisely the vision which must inevitably be lost sight of in any clamor for "collective rights"—for so soon as people view rights collectively, as attaching to them because they are part of a group, they are ceasing to look on anyone as a full, sovereign individual, either those from whom they are seeking their "rights," who become simply the hated and despised "others," or for that matter themselves. However unconsciously, the clamor for "rights" becomes simply a series of unilateral, egocentric demands, which may or may not be granted according to the amount of duress the claimants can muster in their own support.

In fact, except in the strictly legal sense, the whole notion of "rights" is a misnomer, a pure expression of wishful thinking. It is merely a synonym for "demands"—"this is what I want," "this is the way I think I or other people should be treated."

There has been no more beautiful demonstration of the illogicality behind all this than the slogan popular in Britain in recent years, "the right to work." If society were to pass a law stating that everyone *did* have such a right, and what is more, made practical provision to ensure that work was at all times available for everyone, then the phrase "the right to work" would have some substance. But until that time, the slogan is as meaningless as "the right to $100,000 a year" and as likely to remain so.

The harsh but inescapable truth is that no one on this earth has inalienable, God-given rights to anything—not to food, not to justice, not to life itself. The very fact that men can be deprived of these things, and so frequently are, shows just how truly "inalienable" such "rights" are. What every human being *does* have—and this really is something inalienable and divinely-ordained, because it is part of the way we are made—is not a right but an obligation: to treat other human beings precisely as we would wish to be treated ourselves. If we are rightly distressed by the treatment of Scharanksy and Ginsburg in recent days, it is not because their "rights" have been abused: it is because those who are trying them have failed in their fundamental human obligations, to justice, to mercy, to love, and to truth. They have by this measure failed in that obligation attaching to all of us, as Solzhenitsyn puts it, "to leave life a better human being than when we started it."

We do have the right to speak of universal obligations because it places the emphasis back where it belongs: not on what you, or anyone else (even the universe itself) owes *me*—but on what we all owe to each other.

12

Ex Africa Semper Id

November 11, 1978

To anyone who sees the story of modern man as that of a kind of Faustian delving into dark, "forbidden" realms from whence heaven knows what strange monsters may erupt to engulf him, the story of the relationship between European civilization and the "dark continent" of Africa may provide an unexpectedly rewarding field of study.

Let us cast our minds back briefly to those crucial decades around the turn of the last century. As we can now see, something very odd was happening to Western man, as he stood on the edge of the fateful twentieth century. On all sides, as men unlocked the secrets of nature as never before, astonishing new inventions were bursting forth—airplanes, motor cars, radio, even the first breakthroughs in nuclear physics which were to lead eventually to the H-Bomb. In music and painting, the European unconscious was incubating that tremendous eruption of disintegrative forces which marked the rise of twentieth-century art. In view of these, and the many other developments then laying the ground for our own explosive century (e.g. the eruption of workers' and womens' movements), it was scarcely inapposite that in the very last year of the old century, Freud should have chosen to preface the first dramatic announcement of his researches into the dark forces of the unconscious, *The Interpretation of Dreams,* with a quotation from Book VII of the *Aeneid: "Flectere si nequeo superos, Acheronta movebo"*

109

("If I cannot bend the gods above to my will, I will stir up the waters of Hell").

It was equally apposite that the same years should have seen the powers of Europe taking part in that other conspicuous act of intrusion into an age-old heart of darkness known as "the scramble for Africa." For more than 2,000 years, the mysterious dark continent had for European civilization been a gigantic, timeless metaphor for a dark, unconscious realm. It was out of this strange, unknown place that for the Greeks (and Pliny) one could "always expect something new." Despite da Gama's circumnavigation, Africa's shadowy interior had still, for post-Renaissance Europe, been the place where lived "the Anthropophagi and men whose heads do grow beneath their shoulders," not to mention those more tangible freakish creatures—giraffes, elephants, hippopotami—who in the eighteenth and nineteenth centuries were the wonder of Europe's fashionable new zoological gardens. Right up to the second half of the Victorian era, the great African explorations, the wars of conquest (e.g. the Zulu and Ashanti campaigns) and a spate of such popular fiction as *King Solomon's Mines* had continued to delight a seemingly increasingly safe and cosy European civilization with tales of heroism in the face of dark, mysterious forces.

In the very act of exploring and opening up the interior, however, Livingstone, Speke, and Co. had finally prepared the way for the opening up of that quite different relationship with Africa which has characterized the past 80 years. As never before, the once dark continent has been brought into our conscious awareness. And it is an unvarying rule of human psychology that whenever some important, previously buried or unconscious element is brought partially into the light, the process is likely to bring about a potentially catastrophic split between the new, one-sided state of consciousness thereby achieved, and those elements which remain, now inevitably repressed and distorted, back in the unconscious. For those to whom this sounds the merest psychobabble, may I hastily proceed to illustrate something of what I mean. Doing so, I hope, may shed a little illumination on just why, in the twentieth century, Europe's relationship with Africa has proved, through two quite distinct phases, to be so fraught with psychic confusion and one-sidedness (and thus, as their inevitable political corollaries, by the kind of hypocrisy, self-deception and double think of which both Dr. Owen and Ian Smith are in their opposing ways, such conspicuous practitioners).

The first phase, from the 1870s to the 1950s, saw Europe in the age of imperialism conquering, dividing up and imposing its rule over almost the entire continent. From the "light" or conscious point of view, we were bringing the inestimable blessings of civilization and Christianity to a lot of ignorant, barbarous savages, developing rich natural resources which only Western technology could exploit, and generally dragging a "backward" continent into the mainstream of human progress. In reality, the unconscious or dark side of what we were doing was utterly different. When we arrived, to complete and immeasurably extend the process begun by the earlier Portuguese and Boer settlers, here was an unspoiled continent, full of thousands of tribes, living under age-old, organic social systems, infinitely more at one with themselves and with nature than European man had been for centuries. Into this rich, unconsciously-integrated *matrix* had intruded the greedy, psychially-disintegrated, *ego*-driven white men, with their guns and their Mosaic-Evangelical version of Christianity, ruthlessly destroying the tribal infrastructure, imposing their alien culture and institutions, and in general smashing up beyond recall a harmony between man and nature, in order to exploit the earth of Africa for its metals, precious stones, and other "products" to gratify the ego-drives of a civilization now more than ever emerging in its true colors as the ultimate cuckoo in the nest of creation.

So much for the fundamental hypocrisy of phase one. But then, in the fifties, came phase two, when with a combination of forced, foot-dragging reluctance and smug self-congratulation the Western nations began to "liberate" the new "nations" which they had artificially imposed on the old map of Africa. In terms of the great political cycle described by Plato in Book VIII of *The Republic*—Monarchy, Oligarchy, Democracy, Tyranny—the Western nations had now firmly reached the stage of Democracy, where freedom was the highest value. Their imperial conquests in Africa, however, had got stuck at the stage of Oligarchy, where a tiny minority of which outsiders (the Oligarchs) enjoyed a handsome standard of living by virtue of having neatly divided society into themselves, on top, and below them, as a helot class, the blacks—now largely alienated from the sense of significance once given them by their old tribal structures, their relationship with the soil, and their ancestral gods.

On the conscious surface, what was intended to happen was that these Africans would now be liberated to enjoy all the blessings of that phase of social organization which at the time seemed most admirable to the peoples of the West. Ballot boxes would be imported, franchise lists drawn up, and the once benighted continent would be filled with agreeable little replicas of the home-grown European democracies, in full working order. Oh blessed self-deception! Once again, beneath the surface, the reality was quite different. For, as the independence movement gathered way, the African peoples had already, to a greater or lesser extent, been turned by the process of alienation not into a heterogeneous collection of autonomous little potential democrats, but into a mass, defined simply by their external characteristic of being black as opposed to white. Their old tribal loyalties had largely ceased to be something life-giving, providing meaning to their lives, but had turned into something potentially destructive, a mere external badge of division. They had in short begun to develop (despite the many striking and admirable individuals thrown up in all parts of Africa) the collective characteristics of a rootless proletariat, with new loyalties centered on the independence movement or "Party." Psychologically, the moment of winning independence thus became very similar to that moment of revolution in the Platonic cycle, the moment when Democracy gives way to Tyranny, when, in the name of the People, the Party finally overthrows the old order and takes control—no longer a heterogeneous, organic people, so much as a mass following that supreme expression of the collectivized or group *ego,* a charismatic leader.

The first well-known example of this phenomenon was Kwame Nkrumah of the old Gold Coast. Full of revolutionary rhetoric and talk of the People, he swiftly took the new state of Ghana along that only too familiar road to Tyranny. The whole point about the Tyrant (as opposed to the old Monarch or his more shadowy later manifestations as Constitutional Monarch or Democratic President) is that he is no longer subject to a belief that he is the symbolic cornerstone of an infinitely subtle framework, relating his society to the patterns of nature and ancestral wisdom. He is simply (like Stalin or Mussolini) a great bullfrog, puffed up by the collectivized *ego* of his people, inflated by the conviction that this glorious new society is all a function of his own will (as Nkrumah put it, "I am the Redeemer"). And of course all over Africa we have seen the same process repeated countless times since, from Equatorial Guinea to the Empire of Bokassa I, from Mobutu's Congo to Amin's Uganda.

Despite all the lessons of the past 20 years, we still see Dr. Owen cavorting about under the impression that "one man, one vote" means something other than just the fact that, sooner or later, there will only be one left in the country whose vote carries any weight—the tyrant. When Dr. Owen uses that phrase "majority rule," meaning a "black majority," he is still of course thinking of majority as it is defined in the liberal-democratic phase of the Platonic cycle—a preponderance of free, autonomous citizens. In practice, however, in Africa just as in many other parts of the world, it all too often comes to mean simply that tyranny of the People, the *demos,* over the mass of actual people—a deadly abstraction which may be used to cloak and to sanctify every kind of atrocity and "civil wrong" practiced by a part against the whole (and in many parts of Africa this has been given a new twist, as the members of one tribe have, in the name of the whole been able to tyrannize over the rest, through their control of the party or state apparatus).

The most interesting thing of all is that, because of the stage of political development the world in general has today reached, it has now become virtually impossible to defend the oligarchic order of the old white-settler domination—any more than it would have been possible to freeze Britain's development at its stage of aristocratic, landowner domination against the rising tide of parliamentary reform, universal suffrage, and welfare egalitarianism. That is why Ian Smith is on the way out and why the white South Africans (amid a bloodbath which could equal that of the 1917 Bolshevik Revolution and its aftermath) are eventually likely to follow.

We need no longer be under any illusion as to where this tide leads. It has nothing to do with democracy. Nor does it ultimately have anything to do with allowing "the blacks to run their own show"—except in the sense that the 1917 Revolution allowed the Russian peasants and workers to run *their* own show. It is no accident that the one white race apparently able to operate most freely in large parts of Africa are the Russians because, having been through the full cycle themselves, they are entirely at home, if not with Africans, at least with the tyrant state. They therefore have no difficulty in deploying the hypocritical terminology of that final phase of Europe's relationship with Africa, which allows the setting up of a new kind of imperialism in the name of anti-imperialism, just as it permits the imposition of new, much worse forms of oppression in the name of popular liberation. When we see, staring-eyed on our television screens, the faces of men like Nkomo, Kaunda, or Amin, we may wonder at these new freaks and monsters who have emerged from the dark continent—much as our eighteenth-century ancestors marveled at those camelopards and river horses of old. But let us not forget who, all unconsciously, summoned these new monsters into being. Poor us. Even more, poor Africa.

13

WHEN THE MACHINE STOPS

May 19, 1979

Last year it was an unprecedented series of tanker-sinkings and pollution disasters creating havoc around Britain's shores. This year, it has been the turmoil in Iran, gasoline up 30 per cent or more all over Western Europe and chaotic scenes around the gas stations of California.

Slowly, almost imperceptibly over the past few years—certainly since the Yom Kippur war of 1973—the signs have been gathering of some great impending crisis over the quite astonishing degree to which our civilization has become dependent on oil.

What is this extraordinary stuff, laid down by the decaying remains of billions of little creatures in the swamps and seas of 250 million years ago, on which the whole edifice of our twentieth-century existence has come to rest? Eighty years ago, we scarcely needed it at all. Yet today, if it were all suddenly to vanish overnight, the whole, vast, complex structure of civilization across large parts of the globe—the end product of 10,000 years of human evolution—would simply collapse. In just a few decades we have constructed in effect a gigantic, world-wide machine, on which more than half the earth's population now depends for life itself—for food, for clothing, for shelter, for the whole apparatus of working and staying alive—and the hidden lifeblood of that machine is oil. Yet the more one contemplates this machine, for our dependence on which we have traded in a

115

great part of that old, direct inter-relationship with nature which sustained human life through countless millennia, the more one is forced to ask—what has it actually given us?

When I was recently reading of the panic and desperation of tens of thousands of Californians as they faced even a temporary cutting off of their supplies, I could not help thinking of a series of calculations which cast a somewhat chilling light on the absurdity to which oil dependence may reduce us all. The average American, the calculation runs, drives 7,500 miles in a year. Yet the same man spends over four hours a day, either driving his car, or earning the means whereby to pay for it—a total of some 1,600 hours in a year. In other words, for each of those hours he drives only 4.7 miles—which works out at little more than the speed of the average walker.

Of course giving up his car and taking to his feet instead would seem no more thinkable for such a man than it would for most of us—for our whole pattern of life (e.g. taking it for granted that we can live 20 miles from our place of work) has been entirely reshaped and distorted by our wonderful ease of travel. We could no more do without our motor cars and long-distance trucks and airliners than we could do without fertilizers for our farms, central heating and lighting for our houses, plastics for our clothes, or any of the million and one other by-products of our wonderful new Universal Provider. Yet the more one looks at the dark underside of this great explosion of energy which has surged through our civilization in the past 80 years, the more dubious a blessing does the dark, viscous muck appear to have been.

A few years ago I spent some time reading about the history of the oil industry, and I could not help being struck by the extraordinarily unhappy lives which seem to have been led by so many of those individuals most directly involved in it. Time after time, from humble Texas farmers who discovered a gusher in their backyard and ended up committing suicide, to the fabulous John D. Rockefeller himself, spending his last years in a state of miserable, frozen paranoia, the story of oil is that its discovery has fallen on its beneficiaries like some fairy-tale curse.

Do we really think that life in Iran has been immeasurably improved by the great upheaval brought to that country in the past 30 years by its vast reserves of oil? Do the Shetlanders view with unmitigated delight the polluting river of oil and oil money oozing from Sullum Voe to affect every part of their ancient island culture? Do we see in the Arabs who flock in such numbers through the streets of London these days, a people who on the whole look contented, at one with themselves and the world? On the contrary, a more rootless, unhappy, be-wildered-looking lot of visitors can never have come to these shores.

And if this is true of the more obvious, direct beneficiaries of the great twentieth-century oil bonanza, how much is it also true of the rest of us? The flow of oil may have permitted us to cocoon ourselves from nature in an unprecedented degree of material comfort, but it has also brought to our lives a restless-ness and rootlessness the full psychic effect of which we can scarcely begin to be aware of.

The most haunting (if, I suspect, exaggerated) parable I ever heard about oil came from a friend of mine who, some months ago, paid a privileged visit to Williamsburg in Virginia, the "living museum" of eighteenth-century life which is financed by Rockefeller money. Near the town itself is a series of great underground storerooms, into which from the salesrooms of the world pours a constant stream of furniture, paintings, harpsi-chords—every conceivable kind of art object which might have been found in Williamsburg in 1776.

The collection is already so great that not more than a frac-tion of it will probably ever be put on public show—but under the terms of the Rockefeller trust, the flood of treasures must continue to pour in because it is virtually unstoppable. In other words, by what horrendous irony, the Rockefeller millions have come full circle. Begun a century ago, when a young man first began to dig dirty black stuff out of a hole in the ground in

Pennsylvania, today those millions are simply being stuffed back into the ground—in the shape of a not inconsiderable chunk of the artistic heritage of mankind.

Yet even more ironically, with the oil age still only a few decades old, we are already today having to contemplate the astonishing prospect that the supply of lifeblood for this Great Mother we have created, the World Machine, may be beginning to dry up. We face the prospect that, in only a few years perhaps, we may see the nations of the world actually battling to the death to get their hands on the dwindling supplies of the stuff—something which would certainly underline more poignantly than ever the irony with which we so glibly speak of oil as our civilization's "lifeblood."

Of course we find such a prospect unthinkable. We would much rather keep our heads buried in the sand, imagining that "more oil will be found," or that we shall soon discover perfectly adequate "alternative energy sources." But at least, amid such wishful thinking (for as yet there is not the remotest prospect that we could find an energy source to replace all the multifarious uses of oil), let us begin to think more deeply about what our grotesque and historically very short-lived dependence on this substance has done to us all. Our civilization did not, after all, do too badly before oil came into our lives. It produced Beethoven, Rembrandt, Shakespeare, Dante, the Bible. And what have we got to show for our dependence since? Little more than an ugly, noisy, polluted soulless wilderness, and the threat of our total destruction. It is a curious trick to have played on ourselves.

Part Three

THE POLITICS OF A SAD LITTLE ISLAND

INTRODUCTION

It would be a mistake to suggest that life in Britain in the seventies was all gloom and despondency. Despite the ceaseless, demoralizing pressures of inflation, the rampant waves of collectivism that swept people up into such phenomena of the age as football hooliganism or some of the more disruptive forms of trade union activity, the passing of the frenzies of the sixties made the later years of the seventies in many ways a less strained, neurotic time to live in. It would be impossible, for instance, to measure the relief which followed from the quiescence of the great development mania which in the sixties and early seventies had roared through our towns and cities like a hurricane. The slowing of the pace of change manifested itself in countless ways. Even the departure of Edward Heath and Harold Wilson as national leaders brought a relief of its own, and there were many signs of the re-emergence of a quieter, more traditional approach to life, from the longer skirts in women's dress to the pervasive mood of nostalgia which hung over the theater, the cinema, and television.

Nevertheless there was one all-important respect in which, despite the discovery of North Sea oil, the seventies could hardly be said to have been a time when things improved for Britain.

Over the past 25 years or so—since that short-lived, illusionary "New Elizabethan era" of the early fifties, when Britain was still able to see herself as one of the international Big Three, still ruled "an empire on which the sun never set," was still (after America and Russia) the third richest and most technologically advanced nation—British political life has been dominated by one thing above all: our painful, often blindly reluctant, but always eventually enforced adjustment to our continual economic and political decline.

In the 1970s, one part of that process—the dismantling of the British Empire—was, with the exception of the "problem" of Rhodesia, virtually complete. Indeed there were those who saw the most intractable crisis which continued to confront the United Kingdom through the seventies, that in Northern Ireland, as a last ghostly epilogue to the whole Imperial story, appropriately centered on the unhappy island where Britain's "overseas expansion" had first begun 800 years before.

But another aspect of Britain's reluctance to accept her declining status in the world came so much to a head in the seventies that it became the dominant factor in our national life: our inability to accept that we were no longer a "rich" nation, certainly in terms of the prosperity enjoyed by North America and by our European neighbors.

In the fifties and sixties, like them, we had been through a tremendous "revolution of rising expectations." We had accustomed ourselves to thinking that we "deserved" the same standard of living as, say, France or Denmark. Yet for all sorts of reasons (some going back a century or more), we were no longer keeping up with those nations in the degree to which our industrial output justified those expectations (by the mid-seventies our "gross national product" per head had fallen to twentieth in the world league, behind such countries as Austria, Iceland, and Finland). The consequences of this gap between our assumption of what we deserved (both in terms of private and public spending) and what we were actually capable of producing was to color everyday existence in the seventies with a sense of strain and instability such as the British had never experienced.

The most obvious symptom of this gap, of course, was the inflation which even officially trebled prices during the decade—though the price of many things, such as houses, went up much further than that, accounting for the curious fact that although on paper we were all more or less supposed to be keeping pace with inflation, many people actually felt by the end of the decade that it was becoming much harder to make ends meet.

Just as debilitating as the more obvious strains caused by inflation, however, were those subtler social and psychological stresses it brought in its wake—envy, the constant awareness of how much "other people were making," the sense of unreality as money literally lost its meaning. As the noughts multiplied in the headlines, and words like "billion" became common-place, this applied as much to the spending of public money as of private. It was perhaps a tiny measure of how far this process had gone during the seventies that the most celebrated public spending cut of the decade was Mrs. Thatcher's decision in 1971, when Secretary of State for Education, to economize on school milk—saving the nation an annual total of £7 million. By the end of the decade one local authority, Southwark, could quite cheerfully contemplate spending ten times that sum, £70,000,000, on just one new council building—while the amount of money the government borrowed annually to finance its deficit rose in just five years from nothing in 1970 to some £10,000,000,000 at the height of Harold Wilson's mid-seventies spending spree (representing a tenth of the entire gross national product).

The most obvious disruptions of all to national life, as the meaning of money evaporated in this way, were those which resulted from the particular inability of the trade unions to accept that our expectations had outrun our will to justify them. This had already in the late sixties begun to create in the unions a new mood of aggression and "bloody-mindedness," a blind "protectionism," a desire to preserve the status quo in every-thing except ever fatter wage packets, which in the seventies, as both inflation and unemployment rose to levels unprecedented since the war, became even more marked.

What it all came down to was a quite straightforward matter of mass psychology. What was happening was that the British people (and the unions *par excellence*) were collectively slipping into a state of infantilism, where they expected the Great Mother (the State, the system, the World Machine) to gratify their desire for a continual supply of material good things, as of right, in precisely the way that a small child makes demands on its mother. As with all adult people who are reduced to this condition (e.g. the unruly students of the late sixties), the result is a state of rebellious dependency, where on the one hand it is expected that someone else shall provide all that is demanded, but on the other there is a continual mood of dissatisfaction, aggression, petulance, born of a fundamental diminution in self-respect, the unconscious knowledge that one is no longer behaving maturely as an autonomous human being. The symptoms of this familiar psychological condition could scarcely have been more obvious in Britain in the seventies.

I have deliberately placed at the head of this section an essay written on the resignation of Harold Wilson as Prime Minister in April 1976 because Wilson was in so many ways the apt presiding genius over Britain's slide into this condition. His two periods in office as premier conveniently defined that era between 1964 and 1976 which, as I argue in the essay "The Age of Mother," can be seen as a kind of self-contained period in English life, marked out by all sorts of rather morbid psychological symptoms which were in no way diminished by the interlude of Conservative government under Edward Heath in the early seventies.

The remaining essays in this section in no way comprise a comprehensive picture of Britain in the seventies. It is a measure of Britain's decline in the world that little of what happens in our somewhat ingrown, depressive society these days could be regarded as of much interest to readers across the Atlantic. I have, however, included in this American edition one or two essays on parochial themes, where they might be considered to have slightly more general significance. The essay on the disastrously misplanned new "city" at Milton Keynes in Buckinghamshire, for instance, provides yet another instance of that near-universal folly of our times—the belief that it is possible, by taking thought, to create large-scale planned environments in which human beings can happily live. The following essay on the great craze for "leisure" also touches on a fairly universal theme of our time.

Two essays then give perhaps some slight flavor of the remarkable and deeply depressing degree to which the trade union movement dominated British life in the seventies. The first was written on the eve of the closure for what turned out to be nearly a year of two of Britain's best-known newspapers, the *Times* and the *Sunday Times* (because of the unions' persistent sabotaging of production and their refusal to accept the new printing technology); the second was written a couple of months later, during what came to be known as Britain's "winter of discontent" in 1978/9, when a whole series of strikes crippled public services for weeks on end.

No account of the British political scene in the seventies would be complete without some mention of the most startling political scandal to erupt during the decade—the arrest and trial of the ex-Leader of the Liberal Party, Jeremy Thorpe, for murder, which ended in the summer of 1979 with his acquittal by an Old Bailey jury. The essay "The Two Faces of Jeremy Thorpe" was written in the wake of his arrest in the summer of the previous year.

The most startling political innovation of the decade (also marking a dramatic switch in the country's political mood) was the arrival in 1979 of Britain's first woman Prime Minister, bringing with her that whole new package of political attitudes known as "Thatcherism." This is discussed in the essay "The Iron Lady."

Finally, perhaps the greatest public shock for the British in the seventies was the news of the murder in Ireland in August

1979 of Earl Mountbatten, the Queen's cousin (with several members of his family), and also, on the same day, of 18 British soldiers in the worst terrorist outrage of the Northern Ireland troubles at Warrenpoint in County Down. Reflections on these events, written the following day, form the final essay in the section, "Mountbatten—The Man and His Murderers."

14

FAREWELL TO WILSON

Written in the week of the "Resignation Honours List" in June 1976, following Wilson's retirement as Prime Minister two months earlier.

The peculiar quality of surrealistic banality surrounding Sir Harold Wilson's valediction—the absurd honors list, followed by howls of "lies" and "orchestrated vendetta," at the slightest hint of criticism, the contract with "Lord Frost" for what the head of Yorkshire TV claims will be "a television landmark as important and fascinating as Lord Clark's *Civilisation*," the frenzied dinner-party speculation that Lady Forkbender is about to marry Lord Weidenfeld—all this has been so entirely typical of the stamp Wilson has imposed on English public life since the early sixties that it can only, once again, prompt reflection on the sheer enigma of this extraordinary figure.

Throughout his reign, as Professor Trevor-Roper pointed out in the *Spectator* last week, Wilson has been nothing if not consistent. In the week of Hugh Gaitskell's death in January 1963, I recall writing a *Private Eye* strip cartoon about "Harold Willsoon, a very clever little politician. The reason why he is called Willsoon is that whenever anyone has said, 'Oh, not even Harold would do a thing like that,' you can be absolutely certain that he will soon." And ever since, his most obvious single trait has been the way in which he has invariably managed to strain our collective credulity by always doing that one more unbelievable thing—like turning Marcia Williams into

Lady Forkbender only weeks after the "land reclamation" affair: with the added refinement, of course, that no sooner have people reacted with entirely predictable astonishment than they are blamed for being part of a plot got up by the Tory Media.

Yet the most incredible thing has been the way in which for all his follies and absurdities, for all the appalling collapse in British self-esteem over which he has presided, Wilson has always managed to trot quietly on, pipe in mouth, unchallengeably the dominant figure of English public life. Right to the end, against all the evidence, he has still managed to preserve a kind of grudging respect from the most unlikely people—"well, you've got to hand it to him, he is the most brilliant political operator"—almost as if it would simply be more than we could bear to admit the full extent of the disaster he has been.

The 13 years during which Wilson occupied the center of the British stage can, I believe, be divided into five distinct phases—each casting its own illumination on the nature of the Wilson riddle.

Firstly there were his original triumphant 18 months of opposition in 1963-64. He had come to power in the Labour Party with little more than a reputation for ruthless deviousness, at a time when, after the somewhat worthy milksop flavor of the Gaitskell years, those qualities seemed desirable rather than the reverse. Through the summer of Profumo, he stood back from the crumbling ruins of the Macmillan government, carefully cultivating an image of disdainful responsibility. And then, with two masterstrokes, he established the effortless dominance that was to carry him to power a year later.

The first was, with little more than a dazzling lick of paint, to erase all the divisions and squabbles which had racked the Labour Party for years past: without so much as a mention of "Clause Four" or "the Bomb," he simply lifted the eyes of the Party to the quite meaningless new dawn of "the white heat of the technological revolution." The second was to harness all that profound yearning in the closing days of Macmillan's "stagnant," Edwardian, grouse-moor Britain for a new age of "classless," "Kennedy-style" "dynamism." Without any meaningful commitment whatever, in the early months of 1964, he created precisely the right kind of vague, exciting, dynamic image for which so many hungered. In his own revealing words at the time, "the Labour Party is like a vehicle. If you drive at great speed, all the people in it are so exhilarated or so sick that you have no problems." In 1964, Wilson drove his vehicle so fast that exhilarated intellectuals and journalists crowded onto it without even pausing to glance at the destination-board—and on October 15, his love affair with the news media at its height, Wilson's first brilliant stage was consummated.

Stage two was the realities of office. There later grew up a legend among his disillusioned supporters that, in his first two years, Wilson did live up to that promise of "dynamism," and was only corrupted by the exigencies of power. But the remarkable thing, looking back to that era, is how totally and instantly he established all the broad outlines of the style which was to mark his successive premierships over the next 12 years: the fundamental lack of any broad strategy or solid achievement; the paranoid reflex whereby anything that went wrong had instantly to be blamed on "the Tory press" or "the speculators" or the "moaning minnies" of the "cocktail circuit"; above all, his obsession with the media and his own image.

Almost immediately, in *Mrs. Wilson's Diary* in the satirical magazine *Private Eye,* Richard Ingrams and John Wells brilliantly captured the extraordinary Walter Mitty-like flavor of the Wilson court: the entourage of seedy and mediocre aides and hangers-on; Wilson's own constant seeing of himself in image terms ("I'm not a Kennedy, I'm a Johnson—I fly by the seat of my pants," or the famous occasion later when Wilson somewhat unguardedly observed to Ingrams himself, looking round the crowd of assorted pop singers and footballers at a Downing Street party, "Jack Kennedy's soirées at the White House had nothing on this"). His arrival at Number 10, in short, was reminiscent of nothing so much as one of those little men who blow their savings on hiring a famous orchestra so that they can play great conductor for a night. And as Britain stumbled through the first year of Wilson rule, through a welter of half-baked measures, U-turns and headline-seeking gimmickry (the Harold Davies "peace mission" to Vietnam, the Beatles' MBEs), it should have become cruelly apparent just how empty all that talk of "100 days of dynamic action" had been.

Nevertheless, somehow the Wilson myth remained intact. During the autumn of 1965, in fact, as he entered into "eyeball to eyeball" confrontation with Ian Smith over Rhodesia ("my Cuba," as he excitedly told one reporter), he seemed even in some eyes to grow in stature. Flying up to Balmoral to consult with the Queen, or gravely informing the nation on one of his many TV appearances that he had the previous evening "talked on the phone to nineteen Commonwealth Prime Ministers," he seemed to be quite consciously slipping out of the gritty, dynamic, man-of-the-people role of a year before into a new silvery-haired, statesman-like pose (indeed he confirmed this a few months later when he advised the Irish Prime Minister that "a political leader should try to look, particularly on television, like a family doctor—the kind of man who inspires trust by his appearance, as well as by his soothing words").

The election landslide of March 1966, and the opinion polls which two months later showed him the most popular Prime Minister since records were kept, were the high-water mark. And then, all of a sudden, through the seamen's strike—engineered by that famous "tightly-knit group of politically motivated men"—and the great economic crisis of July 1966, the whole edifice collapsed. The *Observer* mourned "The Lost Leader" whose "reputation as a political magician" had vanished overnight. The Walter Mitty Superman was no more. And we were into the third phase of Wilson's reign, the four long grinding years of the late sixties when, as the government stumbled through an almost unbroken series of by-election defeats, from one silly mini-crisis to another ("D Notices," "In

Place of Strife"), the Prime Minister very noticeably withdrew himself from view.

Perhaps the most extraordinary feature of these years was the almost total lack of achievement of the 1966-70 Labour government (apart from the invasion of Anguilla, the dive-bombing of the Torrey Canyon, the starving of Biafra, and the quite unnecessary pulling down of hundreds of thousands of sound houses to make way for high-rise buildings). In his almost endearingly Mitty-like memoirs, for instance, Wilson at one point proudly lists the great reforming measures which were announced in the Queen's Speech of 1968. The chief items were: legislation to convert the Post Office from a department of state into a public corporation, and to transfer London Transport to the GLC; an Act to set up the new computerized vehicle licensing center in the "Welsh Development Area"; the Decimal Coinage Act; legislation on "the composition and power of the House of Lords"; a Bill to lower the voting age to eighteen; and a Bill to "encourage tourism."

It would be hard to conceive a more bankrupt list of mere administrative tinkerings—the only concrete results of which were to accelerate inflation by decimalization, and to subsidize the property developers into filling London with a mass of hideous new tourist hotels.

Indeed by 1970 Wilson was at a pretty low ebb. After years of talk about his "credibility gap," he was probably more widely despised than at any time before or since. He had achieved virtually nothing (except Chancellor Jenkins's rather laborious effort, at the expense of any economic growth, to bring the balance of payments and the budget into surplus). Even so, he was obviously shattered by his defeat at the June election. For months he looked tired and ill, there were rumors of his resignation. He virtually retired from public life to compile those memoirs, Nixon-like in their relentless self-justification. And over the next three years, he seemed to have lost almost all zest for his one-time favorite role as scourge of the Tories (presumably, like all self-fantasizing climbers, having once achieved power himself, he no longer saw Heath, as he had once seen Macmillan, as a giant to be toppled, commanding all his adrenalin). By far the most significant development of this fourth phase of his reign was the way his semi-abdication was used by the Labour left as an opportunity virtually to dictate the Party's new manifesto.

The final phase began in March 1974. No one seemed more visibly surprised and bucked up by his sudden return to Number 10 than Wilson himself. Within weeks he was almost back into the swing of his old familiar style. To the seedy and dubious land deals saga, his typical reaction was to envision cohorts of Tory journalists combing the country to dig up any untruth which would embarrass him, swiftly followed by the most ludicrous example of his abuse of the honors system since the ennoblement of Lord Brayley.*

Much more seriously, however, and worse than any of the faults of the first two Wilson governments, the years of his last two in 1974-6 will almost certainly be looked back on as the time when, thanks almost entirely to Wilson's most characteristic weakness, his invariable wish to avoid immediate trouble at the cost of storing up much worse for the future, Britain was allowed virtually to dig its own economic grave. With the country already reeling from the effects of the "Barber bubble," rocketing commodity prices and the four-fold rise in the price of oil, 1974-6 will be remembered as the years when, under the appallingly cynical and typically Wilsonian "Social Contract," wages and government spending were allowed to go through the roof. As other countries took desperate measures to cut back and fight off the crippling effects of the international inflation, Britain alone did nothing. Perhaps the supreme memorial of the whole Wilson style of government was the way in which, in those years, almost any ludicrous pay claim, almost any pressure for new public spending was given way to without a

---

*This was of course a reference to the award of a life peerage in June 1974 to his secretary Mrs. Marcia Williams, now Lady Falkender.

murmur—until finally in the spring of 1975, as the differential between Britain's rate of inflation and others at last yawned into an unbridgeable gulf, the pound began to collapse. Again, Wilson's response was utterly characteristic. On May 23, 1975 he was telling Robin Day that "to ask for a package that would counter inflation is like a child going round asking Mummy to do something to stop it raining." Five weeks later, as he ate strawberries and cream at an agricultural show in Warwickshire, he was saying, "We reject panic solutions." The following day the pound collapsed to its lowest point ever, and a panic-stricken Mr. Healey was announcing his "package to counter inflation."

It is hardly surprising that many people interpreted Wilson's sudden decision to resign, after all his Mitty-ish talk about wanting to be the longest-serving Prime Minister since Gladstone, in the most cynical light—as simply a recognition that the game was up. Having enjoyed the indulgence of allowing inflation to let rip, and the public sector borrowing requirement to rise to £10,000 million, Mr. Wilson was getting out before the catastrophe.

Such an interpretation, I suggest, does too much credit to his vastly overrated powers of political calculation. The real explanation, I believe, was simply that, deep down, Harold Wilson was bored. After all, in all his 13 years, he has never given an indication that his ultimate political motivation was anything more than an intense and rather naïve kind of egotism. It has long since been obviously pointless to consider his conduct in the familiar terms of honesty, or vision, or executive ability, or a genuine desire to improve the condition of the country, that one might have applied to previous Prime Ministers. He simply wanted to be Prime Minister, in the way that David Frost (a not dissimilar character) wanted to have a chat show on American television, or a poor man might want a Rolls Royce—and just as that man, having won his toy, eventually finds that it is no more than a car, so Wilson, after two years of his second term in office, simply decided he had had enough.

As for Wilson's chief legacy, it is clearly that he trivialized and debased the currency of English political life—from his abuse of the honors list to his abuse of meaningful language—in a way that has been true of no other Prime Minister in history. Kierkegaard once made a profound observation to the effect that revolutions fall into two categories: there is the really passionate kind of revolution, which tears everything down in a welter of blood and destruction; and there is the other bloodless, passionless kind which leaves everything standing, but "cunningly empties it of its significance."

When we think of the almost unbelievable changes Britain has been through since World War II, it is really quite extraordinary how little the outward forms of English life have changed. The Monarchy still rules. The Guard is still changed. The Mace still rests in the Mother of Parliaments. The Lord Mayor still has his Show. The Bank of England still presides over the Pound Sterling. We still have an Archbishop of Canterbury, a Royal Navy, a Foreign Office in its Renaissance palazzo. And yet in a million ways, large and small, the whole show has been "cunningly emptied of its significance." The Pound Sterling has become a laughing stock.* The Church of England dwindles, amid meaningless liturgies and gay priests. The Royal Navy, once used to quelling upstart little nations by sending off the odd gunboat, is now cut to ribbons by Icelandic gunboats in the squalid and unworthy dispute known appropriately as the "Cod War."

For the British, it has been a depressing time to live through—and over the latter stages of this steady declension of English life into a kind of seedy, Peter Simple dream world, the most appropriate presiding figure was Harold Wilson. It would of course be absurd to lay at Wilson's door the responsibility for all that has happened to Britain in the past 15 years. Partly it has been something inherent in the decline of any world power

---

*Written in 1976, the year when the pound briefly dropped to its all-time low of $1.54. Three years later, of course, thanks to such factors as North Sea oil and the weakness of the US economy, it had risen back to the seemingly incredible level of $2.30.

to comparatively insignificant status (if a very fat man suddenly loses 140 pounds and continues to wear the same clothes, he is bound to look ridiculous). Partly we are speaking of something which has happened all over the world, connected I suspect with the omnipresence of the television camera, which has played such a subtle part in diminishing, trivializing and making everything seem less "real." Partly it has been to do with the pace of technological and social change which has obviously driven everyone slightly dotty (you can only have a feeling of real social significance in a stable society).

For all this, perhaps the kindest thing that can be said about Harold Wilson is a remark Chesterton made of Lord Northcliffe in 1922: "It was the fault of his age, rather than himself, that he lived among shadows, fighting in a shadow pantomime." But Chesterton went on to say that "publicity consists not of things, but of their vast shadows thrown upon a wall. To make them so vast, the light must be held very low down." And in the case of Harold Wilson, there was never a moment's doubt as to who it was that was holding the light so low down.

15

THE AGE OF MOTHER

October 22, 1977

Reading the plethora of comment on the two books chronicling the rise and fall of Jim Slater,* I was struck by the implicit assumption in so many of the reviews that the years of Slater's success, between 1964 and 1975, constituted a kind of self-contained era in English life which has now receded into the past. Increasingly, those years, the Wilson-Heath-Wilson era, do seem to have had all sorts of qualities which mark them out as a distinct historical, political, and social subperiod—just as the years between 1956 (*Look Back in Anger* and Suez) and 1963 (the fall of Macmillan) formed such a previous distinct entity. Undoubtedly the prevailing climate of that strange and rather unpleasant time has now passed away; its heroes, such as Wilson, Heath, David Frost, the Beatles, Jim Slater, have lost their glamour and faded, if not into obscurity, at least into eclipse. And we can perhaps begin to see the distinctive quality of English life in those years in a new light.

I believe that an important clue to the nature of that period was contained in a fascinating recent article in the *Spectator* by

---

*The most celebrated British financier of the postwar era, who built up a huge financial empire between 1964 and the early seventies. In 1974-5 it crashed (rather like the Bernie Cornfeld empire before it) and was found to have been "an edifice consisting almost entirely of paper." But during his years of glory Slater exercised enormous influence and was widely portrayed in the media as a figure of superhuman acumen and great personal magnetism.

Leo Abse—which suggested that a great many of the more puzzling phenomena of politics could be explained, or at least illuminated, by recognizing the enormous unconscious influence of the psychology of "Father" and "Mother" on political attitudes. Right-wing politics, Mr. Abse suggested, with their emphasis on discipline, tradition, individualism, and leadership, are "father-oriented." Left-wing attitudes, with their emphasis on permissiveness, welfare, and corporatism, are "mother-oriented." One can see the truth of such an observation all over the political history of our times. One of the supreme examples of a society dominated by the attitudes of the "Terrible Father," for instance, has been Afrikaner South Africa—brutally "masculine" in its orientation, drawing its strength from a sense of historically-ordained hierarchy which must be maintained at all costs against a hostile, namby-pamby, decadent, "effeminate" outside world. Whereas the attitudes which spring from domination by the "Terrible Mother" can be seen at their most extreme in the politics of protest—the attitude of children who cannot grow up, who expect society to protect and shelter them indefinitely, while at the same time shrilly rebelling against anyone or anything which can be represented as the brutal tyranny of "Father."

Certainly an awareness of the unconscious influence of these two great opposites, these two irrational poles, can help to illuminate a great deal more than just politics; for instance, the world of finance and the City of London. Normally those serried ranks of soberly-suited men who inhabit the banks, stock exchanges, and finance houses of the world are heavily under the influence of "Father." "Masculine" qualities such as prudence, firmness, and conservatism rule. But from time to time, even such citadels of patriarchy are swept by irrational eruptions of more "feminine" qualities. Prudence and conservatism are swept aside. There is a sudden heady fascination for intuition, dash, youthful glamour. "Mothers' boys" emerge as heroes of the hour, who seem to have discovered the secret of conjuring money out of nothing, with none of the stuffy, prudish restraints which normally govern the world of the bank manager. And as the long history of financial scandals shows, from Wall Street in the twenties to the crash of the Cornfield and Slater empires in recent years, such heady intuitive spasms invariably end in disaster, with the re-emergence of the gray virtues of "Father."

Reading Jim Slater's autobiography, one is left in no doubt that he was psychologically a classic candidate for the role of hero in such an hour. He obviously has a very strong relationship with his mother (that vital ingredient in creating the irresistible self-confidence of so many would-be "world-conquering" heroes, from Napoleon to David Frost). Her presence is rarely far away throughout Slater's account of his life, from the early index entry "encourages Slater to work hard" to the moment of the final crash in 1975, when he writes, "My mother also gave me tremendous moral support." For such a man no disaster can ever seem so final as to become real. And anyone who might still be wondering why the proposed merger in 1973 between Hill Samuel and Slater Walker to make "the largest merchant bank in the world" did not come off, need only look at the picture showing Sir Kenneth Keith, the absolute embodiment of the heavy physical presence of "Father" (a slightly less grim version of Dr. Hans Martin Schleyer*), and Jim, the smiling "mother's boy," to see why in psychological terms alone the merger was bound to be a non-starter.

But of course it was not just in the City that English life between 1964 and 1975 was so clearly dominated by heroes and qualities with a very pronounced "feminine" aspect (I hasten to add here that I am not talking about homosexual tendencies, but something quite different, and rather more subtle). It was a period which began with the transmutation of Harold Macmillan from the "Supermac" of 1959 into the absolute stereotype of a bumbling, unimaginative, tradition-bound "Father" who had

---

*The West German industrialist who had been recently kidnapped by a terrorist group, and was later found murdered.

to be pushed out of the way in 1961-3. And for the next 11 years English life was ruled in countless ways by the very worst qualities associated with an "age of Mother"—narcissism, self-love, weakness, irrationality, and permissiveness in all its aspects, from morals to money. Think of the celebrities of that era—Harold Wilson, the Beatles, Frost, George Best, Slater, Heath. Despite Mr. Heath's petulant parodies of masculinity in his "Selsdon phase" and again in the disastrous winter of 1973-4, it was a time when real firmness, rationality, authority and other "male" qualities were at a very low ebb in English life. Under the supreme guiding star of Harold Wilson, the attributes at a premium were all those of the man with a very strong "feminine" side—the pursuit of the outward appearance, guile, winning ways, intuition, conciliation, and outward show, punctuated by outbursts of petulance, were the very essence of "the age of consensus," when no one should take too firm a stand or display too rigorous a set of moral principles on anything. It was altogether an age when "personality" took precedence over "character." And the only really conspicuous flag-bearer for a kind of irrational extreme "masculinity" of his own in English life during those years was Enoch Powell (with his attendant chorus of racist dockers and "Father-dominated" Tory ladies).

The symptoms of the collapse of the "masculine" during this period could be seen in almost every walk of national life—from the reign of a kind of effeminate, unstructured permissiveness in morals, education, and the arts (not for nothing was this the heyday of "Pseud's Corner"*), to the craze which swept politics and industry for every kind of "corporatism," for building up ever larger, more amorphous groups into which everyone could huddle for protection. The search for "pseudo-Mothers" in these years took every kind of form, from Wedgwood Benn's setting up of British Leyland to Edward Heath's craving for Britain to

---

*A regular column in the satirical magazine *Private Eye* chronicling the high-flown absurdities of art critics, intellectual jargon-mongers, and all those who found significance in the trivial.

become incorporated into the large, sheltering bulk of the European Community, from the "corporatization" of local government to the bureaucratization of the Health Service and the desire to close down as many small, local, independent hospitals as possible, in order to merge them into huge "maternal" entities. Now of course we can look back from the vantage point of the more sober late seventies to see how absurd and irrational all this pursuit of bigness for its own sake was. The prevailing climate has changed here as dramatically as it has toward the tower block in architecture or the vast permissive comprehensive school in education, but the damage of the "age of the Terrible Mother" is done.

One of the most conspicuous symptoms of this weak, self-destructive age was the almost complete collapse of "fatherly" financial prudence. The belief that money was to be had for nothing infected every kind of group in society, from the City hypnotized by Slaterism to the town halls on their spending spree, from the get-rich-quick property developers of the "Barber bubble" to the unions in the age of Jack Jones and Mick McGahey. Obviously the bubble of collective financial fantasy which was so sharply and disastrously deflated in the great crisis of 1974-6 originated in some ways in the early days of affluence in the mid-fifties and had just gone on growing ever since—but it undoubtedly reached its height in the years between Barber's "easy money" policy of 1971 and the wages spree of 1975, the time when the collapse of "masculine common sense" in money matters finally became so widespread and so complete that even Roy Jenkins could in retrospect seem to have played the role of a thoroughly conservative "Iron Chancellor" in the late 1960s.

Today there are certainly plenty of signs of what the Jungians might call a change in "the prevailing archetype" in English life. The "age of Mother" is discernibly in retreat on all fronts, and, whether Moses Callaghan fits his own bill or not, the virtues of masculine rationality and firmness are more in evidence than they were. But perhaps a last epitaph on the period 1964-75 should be left to Antonio Gramsci, in the comment from his *Prison Notebooks* which is quoted by John Fowles at the opening of his new novel *Daniel Martin:* "The old is dying and the new cannot be born; in this interregnum a great variety of morbid symptoms appears."

16

THE BRAVE NEW WORLD OF MILTON KEYNES

July 6, 1974

These are bleak days for the monster £1,000 million "prestige projects" which were such a disastrous legacy of the overblown fantasies of the sixties. The dinosaurs of Concorde, Maplin,* and the Channel Tunnel seem on the edge of extinction. But there is one project—more expensive, more grandiose, and potentially more disastrous than any of them—which, away from the headlines, is still quietly taking shape. Last Sunday I went to look at it.

An hour out of London up the M1, across 40 square miles of countryside, amid the trees, farms, and old villages of north Buckinghamshire, it is now becoming for the first time possible to discern the outlines of the "city of the future," Milton Keynes. To drive through this vast area today is an eerie experience. The first indications are in the sad little town of Bletchley—a tatty high-rise building, new industrial estates, a forlorn new futuristic "leisure complex," with its "freeform leisure pool."

Beyond, the rolling farmland is crisscrossed with mile upon mile of half-finished roads, labeled V8 or H7. Huge signs indicate "Milton Keynes Central," and a newly-built road leads to an abrupt halt at a pile of earth in the middle of a wheatfield.

The car stops. Yellowhammers and larks sing. All is still

*A huge scheme to build a new London airport on a reclaimed area of the North Sea, finally abandoned in 1975.

141

remote rural peace, on the site of what in three years' time is destined to be "the largest City Center complex in Europe," a mile long and half-a-mile wide.

On nearby hilltops stand the first housing projects of the new city. Not the sprawling, leafy, affluent suburbia of a Los Angeles, but hundreds of grim little misshapen boxes, in brick or corrugated metal, turned out by machine. It is hard to conceive that one is standing at the middle of what, in 15 years' time, is to be one of the major cities of Britain, housing a quarter of a million human beings.

Even harder is it to conceive, however, when one turns to the vision of "MK" conjured up in the mass glossy leaflets and promotional material available from the headquarters of this whole fantasy operation, aptly named Wavendon Tower. The message beamed forth from Wavendon Tower is two-fold. First, that MK is to be a city planned as no city has ever been planned before—right down to the last tree. Second, that it is to be a city dedicated as never before to "leisure." "One of the first European City Centers ever to recognize," proclaims a typical pamphlet, "that the car is a leisure instrument."

"The Linear Parks network in Milton Keynes," runs another, "is to form a continuous mesh across the city. The basis of this mesh is a movement pattern."

Clearly one of the problems most worrying the planners is that the wretched citizens will never know where they are. At one point they hope that the "road network," running "in vertical and horizontal curves corresponding closely to the land form with a reservation of about 100 meters" will be "clearly the identity-giving factor at City scale."

At another, "to aid navigation, complete areas of the development will have cladding colors in either red, yellow, or blue."

At a third, "an advanced tree-planting program is proposed to emphasize the movement pattern of the square so that when the houses are built the green infrastructure of the grid square will have matured sufficiently to form a recognizable overall pattern by which the inhabitants can locate themselves."

Admittedly, any difficulty the inhabitants have in locating themselves may be hardly surprising when it is borne in mind that "a system of street furniture which embraces all equipment (from lighting to ... bus shelters) are [*sic*] proposed with a family solution of structures throughout the city."

And, as if this is not enough for the home of the Open University, "at the apartment block it is the focus of the cube in its green square which is the architectural composition. This was Le Corbusier's point."

While for those office workers who want the opportunity to be "part of the glitter and the action" at the city center, "office buildings are likely to be low-rise and of the Burolandschaft or open plan type, although there will be some "shiny towers" at locations associated with transport nodes."

Finally, in this amazing catalogue of "Linear Parks," and "scarce resources centers" and "activity centers" ("where the man can talk about the problems with his car") and a stadium and ten golf courses and 63 tennis courts and countless "leisure complexes," and, of course, buildings just to live in, built of "white Forticrete block" on "power floated ground slabs," comes the incredible statement: "Milton Keynes is derived from the needs and aspirations of its inhabitants, rather than from an intellectual preconception of life."

Here, in short, is the ultimate monument to that schizoid science-fiction dream which has haunted the imagination of twentieth-century man—the "city in the park," the anthill of shining towers and mass leisure and humming new modes of transport, the utterly depersonalized nightmare which haunted Aldous Huxley in *Brave New World* just 40 short years ago.

Of course there are already signs that this custom-built city for the Deltas and Beta Minuses of tomorrow's Britain is far from living up to its planners' dream. In fact, in the present economic climate, with its gigantic call on public and private resources, the chances must be high that over the next decade Milton Keynes will simply become a pathetic national joke, falling ever further behind its ambitious schedule and finally grinding to a stop in a sea of mud and rusting contractors' equipment, unsold houses and half-finished factories.

But, in the name of the poor people who will actually have to live there, such a horrible mistake must never be made again.*

---

*Six years later, by the end of the decade, these gloomy forecasts were already some way to being realized. It had become apparent that the whole of the basic assumption on which "the need for Milton Keynes" had been posited—i.e. that the population of Southeast England was rapidly rising and that there would be two million more people by 1991—was a typical example of the folly of extrapolating from statistics. In fact the 1971 census had already shown that the population of Southeast England was static, and later figures showed that by the end of the decade it was in fact falling. In 1976 the government accordingly called a halt to its "New Towns policy," and the target figure for the population of Milton Keynes was lowered from 250,000 to 200,000. But already the whole city had been carefully planned *only* to work properly if it was fully developed to the original target figure (and so long as fuel prices made public and private transport cheap and viable). Instead of building outward from existing centers of population, such as Bletchley, the planners had deliberately placed the "largest city center in Europe" (opened August 1979) right in the middle of the "city," surrounded by vast tracts of open countryside. Instead of using the whole site of the city to the full, the planners had placed the greater part of the housing in cramped little estates, miles from anywhere, and the continuing, lavish publicity campaign to persuade people to live there seemed increasingly like a cruel hoax (particularly on those unfortunate council tenants from London who, having relinquished their own tenancies, now found it impossible to move back).

17

THE BRAVE NEW WORLD OF "LEISURE"

August 1973

Lenina looked down through the window in the floor between her feet. They were flying over the six kilometer zone of parkland that separated Central London from its first ring of satellite suburbs ... Forests of Centrifugal Bumble-puppy towers gleamed between the trees. Near Shepherd's Bush two thousand Beta-Minus mixed doubles were playing Riemann-surface tennis. A double row of Escalator-Fives Courts lined the main road from Notting Hill to Willesden. In the Ealing stadium a Delta gymnastic display and community sing was in progress ... Ten minutes later they were at Stoke Poges and had started their first round of Obstacle Golf.

When Aldous Huxley conjured up his horrendous vision of the Brave New World, he thought that his nightmare Utopia of genetic engineering, free love, and a constant supply of "happiness" drugs was still 600 years away. Fourteen years later, when he came to write a new introduction to the novel in 1946, he had brought down the timescale of his predictions to a century or so. Today, we recognize, we are in many respects already living in the Brave New World he describes—and in perhaps no respect was his intuition more accurate than in his perception of the central place that would be accorded by the inhabitants of his Brave New World to the mindless pursuit of organized, mass-produced "leisure."

Let us, like Lenina Crowne in the passage from *Brave New*

World which I quoted at the beginning of this article, take a helicopter ride across contemporary London. There are the gleaming towers, rising through the trees. There are the satellite suburbs, spreading as far as the eye can see. And there, just below us, is the delightful district now known by the Brave New World name of Havering.

What is this that is about to arise in the center of the charming old world town of Romford? It is a "£3.5 million new arts and recreation complex." "The architects and leisure specialists Gillinson Barnett and Partners," according to a handout lovingly prepared by the town's public relations officer, "are suggesting the creation of . . . a 30,000 sq. ft. civic arts center with flexible purpose hall . . . scores of recreational outlets in a new sports hall . . . and a leisure swimming pool that would be the first in Southern England."

"The facilities," he continues, "in low blocks with interesting pedestrian flows, will blend in with existing surroundings." Just what an "interesting pedestrian flow" might be, I leave to your imagination—but more interesting is the way in which these "facilities" will "blend in with existing surroundings." It appears that the "first leisure swimming pool in Southern England" will be situated just next to the New Market Place, with a wall of glass in between so that shoppers and swimmers will be able to goggle at each other as they go about respective pleasures.

This is not the only treat promised to the lucky swimmers of Havering. The leisure pool will have "a transparent roof, shallow beach areas, an irregular shape, a sunbathing solarium, a wave machine, waterfall and play chute." It will also apparently be stuffed with exotic poolside plants—"with selected planting inside," say the leisure specialists, "the leisure atmosphere should be unique."

The citizens of Kirby, Lancs., are made of altogether sterner stuff. Not for them any such sybaritic comforts as a "leisure pool." For them, amid the glories of their Urban District Council's proposed new £350,000 sports complex, it is proposed that there shall be "an assimilated rock wall in Quettabond, which is achieved by anchoring protruding concrete overhangs to the reinforced brickwork, and includes recesses to resemble niches and chimneys, the whole planned to allow would-be rock climbers to practice in their own neighborhood."

The enlightened Borough Council of the Rhondda Valley has lashed out even more extravagantly. In April this year, Major Clifford Jones, "well known for his great contribution to the international rugby scene," mounted a traxcavator to "cut the first sod" of a £750,000 new leisure complex to include not just "a sports hall and lesser halls" but also what are described as "projectile halls," apparently so that the local miners can indulge in such pastimes as "archery, badminton or yoga." The design for this pleasure dome has been decreed by a firm known as Module 2 Ltd, which lives in Piccadilly, London W 1.

At Holmes Pierrepoint in Nottinghamshire, the press was invited in May this year to inspect the £1.5 million "multipurpose sports center," jointly owned by the Sports Council and Nottinghamshire County Council. This "new national water sports center," which was to be opened by the Prime Minister on July 27, offers some of the finest rowing, canoeing, power boating and water skiing facilities in the world," linked with a "330-acre country park area which can accommodate up to 50,000 spectators in picnic-style comfort."

All over Britain, in short, the "leisure complexes" are sprouting like mushrooms. A "floodlit £20,000 dri-ski run" for a New Town here; a "10-acre inflatable multipurpose sportsdrome" for a West Country town there. Even the inhabitants of our prisons cannot escape the flood—for the denizens of Wormwood Scrubs may now take their leisure in two "glass reinforced polyester, folded plate structures" which are planned on "a 4 ft. modular grid, each module made of four separate mouldings of GRP jointed at the ridge and hips and erected as three pin portal arches"—not to forget the "Hume Atkins special Gymnasium fluorescent strip lighting mounted at hip level," and of course the "two to six air changes an hour" clearly laid down by the Home Office's specification.

Just what the burglars, murderers, and assorted rapists of

Wormwood Scrubs are expected to get up to in their "modular structures," I am not quite sure—but one thing quite certain is that the leisure craze is the "innest" thing of the seventies after inflation and playing the environment game.

It was no coincidence that this year's first international UNESCO architectural prize (launched as you will recall during the XIth Congress of the Union Internationale des Architectes held last year in Varna, Bulgaria, and won by Russian student V. Kirpichev) was based on the theme of "Space for Collective Recreational Activities." Or that the RIBA should have held a special two-day conference in May this year to discuss the whole "leisure problem," under the heading "Building for Recreation."

Among the subjects discussed at the conference were "the Leisure Revolution"; "Recreation in Cheshire"; "Planning Dual Use Facilities in the Urban Environment"; and "Sporting and Recreational Facilities in the Private and Commercial Sector." It must have been difficult at times to recall that what was being discussed had any connection with simple fun and games.

The questions posed by the speakers ranged from R. Pickering's challenging, "In the planning of recreational facilities are there anomalies which exist between the provision of facilities for the uncommitted at grass roots level and the needs of sport's elite?" to the dire warning in Norman Collin's, "If the local authorities ignore the serious shortage of leisure facilities and fail to give priority to provide the required facilities, what will be the consequences?" What indeed? Might we have seen steelworkers rioting in the Rhondda, for lack of a place to practice their yoga and badminton? Would the citizens of Romford rush into the streets crying for the administrators of Havering to be hung from lampposts, all for the lack of a mere "leisure pool" (complete with play chute and exotic plants)?

Nevertheless, the conference's winning entry was undoubtedly the thoughtful paper contributed by Colin Bonsey on the theme of "picnic areas." Mr. Bonsey addressed himself particularly to the problem that "people like to picnic as near to their car as they can." Obviously "to allow cars to drive about indiscriminately" on a designated picnic area can "wear out the grass and turn the area into a mud patch." This naturally "calls for some stage management" by the expert picnic area designer. "The typical picnic area," Mr. Bonsey concludes, "should preferably be a collection of small grassed areas or 'nesting sites' sheltered by informal groups of trees and bushes." These "individual picnic spots or 'nesting sites'" should be connected by a "simple graveled circuit track winding round the area." No detail is spared: "The layout of the road is important as it should meander from feature to feature, and never be straight." "Popular picnic areas might include a lavatory, a drinking water fountain, a limited number of picnic tables . . . a barbecue fireplace . . . and somewhere for the children to play."

Even the uniform of the ideal "picnic area warden" does not escape Mr. Bonsey's remorseless gaze. "Obviously we should avoid the park-keeper style with peaked cap, and I would settle for a workmanlike rig, perhaps battledress with shoulder flashes in the winter, and shirt-sleeve order with shoulder flashes in the summer." Nor should we expect our warden to be "a born naturalist or scholar, because if he is he may tend to fight shy of some of the more menial parts of his task, such as picking up litter."

What on earth is happening to our civilization? The most horrific program shown on television so far this year was nothing to do with the impending "eco-doom," nor the "energy crisis," nor even Watergate. It was the film of a whole city in the Arizona desert, entirely devoted to the playing of golf, morning, noon, and night. Here the senior citizens come to live out their last days, living in luxurious bungalows built in a series of huge concentric rings—each ring an emerald-green, well-watered, eighteen-hole golf course. Here each morning every single citizen issues forth in his electric golf cart, to spend every waking moment on the greens—and there was not one who did not hope to die there, too, preferably of a heart attack while still 3 up at the thirteenth.

We should not be surprised soon if we read a little item in the press announcing that Hammersmith Council is to spend £750,000 on building a Riemann-surface tennis court complex for Beta-Minuses at Shepherd's Bush. Or that the mammoth new leisure complex designed by Colonel Seifert for Stoke Poges is to include the latest electronic equipment for playing Obstacle Golf ("you can play any of the Great Courses of the World—just set the indicator, press the button and a film of St. Andrews or Sacramento will unfold before you as you play").

The point about Brave New Worlds is that they do not just spring up overnight, or people might see them for what they are. They develop slowly, in such a way that all seems quite natural. A "leisure pool" here, a press handout announcing that the Duke of Edinburgh is to open a new "350-acre picnic complex" there. And before we know where we are, we are taking the whole thing for granted, scrambling happily up our Quetta-bond replicas of the North face of the Eiger, driving into our allotted place in the Snowdonia "leisure park," dry-ski running down the slopes of the St. Paul's "fun area." As with Huxley's Brave New World, all passion, all adventure, all truth and tragedy and profundity will have gone out of the world. We shall be nothing more than a lot of beautifully fit, tanned, and healthy vegetables, pursuing the sacred cause of "leisure" all our lives long. And we won't even know what we're missing. Or will we?

18

Upstairs, Downstairs at The Times

November 25, 1978

As I watched last week's brilliant, infinitely depressing *Panorama* film on the battles behind the scenes in Gray's Inn Road as the great Times Newspapers dispute worked toward its present climax, I found a particular image coming more and more strongly to mind. It was of that strange, bleak, intangible mood of despair which hangs over H. G. Wells's vision of the England of the distant future in *The Time Machine,* in which society has become irreparably divided between the "upper-world" of the weak, pleasure-seeking, powerless Eloi, and the grim, resentful tribe of Morlocks, who live underground amid the constant throb of machinery, making regular forays to the surface to wreak futile havoc before retiring once more into their subterranean depths: "The Upper-world people might once have been the favored aristocracy, and the Morlocks their mechanical servants, but that had long since passed away. The two species which had resulted from the evolution of man were sliding towards, or had already arrived at, an altogether new relationship."

In the past decade or so of Britain's decline, the new bitter, disruptive mood of the "workers" has become the supreme, all-pervading issue of our society, hovering menacingly behind almost everything else—like an ever-present migraine which simply will not go away. On television, few images have become nightly more familiar than those of one group of workers or another, asserting their power and their "rights." Like the Hydra heads of a great subterranean dragon, the faces of men like Joe Gormley, Alan Fisher, Clive Jenkins, Sid Weighell, have become as familiar as any in the land. Scarcely a week goes by without a bread shortage, a crisis in the hospital service, or a plethora of disrupted rail services, as evidence of the monster's ceaseless stirring into angry, or just petulant activity. As for the shadow this mighty, brooding new power casts over the country's future, it has already reduced significant parts of the motor industry, the largest in Britain, to a state of almost catatonic paralysis. Where will it all end?

Part of the importance of the Times Newspapers dispute, after years when the particularly acute version of the national crisis on Fleet Street's own doorstep has been virtually the Great Unmentionable, is that it has brought into clearer focus than ever the sheer intractability of this wasting disease which has Britain so painfully on the rack. Certainly the picture the BBC gave last week of goings-on behind the scenes on almost any recent Saturday night in Gray's Inn Road showed a kingdom utterly divided into two, quite separate worlds—the "upper world" of smooth-talking, well-dressed, public-school-educated executives like Mr. Marmaduke Hussey, apparently talking the language of reason, progress, and efficiency, and the "lower world" of the printers, the machine minders, talking in the uncouth accents of aggression, negativity, envy, and distrust. And certainly it would have been possible for many viewers to see this division, as so often when we are presented with conflicts between two, utterly contrasting opposites, as simply a battle between "white" and "black," "goodies" and "baddies."

But there was another aspect to this division, caught by the film, which again has much wider resonance to the more general state of Britain today—and that was the extent to which the management, with their new electronic technology clicking away on the third floor, ready to go, represented a kind of computerized, dehumanized, West Coast future; while the printers, desperately trying to preserve with their clanking, oily old machines their notion of belonging to a craft, represented a past which, although undeniably inefficient, dirty, and obsolete (like steam trains and Victorian city centers), still symbolized that style of life created by the first machine age of the nineteenth century which, although it may have seemed in many ways horrible and inhuman at the time, has now in the computerized age of high-rise buildings, come to seem human, colorful, and an almost universal object of nostalgia.

In this respect, there was one moment in the *Panorama* film more evocative than any other—when the printers went through their traditional ceremony known as "banging out," by which they mark the retirement of one of their members. Everyone in the print shop rhythmically bangs the nearest piece of metal, producing a sound which for Wagner lovers is irresistibly reminiscent of the hammerings of the anvils in the cave of the Nibelungen in *Das Rheingold*. And mention of the Nibelungen may remind us that the notion of a world irreparably and catastrophically divided into two warring realms, an "upper" and a "lower," long predates H. G. Wells or even the industrial society of the nineteenth century.

One of the most powerful, mythical images ever created is that of the conflict which runs all the way through the story of the Norse Eddas, between the upper, daylit world of the gods in Asgard and their perpetual shadowy enemies, the giants and the dwarfs, who live below the earth and in the shadowy realms of Jotunheim. As one reads the Sagas today it is hard not to be reminded of our own society—and particularly by the giants, dependent on brute strength and cunning, deeply conservative, always causing trouble, racked with envy of the agreeable life they imagine is lived by the gods, constantly stirring in rebellious forays to seize gold or some other treasure from Asgard.

But not every literary reflection of a society divided into upper and lower halves is quite so catastrophic.

I do not believe it is wholly accidental that one of the most popular TV serials in the Britain of the seventies has been that cosy, nostalgic evocation of life in an aristocratic Edwardian household, *Upstairs Downstairs.* Viewers have obviously derived some obscure comfort from this daydream vision of a world in which the two realms, upper and lower, could still coexist in happy, interdependent harmony—such a striking contrast to the bleak, envious, divided, class-racked society of today. And the real point of how and why the world of *Upstairs Downstairs* did "work," apart from the fact that "everyone knew their place," was that, as in any large human organization which functions smoothly, such as an army at war or a ship at sea, this microcosmic society contained in effect not just two classes but three.

As I watched that *Panorama* film about Times Newspapers, the question I found myself asking more than any other was "what has happened to the NCOs?" It seems to be a law of collective human nature that any efficient organization should be made up not of two, completely separate groups of people (who will only fall to battling with each other) but of two interlocking hierarchies, like two cones, placed one inside the other—and the senior members of the "lower hierarchy," Hudson and Mrs. Bridges of *Upstairs Downstairs,* the RSMs and Chief Petty Officers of the armed forces, are people of very considerable stature in their own right (held in awe, for instance, by junior members of the "upper" hierarchy) whose loyalty, experience, and wisdom are absolutely crucial to the whole operation functioning smoothly.

What has happened to the newspaper industry (as it has happened to a greater or lesser degree throughout our society) is that the old NCO class (Chief Printers and the like) whose pride in their job was a cornerstone of the whole organization, have been devalued—and replaced as chief spokesmen and representatives of the "lower world" by shop stewards and trade union officials, who in old service language, are little more than "barrack room lawyers," motivated by a love of power and the sound of their own voices and incapable of exercising their function except in a perpetual trial of strength with the now completely split-off "upper world" represented by the "management."

The real tragedy of what has happened to Britain today is that once this split between the lower and upper worlds has occurred, *everyone* becomes powerless, at least in any meaningful sense. The workers become mere "giants," Morlocks, able to exercise their powers destructively, through envy and brute strength—which may give them the temporary illusion of self-importance and having more money in their pockets, but it is ultimately, because it is so negative, utterly soul-destroying. The Management is reduced, Eloi-like, to a kind of effete impotence, dreaming dreams of computerized efficiency—in effect, a world in which workers have been abolished altogether. And the ultimate irony is that no one has ever devised a world in which either workers *or* managers can be abolished. Even if the most extreme of the workers were to get their way, and bring the whole house of "capitalism" (as they laughably describe the inevitable structure of technological industrial society) crashing down, they will only be faced with a new, much grimmer kind of "management." They will still find themselves playing the part of "workers," at the bottom of a new, much more rigid, much more oppressive form of industrial hierarchy. And the new all-powerful state will presumably not even let them see *Upstairs Downstairs* on TV—so that they can at least dream, when they stagger home in the evenings, of a cosy, long-lost world in which Hudson and Mrs. Bridges somehow kept the family together and the whole show happily on the road.

19

EAST, WEST, IS HOME BEST?

I hope you all enjoyed Christmas 1978 as much as I did—but I must admit that the experience has left me in thoughtful mood. Three weeks ago I left you all behind in a country which seemed to be falling apart. Garages were already closing for the threatened gasoline strike. Radio and television programs were in chaos and threatened with complete closure. I arrived in Heathrow to find the airport almost paralyzed by an engineers' stoppage. A thick blanket of fog settled outside the windows. Thousands of passengers settled in for a seige which for some was to last more than 48 hours. As discomfort and frustration multiplied, and a sense of sheer, temper-fraying helplessness mounted, it seemed an all too familiar vignette of life in Britain today.

Then, miraculously, our flight was abstracted from the universal sea of "Delayed," "Canceled," "Non-Operational" on the departures board, shot to the top of the list, and we took off into a sun-drenched blue sky above the clouds, which shrouded a gray Britain below. Two hours later we were in a country where there are no strikes, no industrial troubles, no trade union officials coming on television to explain why it is essential that their members should inconvenience everyone else's lives. For ten days we enjoyed one of the happiest, most traditional Christmases imaginable—singing carols, telling stories, lighting candles on the tree, eating steaming bowls of carp—occasionally venturing forth into a city where churches were packed for magnificent Christmas services. Trams, buses, and public services were functioning efficiently. People warmly wrapped up, in fur hats, in the streets looked noticeably as cheerful, if not a great deal more so than their counterparts in Britain. No one gave any thought to the television or radio. It was altogether a model of how Christmas can be celebrated without recourse to outside resources—apart from the wonderful singing of the Christmas masses or a box for *The Magic Flute* in a little eighteenth-century opera house at less than 30 shillings a head. But then, of course, I was behind the Iron Curtain, in the People's Republic of Czechoslovakia.

As we left this haven of light, warmth, and jollity to return to Britain, a friend driving me along a freezing, snow-covered road to the airport, said, "Of course you will be going back to a country where they would have put grit on roads like this by now." We arrived back to a gray, depressed-looking London, headlines of "Grit-spreaders' Dispute Brings Traffic Chaos," delays on the underground and the general bad temper of a traditional "Britain Gets Back to Normal"—back in short to a scene not dissimilar to the one we had left, with news and conversation dominated by industrial troubles, petrol lines, truck drivers on strike, food shortages, and an unending trail of further troubles stretching over the horizon into 1979, from the miners to the power workers. Somehow to cap it all was the spectacle of Clive Jenkins* on television intoning one of those famous Jenkins litanies in which every sentence begins with the words "I blame..." almost everyone in the world other than his beloved, saintly self.

My first thoughts in reflecting on the contrast between these two experiences ran on the extraordinary sense of relief one now feels when given respite from the perpetual state of disintegration which prevails in Britain. There was a time, only a few years ago, when the main sense of relief one experienced

---

*A prominent trade union leader, much hated by the British bourgeoisie in the seventies for his frequent appearances on television expounding extreme left-wing views in a whining Welsh accent.

going to Eastern Europe was the freedom from the more garish blandishments of consumer capitalism—the constant, subliminal bombardment of advertising, of semipornography, of invitations to spend money, and of all those things which Solzhenitsyn in his Harvard speech last year summed up as "the revolting invasion of publicity, TV stupor and intolerable music." It is still a relief to get away from headlines about punk rock stars, corrupt football managers, unhappy heiresses, and obsessive talk about last night's TV serial—but even greater is that which comes from escaping that perpetual blanket of psychic strain created by the awareness that on all sides one group of people or another is trying to disrupt the workings of society, by stopping newspapers, hospitals, trains, electricity, airplanes, docks, or whatever little cog in the whole complex technological machine they happen to have their little bit of power over. It is only when one has been in a country where such things simply never happen that one really notices how depressing it is to the spirit to see night after night on television the faces of trade union leaders, distorted by that deadly combination of self-righteousness and negativity which is inseparable from their role. When did you last see Mr. Alan Fisher, Mr. David Basnett or Mr. Sid Weighell looking open, warm, relaxed, in a word human? Such men are in the grip of a collective psychic condition which subconsciously depresses us all even more than we realize.

Of course not the least irony of the terrible price that has been paid for the absence of such disintegration in Eastern Europe is that it has been imposed by men by no means dissimilar in temperament or political background to our trade union leaders—their role in society suitably metamorphosed, but unmistakably wearing the same gray-faced, unhappy, negative look. With the hidden threat of power such as we can scarcely conceive of, they have lowered their gray pall of bureaucratic restriction, drabness, shortages over whole societies. Uniformed men are only too evident in the streets. The ever-present fear of stepping out of line so pervades everyday life that it is almost impossible for an outsider to appreciate. Private conversation continually harps on the success of this person in getting an exit visa for the West, the failure of that.

But in the interstices of this congealed authoritarianism, people manage to carve out their own warm, intensely private little worlds, preserving their own notions of what is true, what is false, what is important, and what simply does not have to be bothered about. What to a Westerner is most lacking in Eastern Europe is the endless public hubbub of our own society—the din of publicity, of meaningless political argument, of whining and self-assertion, of sex, crime, discord, and shouting headlines. Life is so much *quieter,* more withdrawn, more isolated. One is no longer plugged in to that vast, all-pervasive, raucous *thing* which gives our society such a false sense of unity, by bombarding us through television and the newspapers with a constant stream of rubbish and trivia, in which politicians, singers, criminals, television personalities, sportsmen, and other "celebrities" are all blurred together as the supposed center of our lives.

Never before on a visit to "the Socialist world" have I felt more acutely the horrors of our own way of life as it has developed in the past decade or two, or been more ready to understand the shock described by Solzhenitsyn in his Harvard speech as he at last came face to face with the reality of life in the West. We have so much, and we make the worst of it. They in some ways, have so little, and many of them make the best of it. Above all, as never before, both in East and West, I have found myself looking at how individuals react to their circumstances. I do not think I have ever more greatly valued cheerfulness, those people who regardless of circumstances refuse to look depressed, bad-tempered, self-pitiful, self-righteous, but preserve around them little islands of warmth and good humor. I think of an elderly lady tramdriver in Prague, cheerfully sweeping snow from the tracks at 18 degrees below zero—or the smiling station master on a Piccadilly Line station trying to keep up the spirits of a fractious, glum crowd of passengers who had just been turned off a train "taken out of service" in mid-journey. Godfrey Winn I may sound like, but, by golly, if every-one behaved like Clive Jenkins where on earth would any of us be?

20

THE TWO FACES OF JEREMY THORPE

One of my earliest and most vivid memories of Jeremy Thorpe dates back to 1957. As a young barrister, he had come down to Dorset for the weekend after attending the most famous murder trial of the year—that of the South Coast doctor who was accused of killing off some of his elderly patients. On the evening of his arrival, Jeremy held a drawing room full of people entranced with a blow-by-blow re-enactment of the high points of the trial. Striding about the floor, he brilliantly mimicked in turn each of the main actors, such as the chief prosecuting counsel, the Attorney General of the Day, Sir Reginald Manmingham-Buller. It was an astonishing tour de force by a young man, still in his twenties, who was already fast becoming the *beau idéal* of Liberals all over the country, a suitable Crown Prince to the Party's glamorous new leader, Jo Grimond. They were heady times for Liberals—and for Jeremy Thorpe in particular the future could scarcely have seemed more sunlit.

Most of those present in that Dorset drawing room that evening would probably have predicted that in 21 years time Jeremy himself might well be Attorney General. The thought that he might be standing trial for conspiracy to murder would have seemed beyond the furthest reaches of fiction. And it is only because we have been inured by the shadows of rumor progressively lengthening over the past two or three years that we are any of us, even today, prepared to contemplate anything so incredible. Even last weekend, after those first, shattering

163

evening newspaper front pages—THORPE CHARGED—the media still seemed fairly nonplussed as to quite how to cope with such an earthquake at the center of our cosy, familiar British political scene. The television crews hung baffled round the Thorpe cottage, trailed him in and out of Barnstaple, earned themselves some familiar Thorpe satire at the Bishops Nympton flower show. Thorpe himself peered grimly at the pots of marrow jam as if trying to pretend that it was just any other Saturday in the constituency year. Perhaps the full measure of just what an extraordinary thing it is that has happened was caught by the *Sunday Telegraph* editorial, which claimed that Thorpe was facing "one of the gravest charges brought against any British politician in modern times." *One* of the gravest charges? What on earth was the *Sunday Telegraph* suggesting could possibly be compared to the gravity of a charge of conspiracy to murder? John Stonehouse's obtaining of passports under false pretenses? Edward Short's receipt of £250 from T. Dan Smith? Hugh Dalton's budget leak?

Undoubtedly the most perceptive and interesting press reaction of recent days has been a two-page profile of Thorpe in last Saturday's *Daily Mail*. Written by Peter Lewis, under the title "Man Behind the Actor's Mask," its theme was the remarkably two-sided nature of Jeremy Thorpe's personality. On the one hand, there is the familiar extrovert, the "Card in the Brown Bowler," the darling of the North Devon Liberals and of constituency workers up and down the land: the actor who can dress up as a Fleetwood fisherman, or a Nottingham milkman, or a West Country farmer: the votewinner, with his "amazing memory, leaping stiles and walking village streets," who has a joke for every occasion, and "seems to know everyone's names, their cars, their dogs, their piglets." On the other hand, one has to accept that there is another side to Thorpe, known to many of those who have worked with him most closely at Westminster— "another face, sometimes seen, which is dark and sombre. His witty tongue also has a cutting edge, which workers at party headquarters have sometimes felt . . . he can tear someone to shreds verbally. He can go on and on, then break off without giving you the chance to defend yourself. Among his favorite phrases is 'a child of three would not have done what you have done.'"

Certainly one of the more surprising things in recent months, as the net of fate has seemed to close round Thorpe, has been the *schadenfreude,* almost the vindictive glee, which normally quite sober and charitable people who have been Thorpe's senior colleagues in the past have shown at his discomfiture. One, with whom I had lunch a few months ago, said, "I cannot think of anyone I have ever worked with, or any one in public life, whom I would be more delighted to see brought down." As someone who has on the whole seen only the "public face" of Jeremy Thorpe, the charm and good humor, I was quite shaken by such vehemence—but as Peter Lewis's profile amply brings out, one must accept that Thorpe is a particularly dramatic example of that age-old psychological condition to which every one of us is prone in some degree or other: the split between what Jung called the *persona,* the outward personality that is turned toward the world, and the inner, hidden personality which, for the very reason that it is repressed, usually takes on a dark and negative (though of course not necessarily criminal) form. It is hard to think of any politician who does not suffer from the "*persona* problem" in one respect or other—it is the occupational disease of politics, just as it is of any profession whose members are in some way in the public eye, whether they are television personalities, film stars, writers like Ernest Hemingway, or even doctors and clergymen.

The chief peril which arises from the growth of an elaborate *persona* is that the split between the two halves of the personality is likely to worsen. It may be vainly or temporarily repressed, by means of alcohol or other forms of escapism, but it may eventually become intolerable. In the worst cases, the "dark side" may overwhelm the conscious personality altogether, as with Churchill's horrendous depressions, or even the suicides of such obvious "*persona* victims" as Marilyn Monroe or Hemingway himself. While the split remains, such people are incapable of true depth, nor do they understand what is happening to them—because it is only when the two halves of the personality, outer and inner, light and dark, are consciously faced up to and reconciled that anyone can begin to reach real self-understanding.

However the Thorpe affair ends—even if he is eventually cleared of the charges which have been laid against him at Minehead—it seems certain that one of the most dazzling careers in postwar British politics has been brought to an end, and that the shadow of these past few years will continue to hang over him for the rest of his life. As it has so far been publicly presented to us, it is one of those real-life dramas which uncannily echo the dream-turning-to-nightmare pattern of tragedy.

Yet again we see a particularly vivid example of that great psychological conundrum of our age, the boy hero who eventually comes unstuck, and many of whose inmost problems can be traced back to having a strong mother and a weak father (e.g. Jim Slater, David Frost, Harold Wilson, John Stonehouse). It may be that, as Freud puts it, "a man who has been the indisputable favorite of his mother keeps for life the feeling of being a conqueror, that confidence of success which often induces real success"; but it may also present such a man with appalling difficulties in relating both to his own masculinity and to the opposite sex. Such boy heroes may indeed conquer the world in terms of outward impact (as did Napoleon, one of the supreme examples in history). But such men are happiest when they can bask in the admiration of others, can show off like precocious children without having to take real, grown-up responsibility—which is why so many of them are attracted to the glamorous world of showbusiness (e.g. Frost or Groucho Marx). They live in an infantile fantasy of masculinity (for example Groucho's behavior in his films toward Margaret Dumont, Stonehouse's financial operations, Slater's likewise) which can cause no end of trouble.

Like Anthony Eden during the long years when he stood in the shadow of Churchill, such men are often seen to best advantage when they can play heir apparent to some more obvious father figure, but come a terrible cropper when they have to succeed to the role of Father or leader themselves—as did Eden or that other prime example of the phenomenon, the late Duke of Windsor. Similarly Thorpe, with his show-off gifts of wit and mimicry, never shone to such advantage as during the years when he could play chief lieutenant and heir apparent to Jo Grimond. His succession to the leadership in 1967 coincided with his first marriage and becoming a father—that brief sunlit period which was to end so tragically in his wife's death in 1970. But despite the Liberal Party's successes in the two general elections of 1974, Thorpe never seemed wholly at ease in the Liberal leadership. Even before his electoral triumphs of 1974, his weakness on the masculine side of his personality had led him to his foolish involvement with that very dubious financial operation, London and Counties Securities, the first of the fringe banks to come crashing down in the post-November 1973 financial collapse. While his private world had already become shadowed by that growing nightmare which has now erupted into the open, first bringing him down from the leadership, then leading him to this present crisis, unimaginably the worst of his life. Until the outcome is clear little more can be said, except perhaps this. So long as he has the support of the two women who are close to him, his mother and his wife, both of whom have strong personalities, all will never seem lost. But at the same time, in the face of this horrendous public ordeal it will be harder than ever for him to face up to that inner split. The urge to preserve the *persona* to the last will be strong indeed, even though it becomes nothing more than an empty and lifeless mask. Truly has this been a tragedy of our times.

21

THE IRON LADY

By the end of the seventies, the British appeared to have taken with surprising equanimity to the fact that for the first time in history there was a woman presiding over their affairs at 10 Downing Street. Yet they were still puzzled by her as a politician, as a personality. They could not quite "place her"—and this was indeed a consequence of her somewhat enigmatic gender.

From the moment Margaret Thatcher became leader of the Conservative Party in February 1975, a strange misconception grew up that, because she was a woman, she might somehow bring a female influence to bear on the running of our national affairs. Just how this would express itself—in greater compassion, in showing the kind of housewifely prudence that led her to pile up her larder with cans during a food crisis—was never quite clear.

But what people who held this view failed to grasp was the simple psychological truth that women who get on in politics do so because it is the male element in them which is hyperactive. What was ever truly feminine about such raging viragoes as Mrs. Barbara Castle or Mrs. Judith Hart—let alone about Mrs. Thatcher's prime-ministerial predecessors abroad, Golda Meir or Indira Gandhi?

Mrs. Thatcher's driving force throughout her career has always been that masculine element in her, which led her to become a lawyer and an industrial chemist, which gave her such a careful, legalistic mind and her habit of always seeming, even in the most friendly interview, to be straining to make some overinsistent, contrary point. If there was any single achievement which convinced her fellow Conservative MPs in 1975 that she would make their best leader, it was her performance, just prior to the leadership election, in outdoing all the men at their own game as she fought the Labour Party's Capital Transfer Tax and other financial provisions, detail by detail, through a parliamentary committee. In her first year as leader, a lot of her success in the House of Commons and in the country at large was due to the fact that she seemed more of a "man" than her opposite number, the wily, placatory, rather "feminine" Harold Wilson. It was certainly not her own feminine qualities which led the Russians in 1976 to dub her "the Iron Lady," any more than they had given rise to her earlier political nickname, "the Milksnatcher." When she reached office as Prime Minister, she seemed more than ever to cut a forceful figure alongside most of the rather emasculated group of senior ministers, Keith Joseph, Willie Whitelaw, Jim Prior, who surrounded her. And on issues where compassion might have been called into play, such as immigration or the admission of the Vietnamese refugees in the summer of 1979, it was conspicuously Mrs. Thatcher who appeared to take the tough, unfeminine line, while some of her colleagues such as Lord Carrington were way ahead of her in urging a softer, more humane approach.

Nevertheless in the new mood which overcame Britain in the late seventies, it was precisely this masculine element in Mrs. Thatcher, her insistence on financial rectitude and that people should be manly enough to stand on their own feet rather than rely for everything on the "Nanny State," that was her chief strength. The chief fear was not that, once in office, she would behave in a weak, womanish way, but that her attempt to take a tough, manly line would—as is usual when women are dominated by their masculine element, their *animus*—simply lead her to become bossy; that she might antagonize the unions and others by attempting to play a man's role without that full weight of masculine authority which is necessary for true, persuasive leadership (and which, curiously enough, can only be effective when it is tempered by precisely those softer, more feminine qualities, such as sympathy for others and a sense of humor, which the bossy woman so conspicuously lacks).

As the seventies came to an end, these fears were still largely unresolved. Despite her determination in the face of a gathering economic storm, despite her apparently skillful opening moves in the international chess game over Zimbabwe-Rhodesia and her courage in flying to Ulster in the wake of the Mountbatten and Warrenpoint murders, she still had not really been put to the test. But as the eighties began, there was perhaps a further fear which, although not widely expressed, ran even deeper than these—and it was one which stemmed from the whole of her philosophy and approach to politics.

At the heart of Mrs. Thatcher's "New Conservatism" was the belief that most of Britain's troubles stemmed from the fact that we had as a nation become soft, economically stagnant, overreliant on the State—and that if only we could get production going again and produce more wealth, a large part of these problems would simply vanish. As a general diagnosis, this might have had some considerable truth—but in the climate of growing fears over the future of the world's resources, above all energy, was it any longer realistic to base a political prescription for the future of any country on the premise of boundless economic growth? Even if, in the short run, Mrs. Thatcher's drive for "more private incentives, less public subsidies" *did* come off, sending a wave of new vitality coursing through the economy (which in itself seemed highly dubious), was it sensible to place all bets on such a proposition when it seemed that the real problem of the future might be to persuade, cajole and force people into *lowering* their expectations, in as fair and orderly a way as possible?

From one point of view, of course, it would have seemed the purest defeatism to talk in 1979 in this kind of language. For 30 years since the war, the whole of Britain's domestic politics had been centered on the promise of ever increasing growth, ever rising expectations. The two great ideological driving forces of the age, Socialism and Consumer-Capitalism, were so allied on this matter that they were indistinguishable, except in their prescriptions of how best to arrive at the common goal. And certainly the notion that there might simply not be the natural resources available to sustain unlimited growth throughout the world no more crept in to color with caution the utterances of politicians, of any party, in 1979 than it had done in earlier election years.

In the short term it may well have been that Mrs. Thatcher's policies were by far the more realistic of the two alternatives held out to the British people in the late seventies. But in the long term it may prove that she was simply holding out yet another version of the unobtainable Holy Grail; indeed that in doing so in quite the way she did, she was ensuring that when real economic storms blew up, of a world-wide nature, she would be particularly ill-equipped to give the British people the kind of leadership that might help them to adjust to such cruel realities. In this respect, it might well be in the end that such feminine qualities as compassion and an intuitive insight into the deeper realities of the situation would have stood both her and Britain in better stead than the impressive, but rather too one-sided reliance on the "masculine" that in May 1979 had carried her triumphantly to power.

22

MOUNTBATTEN: THE MAN AND HIS MURDERERS

September 1, 1979

In the wake of the news from County Sligo and County Down it is hard this week to write about anything else. When Airey Neave* was killed earlier this year, one thought that the Irish troubles had claimed by far their most prominent victim since General Wilson in 1920 and the Phoenix Park murders of 1882. Now it is impossible to imagine how that terrible sickness could have reached higher in British public life, short perhaps of the Queen herself—in an event only made more shocking by its context, a peaceful fishing trip in that sunlit bay on the remote coast of western Ireland.

Indeed in a curious way it took the total shock of such an event to bring home just what an astonishing figure Lord Mountbatten was. As his golden career unfolded in the first-class obituary program put together for BBC television by Ludovic Kennedy, it seemed as much a reminder of Britain's own glorious past, and of qualities and values we have lost, as a tribute to the man himself. It seemed almost unbelievable that one human being could have touched the history of our century at so many points, from the presence of Queen Victoria at his christening, through the resignation of his father as First Sea Lord in 1914; his friendship in the twenties with the young

---

*A senior Conservative politician, close colleague of Mrs. Thatcher and her spokesman on Northern Ireland, who was assassinated by Irish terrorists outside the House of Commons in March 1979.

173

Prince of Wales; staying in Hollywood with the Fairbanks and making a silent film with Charlie Chaplin; polo playing in Valletta under the shadow of the battle cruisers of the Mediterranean Fleet and being the man who brought the Royal Navy fully into the age of radio; the Hornblower-style boy's adventure story of the *Kelly*; the Southeast Asia campaign; the last Viceroy; being appointed First Sea Lord in 1955 by the same man, Winston Churchill, who had accepted the resignation of his father 43 years before; having reluctantly to provide ships for the last ignominious imperial adventure of Suez. As we reached the period of Britain's decline into postimperial seediness in the past 20 years, he seemed more than ever to be a last, sunlit link with that tradition of our national greatness which had run unbroken for hundreds of years and which now seems so hard to connect with our present trivial age of small men. Was there a more telling contrast in the film than that between Clement Attlee calling in the First Sea Lord to tell him that Mountbatten was to be taken back by the Navy after his time as Viceroy ("I haven't called you in for your opinions—I'm giving you an order"), and the associations conjured up by the revelation near the end that in 1965 Harold Wilson had been toying with the idea of sending Mountbatten out to "solve the Rhodesian problem?"

What emerged overall was a man who, within the framework of all the successive roles allotted to him in the public pageant of our time, developed a genuine and powerful sense of personal authority which stems not from mere personality but from character shaped over many decades by training, by self-discipline, by a developed and tested sense of self-reliance. He was a man who had learned how to relate fully and easily to his own masculinity, someone in whom all those human drives such as ambition and the desire to lead, which we have so often seen turned into immature self-parody by the lesser men of recent years, found proper expression. In the past two decades, for all sorts of reasons, we have been particularly ill at ease in this country with the type of masculinity Mountbatten represented. We have lived in an age when it has been hard for men to behave truly like men. We have seen endless displays of rather petulant pseudomasculinity from men such as Heath and Wilson.

But in Mountbatten (and in this he was perhaps fortunate in the time he lived), we saw someone who had been able to develop the "larger-than-life" stature of true maturity and someone who, therefore, in that fundamental sense which challenges and should inspire each one of us in the way we conduct our own lives, was worthy of real respect.

What, on the other hand, can we say of the "other side" of this culminatory drama of Lord Mountbatten's life, of those men who spent perhaps weeks or months carefully planning his murder (and quite incidentally those of anyone else, such as women, children, and the rest of his family, who happened to be around)? The other day I asked an analyst friend of mine over dinner his definition of a psychopath. He replied roughly as follows: "He is a moral defective, quite unable to share the 'objective' view of morality. He is so completely ego-centered that he interprets his own needs, longings, and desires as fundamental reality. Yet he is sufficiently in touch with reality very often to carry others along with him and to persuade them that he is right. He is a pathological liar. He may be purely impulsive, or he may be capable of long, obsessive planning to achieve his ends. He does not learn from punishment or experience. He is cold, unable to form close relationships, always ultimately betrays trust. He is quite untreatable because it is impossible to get through to him and to put him in touch with his own deeper self. He usually ends up in prison."

We tend to think of the psychopath as an individual, lone figure—the Yorkshire Ripper, the Boston Strangler, possibly with one or two accomplices, like Ian Brady. Indeed our prisons are full of such, whether they are murderers or merely confidence tricksters. Nevertheless, far more dangerous than the mere individual mass murderer, as we have seen so often in our times, from Trotsky, Lenin, and the Bolshevik revolutionaries, through to Hitler, Idi Amin, or Pol Pot, is the psychopath who is created not just by his own psychic disintegration but by collective factors in society around him. These are the "schizophrenic psychopaths" who may, in their private lives, be kind to women, children, and animals (invariably with a heavy overlay of sentimentality), may even be "devoutly religious," but who in their other personality "justify" their psychopathic behavior by reference to some collective cause—whether it be the "party," some form of nationalism, or merely that of a criminal gang.

In such a cause, the "collective psychopath" behaves just like the individual psychopath, except that instead of interpreting his own, individual desires as fundamental reality, he merges his own ego into that of the group—and it is in the service of that collective ego that he is prepared to do all the things with which we are familiar from the behavior of the individual psychopath, such as lying, the obsessive planning of terrible crimes, the wanton killing of women and children, and in general the complete suspension of any normal moral sense.

Why should the Irish have developed a proneness to this particular form of collective psychopathology? One thing which strikes one about the psychological make-up of the Irish over the past century and a half is the way they have been inclined to fall into the familiar pattern of the "boy hero who cannot grow up," who is unconsciously dominated by "Mother" (in this case "Mother Ireland," "Mother Church") and therefore remains frozen in permanent rebellion against the masculine world of "Father," represented by authority, by the "occupying British," above all by the British armed forces. Nothing could be more obviously reflective of the boy hero acting out an infantile parody of masculinity than the spectacle of the IRA parading through Belfast with their black berets and sunglasses, playing at being men (unconsciously looking for the approval of Mother for their courage in standing up to Father). And of course the opposite, equally immature form of play acting is that which affects the Paisleys, the ultra-loyalists, who identify with all the symbols of Father-masculinity, such as the flag, law and order, discipline—it was no accident that in his own tortured, lonely search for his own masculinity they should have attracted Enoch Powell.

It was perhaps ironic that, in so far as Lord Mountbatten was known to hold any view on the Irish problem, it was in favor of a federal solution—in other words, the same as the declared policy of the Sinn Fein movement itself. But more important was that, as the most distinguished surviving member of the British armed forces, not to mention as a member of the hated Royal Family, Mountbatten was, as one now sees in retrospect, the ideal target for their particular form of psychopathology, and the fact that he presented himself, undefended and completely vulnerable, in a remote part of Ireland was, as we can now see, asking for trouble. Above all, perhaps, he represented precisely that which his killers most desperately lack and therefore resent most deeply of all—he was a real man.

Part Four

Culture Heroes—Nostalgia and Self-deception

Introduction

In the souvenir shops of London in the late seventies there was on sale a postcard of peculiar poignancy. It showed a group of three politicians attending a Remembrance Day ceremony at the Cenotaph some years earlier—each with suitably solemn expressions and clutching a large wreath. The three men were Jeremy Thorpe, Harold Wilson, and Edward Heath—and the card was captioned, with I suspect wholly unconscious irony, "Lest We Forget."

By the end of the decade, of course, the rather foolish and fantastic period which these men had symbolized in Britain's public life, between the mid-sixties when they had become leaders of the three major parties and the mid-seventies when they departed, already seemed a long way away. Two of them had, for different reasons, passed under a very considerable cloud; the third, Edward Heath, still embittered by the circumstances of his removal from office, seemed more stubbornly than ever in the political wilderness.

But it was not only in politics that the great innovative wave which had thrown these men to the top of English life in the sixties seemed exhausted and part of another age. For 15 years from the mid-fifties on, Britain's great social turmoil had thrown up an absolute plethora of new "stars" and celebrities—playwrights, pop singers, television personalities, dress designers, film directors, novelists, artists. Now, in the seventies, there was no more revealing symptom of the way that turbulence had run its course than the almost complete lack of new "names." It was a

179

decade when fewer "stars" emerged from obscurity onto the national stage than any other of the century.

Indeed, both at home and abroad, the seventies were a time when old reputations crumbled rather than new ones were made. From Richard Nixon to Jackie Onassis, from Marshall McLuhan to David Frost, from the Beatles to Muhammad Ali, there were few celebrities from those heady days of the fifties and sixties who commanded the same respect or exercised anything like the same glamorous sway by the end of the decade as they had at its beginning.

Under its general title "Nostalgia and Self-deception," I do not wish to imply that the heterogeneous group of "culture heroes" who are the subject of this section were all of equal significance, or had much in common—except that, in different ways and at different levels, they all reflected the general exhaustion and confusion of our culture in the seventies.

The first essay, on David Frost, charts the career of the greatest superstar ever to have been thrown up by television, in its sixties heyday. In the ultimate emptiness of the "Frost phenomenon," as it emerged in the seventies, it is possible to read a reflection of the dwindling novelty of that essentially empty and superficial medium itself, which—though still obsessively watched, in "living color," by four-fifths of the population—turned out to have been perhaps the most over-rated of all the new toys twentieth-century man had devised for himself. The following essay, "The Rise and Fall of the Super-Egotists," is a kind of footnote on the sort of fame Frost enjoyed.

The third essay is a more personal look at another very different TV personality and culture hero of the seventies, Kenneth Clark.

Another inhabitant of the world of fashion whom, like Frost, we came to see in a somewhat changed perspective (as it emerged to what extent he had been as much a creation of the fantasy bubble of the sixties and early seventies as its observer) was Tom Wolfe.

Two rather more substantial figures of our times have been

John Betjeman and Arthur Koestler. Yet both in the seventies could be seen as symbolizing in their own way the loss of confidence and direction of an age in which it had become easier to perceive the charms of the past and the follies of the present than to see a healthful way forward into the future.

A somewhat different pair of Culture Heroes of the seventies, in that they were both literary figures of the distant past whose works enjoyed a tremendous vogue during the decade, were the subjects of the next two essays, Thomas Hardy and Anton Chekhov. It may be seen why I have included them under the subtitle of this section, as I try to uncover why it was that these two writers so particularly caught the imagination of our time.

One of the few groups in society which valiantly tried to keep the struggle toward a better, brighter future alive was, of course, the Women's Lib movement. The essay "The Real Failure of Women's Lib" is a retrospective look, ten years on, at the best-selling book *The Female Eunuch* by the lady who became virtually synonymous with the women's movement in Britain, Germaine Greer.

Finally there is an essay on another best-seller, one of the most haunting books of the decade, *Watership Down*—which, as I argue, beyond its cosy, sunlit, innocent-seeming surface could in reality be looked on as an unconscious cry for help, a dream of escape from the growing nightmare engulfing mankind.

23

DAVID FROST: THE MAN WHO ROSE WITHOUT TRACE

Adapted from an article written for the *Observer* in the week
of the first Nixon-Frost television interview, May 1977.

Last Thursday evening, a curious thing happened. Millions of
people in Britain turned on their television sets to watch what
most of them knew was likely to be a spectacular media non-
event. It was highly unlikely that any startling revelations
would emerge from the lavishly-publicized interviews between
David Frost and ex-President Nixon. Yet the very fact that they
switched on was a last fading tribute to the man who was once
the biggest superstar ever produced in the short history of
television.

The real shock, as the two wraith-like figures from what
seemed like another age hove into view, was the sheer stumbling, incoherent, sentimental, embarrassing amateurishness
of it all. Was this really the man who was once President of the
United States? Could this really be the man who was once
kinown as "the most ruthless TV interrogator of the Western
world?"

Shortly before Christmas 1970, the entire Establishment of
Nixon's America gathered at the White House, in full evening
dress. For the best part of two hours, the President, John Mitchell, Billy Graham, H. R. Haldeman and the rest were held
more or less enthralled by a selection of "Christmas readings,"
interspersed with such ancient jokes as the notice supposedly
seen outside a "New York church" reading, "If you are tired of

183

sin, come inside"—against which someone had penciled, "If you are not, ring this number."

Such chestnuts did not go down too well with all that august audience (Billy Graham in particular was reported to have been fairly tight-lipped about the whole affair, despite the Bible readings thrown in), but for the show's star, David Frost, just 30 years of age, that evening at the White House in the high noon of the Nixon Presidency was the peak of his astonishing career. A few months earlier an opinion poll in Britain had shown that he was better known than anyone except the Queen and Harold Wilson. In America, where his new five-nights-a-week chat show had swamped all opposition, he was described as "the best-known Englishman since Winston Churchill." Indeed his fame at that time was literally world-wide. In 1971, when Bangladesh became an independent nation, Frost was personally welcomed by Shaikh Abdul Rahman, the country's leader, in front of a crowd of 100,000 people. After the death of New Zealand Prime Minister Norman Kirk, Frost flew his widow to London for a special memorial service.

Yet in the past few years, something very strange has happened to the man who had traveled up through the frenzied, image-obsessed sixties like a meteor. His appearances on television, though noticeably fewer, have by no means ceased. The company he has kept has on the whole been just as starry and cosmic as at the height of his fame. But he has become almost like a ghostly presence, totally unreal, so that one is no longer quite sure whether he is really there or not (I recall a particularly surreal moment in 1974 when no sooner had one channel shown a laughing Muhammad Ali, just after winning a world heavyweight fight in Zaire, with a seemingly diminutive Frost clutching a microphone on the edge of the screen shouting "Super, Muhammad, super," than Frost appeared on another channel cosying up knee-to-knee with Senator Edward Kennedy, saying, "It's a great joy to be with you again, Senator.").

Did the "Frost phenomenon" ever have any reality? Or was it always something of an illusion? The answers to such questions, I believe, tell us a great deal about the curious nature of this freakish and unreal medium which in the past 20 years has passed into the center of our public and private lives.

I first met David Frost nearly 20 years ago at Cambridge. It is hard to convey just how "ordinary" he seemed in those days. Cambridge in the late fifties was obsessed with "success." Undoubtedly the dominant personality among the undergraduates of the time was Peter Cook, whose funny voices and "Goon" names (Pules, Rune) were imitated everywhere—and by no one more assiduously than the thin-faced young freshman from Beccles. When Cook introduced a "Macmillan Press Conference" cabaret act, to wild acclaim, Frost quickly had a pale version of his own. Although he never produced anything very remarkable, Frost worked at it all so hard—at his sketches and little bits of journalism, at being everywhere and knowing everyone—that in that highly competitive world, he soon became a kind of affectionately regarded joke. He was so dogged and so open about his desire to "get on" that despite his plagiarism (and despite such incidents as the time a group of his fellow cabaret artists arrived at Great Yarmouth to find posters announcing "DAVID FROST presents The Cambridge Footlights"—of which he was at the time only a very junior member—he explained that he "could not think" how such a poster had been printed), he was impossible to dislike.

By the time Frost came down in the summer of 1961 to work as a humble production trainee for a commercial television company, it seemed he might easily vanish into complete obscurity. For more than a year, while his contemporaries were winning fame in *Beyond the Fringe* and at the new "Establishment Club," he was doing little more than make occasional £15-a-night cabaret appearances and being ruled by one of his TV company superiors as having "the wrong face for television."

The great turning point came on the night of November 24, 1962, when the BBC launched its new Saturday night "satire show" *That Was The Week That Was.* Frost had come to be chosen as the show's "anchorman" almost by a series of accidents (he was originally picked by producer Ned Sherrin as a supporting ad-lib comedian). But in the strange atmosphere of that winter, the twilight of Macmillan's England, *TW3* became overnight the most hypnotically watched TV series in history—and, as its chief star, Frost became, equally overnight, a national figure of a kind television had never produced before.

The transformation in him was remarkable. He even looked physically broader. Suddenly, at the age of just 23, he had entered a magic new world—expensive restaurants, taxis (he helped to run up one of the BBC's largest ever taxi bills, by such devices as keeping drivers waiting for an hour while he underwent his twice-weekly grooming at the hairdresser), newspaper interviews—where every day was like a royal progress through a wash of compliments ("loved the show," "super," "bless you").

Frost was never by any stretch of the imagination a satirist (indeed he scarcely held passionate views on anything), but there was one thing it was impossible not to be impressed by—his extraordinary, intuitive feel for television itself. In the studio, he was instantly, nervelessly at home, as if the very presence of cameras and lights gave him an extra charge of confidence and energy. Yet where could such astonishing ambition, unattached to any specific talent (other than his remarkable confidence on television), turn to next?

In January 1964 came a clue. We were together in New York. Frost was in an unusual state of excitement. He had caught his first glimpse of the American TV "chat show"—and, as he talked of Sullivan, Paar, and Carson, he was more obviously star-struck than I had ever known him. He had at last spotted the Everest of his universe.

The following winter, he took at least a tiny step toward that immeasurably distant goal when, back in Britain, he worked himself (again not as originally intended) into the center of the hugely ambitious attempt to follow *TW3* with a mixture of sketches and chat with modest celebrities, spread over three nights of each weekend, *Not So Much A Programme, More A*

Way Of Life. But then came disaster. As the show's run came to a close amid a storm of public protests, the BBC chiefs panicked. There must be no more embarrassing satire. The chief cuckoo in the nest, Frost, must be sacked—and it was small consolation to him that, as their one concession to his "image," they agreed it should merely be announced that he had resigned, as if of his own volition.

Through most of 1965 Frost was at a low ebb, unemployed and unnoticed. But he then pulled off the coup which was to be the hinge of his entire career. As Daniel Boorstin wrote in *The Image,* "Being well-known for their well-known-ness, celebrities intensify their celebrity images simply by being well-known for relations among themselves. By a kind of symbiosis, celebrities live off each other."

On January 7, 1966, gambling on a sudden hunch, Frost invited 17 people to a champagne breakfast at the Connaught Hotel. They included newspaper tycoons, Fleet Street editors, such celebrities of the sixties as Len Deighton and the Bishop of Woolwich—and the Prime Minister, Harold Wilson. Few of them had the slightest idea why they had been invited (let alone why they had accepted)—but Frost's intuitive sense of the power of television to blur all celebrities into the same dream-like mass was unerring. They came—and from then on he was "the man who invited the Prime Minister to breakfast."

His career now took off like a rocket. Within months Frost had moved into an expensive house in Knightsbridge. He had built up his own team of advisers. By the autumn he had negotiated his own chat show on ITV, *The Frost Programme,* explicitly planned to associate him with "big names" and headline-making coups, like the first TV interview with the rebel Rhodesian Prime Minister Ian Smith (which began "Good evening, Ian"). The series ended some months later with the harrying before a specially invited audience of the fraudulent insurance chief Dr. Savundra. As he left the studio to frenzied cheers, and shouts of "good old Frostie," it was his most heroic moment.

In 1967, after setting up London Weekend Television, by a

series of self-introductory telephone calls to prospective backers, such as Arnold Weinstock of GEC, he won a contract from the ITA for "his own" television company. In October he made skillful use of a speech to 150 American TV executives at the Royal Garden Hotel (billed as "Britain's Number One TV Personality") to win himself a million-dollar contract to interview all the following year's Presidential hopefuls on American TV. And by the end of 1968, after another carefully-timed telephone call to the head of the Westinghouse network (on hearing that their main "talk-show host" was leaving), Frost was finally within sight of the goal he had set himself just four short years before.

There was just one last hurdle. When it was put to London Weekend's managing director, Michael Peacock, that his new company's star asset was contemplating a five-nights-a-week show in New York, in addition to three nights in London, Peacock was flabbergasted. It just could not be done. Eight nights a week on television was contrary to nature. Never was Frost's ambition so pushing, so insatiable. His biographer, Willi Frischauer, has described the extraordinary lobbying, negotiations, and telephone calls that went on throughout a weekend. When Peacock finally caved in, as Frischauer relates, Frost ordered his chauffeur to drive him to Westminster Abbey, where he knew there was "a special chapel set aside for private prayer." It was closed, but, on the way back, St. Columba's, Pont Street, sufficed for this unique moment of thanksgiving.

On July 7, 1969, after a coast-to-coast campaign of mysterious advertisements for "The Great Briton," the "David Frost Show" was finally unveiled (an interview with Prince Charles). Within months, the reports were coming back: "David Frost is now a bigger success on American TV than he has ever been here." In Britain that winter he interviewed Prince Philip, and Harold Wilson from Number Ten Downing Street. In New York he talked to Dean Acheson, Golda Meir, John Lennon, and Yoko Ono. In the space of one week in June 1970 he was awarded the OBE in Britain, made Doctor of Laws in Boston, and given a "Faith and Freedom" award by the "Religious Heritage of America," for "communicating the relevance of Judeo-Christian ethics to twentieth-century America." His agent let it be known that "David" would be prepared to do a TV commercial for £100,000 ("he has always refused before . . . the commercial is now an international service in which he firmly believes").

In December, the ultimate accolade, Frost was invited by President Nixon to give his special White House Christmas Show (his mother Mona, flown over from Beccles to sit between Nixon and John Mitchell at dinner, told them, "I had to give up a training session with the Women's Fellowship Choir to be here").

But the terrifying strain was beginning to show. In Britain that winter, Frost was running for the first time into heavy criticism. Noting that most of his guests on British screens were now American—Spiro Agnew, Woody Allen, Norman Mailer— Milton Shulman commented, "Frost approaches them in the cooing, glutinous, chummy, ingratiating style which obviously appeals to American viewers . . . one senses he has lost his instinctive grasp of what is going on in this country."

Over the next two years, amid a clatter of falling ratings on both sides of the Atlantic, the whole thing collapsed with astonishing speed. In Britain he gradually vanished from the screen. In America, in a last desperate bid to retain his image, on January 12, 1972 he flew 60 guests to Bermuda for lunch, including Professors Galbraith and Schlesinger, John and Yoko, Sargent Shriver and Bobby Fischer. All in vain. On May 6 came the headline "FROST SHOW CANCELLED." The cancellation, according to Frost, was "at my request. I felt the time had come to move on to something new."

In Frost's clipping file there are certain quotations which recur. One, used often in the sixties, and ascribed to a sermon heard in childhood, was "Happiness is a by-product of doing what you like." In 1971 the remark appeared with a significant alteration: "Money is a by-product of doing what you like."

Frost was already a millionaire and had for some years been building up a whole network of TV production companies, some registered in the Bahamas and Curaçao. But in 1971 his fascination with money began to show a new intensity. There was a night-club deal with Bass Charrington, an interest in a two-million-dollar scheme to sell replicas of the Liberty Bell to America, another in a Japanese-U.S. steak house chain ("an all-important attraction is the ballet-like manner in which the chef serves and cuts the food").

Then in February 1972 it was announced that financier Jim Slater had bought a company called Equity Enterprises, as "a sort of investment piggy-bank for 33-year-old David and other friends." Over the next year or two it became clear that Frost had at last found a new world which had almost as much glamour for him as television. In particular his admiration for Slater became a wonder to behold.

I once met David around this time at a party. He came out into the garden, where he saw a senior executive of the *Sunday Times,* which had recently been running some hostile articles about Slater. "Very good articles, Ron," he began. "I've no complaint about that. But if you're going to write about merchant bankers, why do you just pick on one?" He went on to suggest that, when "all this is over," Ron should invite Slater to lunch. "You would be absolutely fascinated by his mind." For dramatic effect, David pointed in the fading light to a nearby rosebush. "I mean Jim is as interested in why that rose should wither and die as he is in a balance sheet."

It was an eerie moment. David was addressing a small group of friends and acquaintances as if it were some shadowy television audience. It was as if, after years of living in the television bubble, he had passed permanently through into the looking-glass world.

In the past three years, although he is far from bankrupt, many of Frost's more grandiose financial projects have come unstuck. The shares of Equity Enterprises, in the wake of the Slater debacle, still stand suspended. And it is hardly surprising that, as a kind of last grand throw, he has returned to television, and to those two retired political stars of the sixties and early seventies with whom in a curious way his own career has been so closely linked. Almost everything now hangs for Frost on the success of his two vast international collaborative operations with Richard Nixon and Harold Wilson (as indeed, like three drunks leaning on one another, they depend on him).

What made Frostie run? For nearly 20 years I have been haunted by that question. He is so completely unlike any other human being I have ever met that I have even sometimes come to think of him as hardly human at all, simply as a phenomenon.

I once recognized the puzzlement of H. R. Haldeman when, in an interview, he was asked to assess Richard Nixon "as a man." He just could not place Nixon in normal human terms. And I have often felt over the years that Nixon and Frost (and indeed Wilson himself) had an extraordinary quality in common. It was as if, as people, they had no "center," as if they had become so completely absorbed and submerged by the demands of their public image, and by the whole shadowy realm of receding mirrors they inhabited, that in any other terms they had virtually ceased to exist.

Despite his universal geniality, from Cambridge on, David's most obvious quality was ambition of an all-consuming and extraordinary kind. With most people it is possible to localize their ambition—they want to be Prime Minister, or write a great novel, or make a million pounds. But David's ambition had a kind of distilled purity. He simply wanted to be amazingly famous for being David Frost. All the guises he adopted along the way—cabaret artist, satirist, fearless interviewer, cosy intimate of the stars—were merely passing means to that one all-consuming end.

Of course he could never have done it except in the age of television. He never had the specific ability as a writer or actor to achieve such unique fame through journalism or the films (he had very little ability, in fact, as either). Only television was sufficiently ill-defined (in McLuhan terms "cool") to allow Frost to become famous simply for being himself—which is why he remains perhaps the supreme symbol of that curious, unreal period, the "McLuhan Age."

Nevertheless it would be a mistake (though one often made) to see David just as an ordinary person blown up large by the media. In fact he has unusual gifts—superhuman energy, compelling charm, an extraordinary memory for faces, great personal generosity. In all these respects, his eulogists, such as Bernard Levin, are completely right. What they forget to add is that the bad fairy who came late to the christening decreed that all these gifts should be used only to serve one end, David's peculiar ambition to be world-famous simply for the sake of being world-famous. That is why, once that ambition finally began to crystalize round one specific goal, it could only be to head for the very heart of the furnace where, in the 1960s at least, "celebrity fame" was manufactured—the American TV chat show. In the context of real fame, of course, it is an astonishingly limited little goal (I remember once, when Frost's celebrity was at its height, asking a Nobel prize winner who spent much time in both Britain and America what he thought of David Frost: he replied, "Frost? Who? I've never heard of this man"). But in prospect, for the minister's son from Beccles, whose world view had been shaped by the *Reader's Digest* and *Time,* it seemed a goal transcending everything else in the world, worth seven years of astonishing energy and will to achieve. Only when it was realized, did it inevitably turn to dust. Because in the end there has to be more to ambition than just the desire to become famous, to whatever superhuman limits it is felt and pursued. That is why the most fitting epitaph on Frost's career remains, alas, that coined as long ago as 1967 by Kitty Muggeridge, when she said, "Frost has risen without trace."

24

THE RISE AND FALL OF THE SUPER-EGOTISTS

Without wishing to add further to the verbiage already lavished on the multi-million-dollar drool-in between David Frost and Richard Nixon, I would just like to offer a kind of extended footnote to my observation that, as public figures, Frost, Nixon, and Harold Wilson have certain remarkable qualities in common. I believe that we have here a type of man, or rather phenomenon, which, while seeming in some ways to be so contemporary, so much a product of the unreal, image-conscious television age, has in fact occurred many times before in history and cries out for some kind of identification.

What are the qualities which distinguish such men? In fact it is of the essence of what we are trying to describe that such men are very *hard* to define in normal human terms. They seem to exist almost entirely in terms of their relentless upward drive, their almost unnatural ability to manipulate others into accepting them at their own self-valuation. They seem to transcend almost all the normal canons of what is acceptable and expected. They seem in a curious way (without necessarily being in any obvious way immoral) to be detached from morality. They display colossal cheek, and get away with it.

First, that curious personal elusiveness. Professor Daniel Boorstin touches on this, when he writes in *The Image* about the celebrity—"his qualities—or rather lack of them—illustrate our peculiar problem. He is neither good nor bad, great nor petty. He is the human pseudo-event . . . made by all of us who willingly read about him, watch him on television . . . his relation to morality and even reality is highly ambiguous."

We can see how this applies to Frost, and the extraordinary way in which it was impossible ever to pin Frost down to any of the various roles he played during his career—comedian, actor, satirist, fearless interviewer, cosy intimate of the stars, big businessman. Was he ever really *any* of these things? If so, he was never much good at being any of them specifically—but what he was always superbly good at was using those various passing roles to play himself, heading relentlessly on toward some mysterious place in the sun, simply for being David Frost.

The same was true in political terms of Wilson and Nixon. What did either of them ever actually *stand* for? Certainly no identifiable point of principle, no philosophy, no fixed position on anything. Like Frost, they played their various passing roles, for or against the Common Market, for or against *détente* with the Russians, like a succession of costumes, chosen in accordance with the mood of the times, simply to serve the supreme end of getting to the top and staying there.

Secondly, there is the element of cheek or *chutzpah,* of always doing the thing which no one would have thought that even they would try to get away with, as if the normal criteria of expected behavior just did not apply. One of the most revealing episodes I recall from my years working closely with Frost was a visit to his hotel when we were together in New York in 1964, shortly after Kennedy's death. His room was almost papered with drafts of two letters, one to David Ormsby Gore, our Ambassador in Washington, the other to President Johnson. Their purpose was to secure for Frost the first, exclusive BBC interview with the new President. It was an extraordinary thing to try on. As a mere 24-year-old member of the *TW3* team, Frost had no official status whatever (indeed Robin Day and a visiting *Panorama* team, seeking the same interview, were absolutely enraged to find that, whatever "usual channel" they tried to get into the White House, the jumped-up young unknown had been there first).

Of course this colossal nerve was characteristic of Frost's career at many points on his upward climb—the outrageous plagiarism of his early days, the embarrassing awfulness of his cabaret acts, and his endless repetition of the same old terrible jokes, above all perhaps that astonishing breakfast at the Connaught Hotel in 1966, when Harold Wilson, the editors of some of Britain's leading newspapers, and a whole crowd of celebrities turned up to drink champagne with a mere "TV satirist" simply because they had been so taken in by his total self-confidence that they never paused until afterward to realize what an extraordinary self-publicity stunt they had all unwittingly given their support to.

Exactly the same suspension of disbelief has attended Harold Wilson's career at every stage—to the point where a sense of reality was almost eroded. Even when he appointed his secretary Marcia Williams to the peerage, barely a month after the squalid "land deals" affair, no one really knew how to react except with bemused acceptance. He "got away with it" just as he had got away with a thousand lesser absurdities before, from his ludicrous *volte face* over the "Bank Rate Leak" of 1957, to his dreadful pop-cultural name-dropping.

Yet however embarrassing such things are to those who know their perpetrators closely, and are not under the spell, the extraordinary thing is just how potent and durable the spell is for millions of others. And here we may see a historical parallel. In Sir Lewis Namier's essay on Napoleon III, he describes the astonishment of those who knew Louis Napoleon well, that such a completely ordinary, mediocre little man should be the Emperor of France. But away from the court, away from Paris, Louis assumed, like the TV superstar of today, an almost divine stature—the millions, looking up, invested him with superhuman qualities which existed solely in their own minds.

Above all, so total is their ambition, these Super-Egotists seem to have missing from their mental make-up that X-Factor which for most of us preserves some sense of our place in society and in the hierarchy of talent or birth or proper expectation. Like Balzac's de Rastignac, they see society simply laid out before them as a series of stepping stones, enabling them to hurtle upward without any inhibition. There is no place so high that they cannot instantly aspire to it, simply because in the end their own ambition is the only criterion of value they know. The only limit to their ambition is the limitations imposed by their own imagination as to how far they can climb.

Obviously one of the greatest examples of such Super-Egotism in history, hurtling up from nowhere in the social shambles that succeeded the French Revolution, was Napoleon I. The way in which, in barely ten years, Napoleon Bonaparte rose from complete obscurity as a young gunnery officer to being first the ruler of France, and then the Emperor of half Europe, has much in common on a grander social and political scale with the meteoric climb of a Frost or other celebrity of our own day. Although Napoleon may have seemed to have more obvious talents, such as his generalship, he still had that same curiously elusive quality as a human being. His incredible climb to the top, even his military successes, were all ultimately achieved by colossal nerve and self-confidence, magnified into a seemingly irresistible force of nature. And when I read of Napoleon enthroned at Erfurt in 1808, giving audience to the crowned heads of Europe, I always think of him as a kind of Super-Frost, sitting with all those celebrities at the center of a kind of Super TV chat show.

Yet, like Groucho Marx not wanting to be a member of any club that would let him in, there is in the hour of triumph of all these men a kind of cosmic frustration, that in having achieved their supreme goals so easily they have in fact rendered meaningless the whole structure and hierarchy of the world they have conquered. So Frost, having become the ultimate TV superstar, sitting on his Everest in 1970, suddenly finds that he has lost his incredible inner drive, becomes inwardly tired and flabby, and finds the whole thing has turned to dust. Wilson and Nixon, having achieved supreme political power, find that they have not got the slightest idea what to do with it (except indulge in public relations exercises and occasionally lash out by invading Cambodia or Anguilla), eventually fading away into nothing more than ghostly caricatures of their former selves. Napoleon III is eventually blown away by the first serious puff of wind and all his grandiose make-believe Second Empire with him. Napoleon I sits on St. Helena, boring Las Cases and the few other wretched survivors of his court to death with his meaningless platitudes about power and life and fortune, endlessly wondering "what happened?," as mystified as Nixon showed himself to be as to why the whole fantasy had mysteriously evaporated.

Finally there is one last, supreme example of the phenomenon who must be considered—the most appalling and destructive of all—Adolf Hitler. Once again we see many of the same characteristics—the utter banality of "the real Hitler," the continuing mystification as to what he was "really like," the astonishing nerve by which he got away with things which no one else would have dreamed of attempting, right up to the invasion of Russia. Once the spark had ignited, his upward drive was unstoppable, his manipulation of others incomparable—but at the heart of the phenomenon which had all Europe in its thrall and left tens of millions of corpses was a little man whom not a lifetime's-worth of home movies of the terrace at Obersalzburg can show as personally anything other than extremely ordinary and boring. Obviously Hitler left a huge legacy in terms of destruction, as in his lesser way did Napoleon (who also left the Code Napoleon and a few triumphal arches scattered about). But ultimately the astonishing thing is how little positive any of these men leave behind. They have all, in Mrs. Muggeridge's immortal words, "risen without trace," even if they eventually fade away without trace as well.

Their last legacy perhaps is that each in his different way has left a void of meaning where he has passed. Wilson and Nixon both emptied politics and political language of significance. Frost emptied television of significance (in so far as it ever had any). Hitler and Napoleon left a dark void which puzzled succeeding generations have desperately tried to fill, with their endless reconstructions of the great stirring days of Napoleonic

Europe, or of the Nazi Empire and World War II. But having sucked the world into the black holes of their egos, the Super-Egotists eventually leave behind nothing but a series of rather depressing enigmas. For true achievement, for substance and for meaning, you have to look at quite other kinds of historical figures altogether.

25

KENNETH CLARK: THE ESTHETE AS HERO

A review of Clark's autobiography, published November 1977.

Just before the seventies began, as I described in Chapter 3, "On Dover Beach," Kenneth Clark's television series *Civilisation* enjoyed a success unique in television history. Millions of people looked on the series with an almost superstitious reverence. It was as if, out of the dark night of the late sixties, with all its frenzied contemporaneity and hideous confusion, people saw in the urbane figure of Clark and the magnificent array of agreeable images he presented, a kind of icon—an emblem of stability and eternity in a world which had become a nightmare.

Yet the most remarkable thing of all was that almost no one seemed to be listening to what Clark was actually saying (a small indication of this was the number of quite elementary mistakes which survived right through to the publication of the book, such as giving the date of the fall of the Bastille as 1792). Had they done so (as I argued in Chapter 3) they would have seen that far from providing reassurance, Clark was in fact quite unconsciously presenting the evidence for an astonishing pessimistic view of the past thousand years of European history—the "centered" certainty of the medieval world view disintegrating, step by step, to an all but total state of catastrophe at the present day. There was almost no sign that Clark himself realized that this was what he was doing. He consciously ended the series, in fact, on a note of somewhat unconvincing optimism (as he puts it in *The Other Half,* "I walked into my library, patted a wooden figure by Henry Moore, as if to imply that there was still hope, and it was all over"). But beneath the agreeable dreamlike surface there unmistakably lurked a quite appalling nightmare.

Lord Clark has done precisely the same thing with his autobiography. In the first volume, he showed us an intensely lonely little boy, born into a rich, loveless, philistine Edwardian household, finding his escape into the "secret garden" of Art— the magical frozen world of pictures and beautiful forms. We left him, in his late thirties, as Director of the National Gallery, having transformed his entire life into such a work of art: its foreground, the brightly-lit world of prewar fashionable London, in which famous names shimmered around the central figure and his wife Jane like exquisite *objets* —while beyond the pool of light a vast, threatening darkness was ruthlessly shut out.

We take up the story in the second volume in September 1939. Having stuffed away the National Gallery's treasures like a Nibelungen hoard into a Welsh cave, he then presents an extraordinarily detached view of the war. The cataclysmic events rocking civilization are reduced to little more than noises off (one feels that Clark would scarcely have been aware of the Battle of Britain had not Air Chief Marshal Sir Cyril Newall been a "close friend" who kept him informed), while we move through a series of carefully composed scenes, from Myra Hess playing Mozart concertos in the empty Gallery, to Clark telling John Betjeman to watch out for a "ravishing" girl in the Ministry of Information canteen called "Miss Joan Hunter Dunn." If Clark sits out an air raid in a cellar, it *has* to be with Arthur Waley, talking of Chinese poetry. He even manages two trips to Sweden, to talk about ceramics with that "human masterpiece," the Crown Prince. While if occasional, disagreeable forays do have to be made into the darkness, like his abortive trips to provincial cities to persuade them to show works from the National's reserve collection, "these well-meant expeditions gave me an insight into industrial England which I would never have enjoyed otherwise, and Jane, who always accompanied me, dressed in exquisite Lanvin clothes, gave immense pleasure to the local mayors."

In May 1945 Clark seems barely aware the war has ended ("we were lunching with Mr. Bevin that day, and the subject was scarcely mentioned"). The magic pageant floats onward, as Clark moves effortlessly from Ruskin Lectures in Oxford and his books (*The Nude, Landscape Into Art, Piero della Francesca*) to the chairmanship of the Arts Council, Sadlers Wells, the chairmanship of the ITA, Covent Garden. The sets continue relentlessly exquisite—his medieval castle Saltwood, Japanese temple gardens, cool green rooms in the Louvre, furnished with "Maya carvings and Islamic pots." The actors remain relentlessly famous—Picasso, Keynes, the Menuhins, Edith Sitwell, Vivien Leigh, Berenson, Gulbenkian, de Gaulle. Even at the very moment when Churchill has his famous stroke in 1953, it is Jane whose hand he clutches for support. It all seems too perfect to be true—and curiously empty, like a dream. Just occasionally the famous names are misspelt—"de Gaspari," "Monteverde," "Parmigiano," "Lawrence Olivier"—as if to show that what we are watching is a kind of eerie masque, below the polished surface of which something is mysteriously, fatally wrong.

In fact "eerie" is precisely the word for this book; this chilling portrait of the "incurable esthete" as hero, desperately trying to keep out any hint of reality from the succession of waxwork animated *tableaux*. Where is the underside of all this glittering, dead surface? A feeling of terrible claustrophobia begins to mount. Every glimmering of life trying to break in is so rigorously excluded. There is even an extraordinary passage on page 108 (which must be read in full) where Clark describes an obviously genuine and powerful mystical experience ("my whole being was irradiated by a kind of heavenly joy, far more intense than anything I had known before") the implications of which he decides are far too embarrassing to face up to, so like everything else it is stuffed ruthlessly back into the darkness.

Then, like an idea whose time has come, Clark makes *Civilisation:* he is transformed in the late sixties into one of the most celebrated men in the world. He goes to Washington, and amid near-riotous scenes, he is mobbed at the National Gallery by a huge crowd. He felt "like some visitor to a plague-ridden country, who has been mistaken for a doctor but is not a doctor." He rushes off to the lavatory where he "sobbed and howled for quarter of an hour." He knows that he is "a hoax," that he has seemed to be offering what he cannot deliver, that beneath the marble surface is nothing but a deadly void.

This must be one of the most unconsciously self-revealing books ever written. What comes through is the self-portrait of a man who, by a steely effort of will, has subordinated everything in his life to the preservation of an almost flawless mask or *persona;* who has remorselessly fought off every temptation to self-analysis (as he says "I cannot go very far in that direction"), to the point where he can no longer even endure going for a walk on his own because his thoughts "are now so melancholy that I cannot face them."

Of course the price that must be paid for such one-sidedness is always colossal. Throughout these pages there is never any doubt as to where the shadow from all this relentless artificial sunlight was falling—on his wife Jane, his other half. Again and again she is said to be suffering from mysterious illnesses. Finally, after an almost *Götterdämmerung*-like scene in Palermo (where the book becomes remarkably like some major tragic novel), Jane collapses altogether. For three years, while she is barely conscious, Clark keeps a lonely vigil by her bedside. After an evening when her mind had suddenly cleared ("We looked through a new volume of photographs of *quattrocento* art and she identified every one"), she dies. As the picture of a man who to the end has never dared face up to "the other half" of himself this is a spine-chilling book, which ends up by casting fatal doubt even on those things where Clark's external reputation has always rested most strongly. Even the magnificent paintings, you realize, were only experienced as backdrops to a stage set (how could anyone speak of Piero's "Baptism" in terms of "good taste?)—and when the lights went out, there was nothing left but a very lonely and silent darkness.

26

TOM WOLFE: SAGE OR VICTIM?

A review of *Mauve Gloves and Madmen, Clutter and Vine,*
published September 1977.

I vividly recall my first encounter with the writings of Tom
Wolfe. It was in 1965, the year when that curious mania known
as the "swinging sixties" was at its height. I was deeply puzzled
by this outbreak of cultural hysteria which seemed to be engulfing the Western world—the insane fashion-consciousness, the
demand for bright colors and loud rhythmic noise, the worship
of certain key figures, dream heroes, whose role was to provide
imagery for the collective dream state—pop singers, pop artists,
photographers, model girls, dress designers. And not the least
extraordinary thing about it seemed to be the extent to which
almost everyone (in the media at least) seemed to be quite
bewitched by what was happening. There seemed to be no one
standing outside the bubble and observing just how odd and
shallow and egocentric and even rather horrible it all was.

Then one day there fell into my hands a new book from
America called *The Kandy-Kolored Tangerine-Flake Streamline Baby* (1965), by a young journalist then in his mid-thirties
(Tom Wolfe was born in 1931). From the moment I opened it, I
was transfixed. Here at last seemed the very man I had been
waiting for—the detached observer who not only saw that
something very odd indeed was happening to the Western
world, but had also (quite a problem) discovered the right style
in which to write about it.

In his introduction, Tom Wolfe described how it happened. He had been sent out to California by *Esquire* to write an article on the custom car cult—the backyard craze for building automobiles shaped like alligators and fish and heaven knows what, in extraordinary designs and colors. He had come back to New York, tried to describe this strange, surreal little world in his usual condescending "totem prose"—and found it simply could not be done. Eventually *Esquire,* with "a two-page wide color picture for the story locked into the presses," told him in desperation just to type up his notes and send them over for someone else to write the article. Wolfe sat down that evening at 8 P.M., turned up the rock'n roll on the radio, and tried to put down every scrap of an impression he could recall, in a kind of stream of consciousness. Forget about main verbs ... finishing sentences ... if you're still groping for a word, just ... leave dots! By 6:15 next morning he had written 49 pages—and *Esquire* ran the story exactly as he had put it down.

Over the next 18 months, in 1963 and 1964, Wolfe used the same vivid, breathless, epithet-drunk prose style to describe Billy the K., the disc jockey who became known as the "Fifth Beatle," and Cassius Clay and Las Vegas (the "new-style-town" *par excellence*) and Baby Jane Holzer, the "girl of the year," who mixed with the Stones and Hockney and all those incredible new pop swingers from Britain ("They're all young and they're taking over, it's like a whole revolution, I mean it's exciting, they're all from the lower classes, East End sort of thing"). And at last there it all was on the page—the whole frenetic, nervous, crazy, egocentric, self-destructive, nightmarish *danse macabre* of the "New Culture"! The "swinging sixties" to the life!

But then came the nagging question. For all his extraordinary perception and ruthless eye for the sham and the egocentricity and the nightmarishness—to what extent *was* Wolfe actually "outside" what he was writing about? How *deeply* did he see—or was he still really inside the bubble, just another brilliantly gifted part of the charade he dissected so mercilessly? Did it matter?

Three years later, when his second collection of essays was published (in Britain as *The Mid-Atlantic Man*), the questions still nagged. The book contained some of the most ruthless profiles Wolfe has ever written, such as that of Bob and Spike Scull, a couple of new-rich New York socialites who had made it big in the sixties art scene on money from his cab fleet. This culminated in a party of truly Inferno-esque quality out in Flushing, for Jasper Johns and Rauschenburg and "Poonsy" and "Andy" and everyone, the climax of which was a Warhol-type film showing the view from underside up into a lavatory pan, with a huge turd crashing in full color into the audience's faces. There was an almost equally horrible portrait of Hugh Hefner, the pasty-faced Masturbation King, sitting at the heart of his horrible Chicago mansion on an enormous round bed, surrounded not so much by beautiful girls as by a mass of dials and video screens and electronic equipment so that he can watch himself on the Ampex while the bed turns ... and turns ... and turns. There was a poignant description of Carol Doda, the San Francisco stripper, who had become the city's biggest tourist attraction by blowing up her breasts with silicone to grotesque size, until ... well, what would happen when the thrill and the silicone wore off, and poor Carol was alone with her withered balloons and no one to treat her even as human any more?

But for all his apparent searchlight eye for the grotesque fantasies by which people seek to make themselves rich and famous and popular and special (until one day they wake up and find themselves miserably alone), Wolfe did not bother to hide his admiration for some of the values and heroes of the strange New Culture he was charting. He seemed to have an obsession, for instance, with physical description, and in particular with the difference between glorious, energetic, sexy youth ("beautiful little high-school buds in their buttocks-decolletage stretch pants") and the hideous deformations of advancing age ("old veiny white ankles, which lead up like a senile cone to a fudge of tallowy, edematous flesh"). Perhaps still more revealing was the essay on Marshal McLuhan which, while appearing to portray him as a kind of wonderful, absurd confidence trickster, could never actually bring itself to the point of denying that perhaps McLuhan was right! Perhaps, after all, he *was* the sage who, alone, had grasped the impenetrable truth about this strange madness which had seized the post-TV, sixties world?

About the time *The Mid-Atlantic Man* (1968) was published, Wolfe wrote what is probably still his most famous essay, "Radical Chic"—the horrific snapshot of a party given by the Leonard Bernsteins for a mixture of New York smart set and the leaders of the Black Panther movement, which more than anything else captured that insane blur in late-sixties America between violence and glamour. In 1975 came that brilliant long article (or short book) *The Painted Word,* showing how the whole crazy fantasy edifice of the New York "modern art world" ultimately rests just on two or three critics, whose word alone decides whether a pile of garbage poured on the floor is just a pile of garbage, or the most wonderful new art sensation, worth $20,000. And now we have Wolfe's first new collection for seven years, *Mauve Gloves and Madmen, Clutter and Vine.*

At first sight it seems to be much the mixture as before, although with rather more fiction and less straight reportage. The title story gets inside the mind of a successful Jewish writer who has become so carried away by all the externals of his new role as a successful writer—the Lobb shoes (to think, his father had come over from Russia with nothing!), the Martha's Vineyard beach house, the smart literary party in their Manhattan apartment, with flowers by "Mauve Gloves" and catering by "Madmen, Clutter and Vine"—that he has virtually forgotten how to be a writer. There is another story about a black baseball player who is conned into making a dreadful TV commercial for aftershave. There are one of two rather jaded little essays on the pornography of violence and the survival in America of give-away upper- and lower-class accents ("Honks and Wonks"). And by far the best piece of reporting in the book has nothing to do with the fashionable world at all, but is a portrait of American pilots flying off carriers into North Vietnam ("The Truest Sport: Jousting with Sam and Charlie"). This completely dispels (certainly as far as I was concerned) any view that those fliers were safely cocooned in a kind of air-conditioned, electronic bubble, murdering in comfort by remote control. Thanks to the unprecedented concentration of flak and supersophisticated SAM missiles which were thrown up against them whenever they stuck a nose in off the Gulf of Tonkin, their survival rate compared unfavorably with almost anything in World War II.

The longest essay in the book, called "The Me Decade: The Third Great Awakening" (already published over here in *Harper's-Queen*) begins with a description of a girl at a "let-it-all-hang-out" therapy session in the Ambassador Hotel, Los Angeles. Everyone has to shout out the thing which deep down most worries them about themselves, and in her case it is . . . hemorrhoids. From here the essay modulates somewhat improbably into an analysis of the great religious revival which has overtaken America in the past ten years, from Hare Krishna and LSD to born-again Jimmy Carter. Wolfe compares this ("the third great awakening") with the previous explosions of popular religious fervor in the 1740s (Wesleyism) and 1825-50 (Camp meetings and Mormonism). And his thesis is that at the heart of this religious revival lies an obsession with "Me"—that the ultimate fruit of postwar money and prosperity is that everyone has been liberated to concentrate on themselves. So recklessly does he mix up soul and body, religion and sex, that almost any movement which has caught on in America in the past decade can be seen as essentially just part of the same mishmash of egocentricity.

Now this is perhaps an arguable, interesting thesis—although the case would have to be put with a great deal more psychological and historical rigor than Wolfe brings to bear. As it stands, it is just a long, confused, breathless attempt to jumble together by sleight-of-hand anything from group sex, Ger-

maine Greer, "honesty sessions," and *Suck* to Gnosticism,
Methodism, and Zen. In fact one feels that the pages of
Harper's-Queen were exactly the right place for it. But in the
end this essay brings us back to the question—just where does
Tom Wolfe stand, and how serious is he?

Because there is no doubt that he sets out to be something
much more ambitious than just a casual observer of the passing
show. He is an analyst, a deep thinker, a man who can use
words like *kairos* and *antanacasis,* consider the nature of
ecstasy, talk about Zoroastrianism. He asks to be taken very
seriously indeed—so let us try.

It was extremely revealing that the one intellectual charlatan
against whom Tom Wolfe was reluctant to pronounce
anathema was Marshall McLuhan. For the point about McLuhan is that once upon a time he was an ordinary, dull little
Conservative Catholic intellectual, influenced by Chesterton,
hating the modern world, and hankering for the lost paradise of
a pre-industrial, agrarian society. Then one magic day, some 30
years ago, he read Poe's story *The Maelstrom,* about the sailor
who, caught in the notorious whirlpool, realizes that the only
way to escape is not to fight the downward pull of the vortex,
but to leap out of his ship and float—like the surrounding
driftwood—UPWARDS, to safety! The lesson was not lost on
the Canadian professor. He decided that no longer would he
fight the whirlpool of modern culture—he would float with it.
Instead of castigating the mindless stream of imagery of television or pop music, he would bless it. He would acclaim
everything—"the medium is the massage"—he would float
with the random sensation flow of "postlinear," "postverbal"
culture—and everything would be OK! Thus, telling people
what they wanted to hear in the crazy late sixties, did McLuhan
win his brief reputation as the prophet of the age.

The parallel to Wolfe himself is inescapable. If you go back to
the introduction to *The Kandy-Kolored Tangerine-Flake
Streamline Baby* (1965), the nearest thing to an explicit credo
he has ever written, his moment of "literary conversion" was

when he realized that the only way to write about the pure sensation flow of sixties culture was not to fight it by trying to describe it in old-fashioned, condescending "totem prose" but simply to flow with it—by creating, McLuhan-like, a prose style which exactly matched it. Deep down, of course, Wolfe made no secret of the fact that, far from dismissing "the New Culture," he was celebrating it—revelling in what he called:

> the new sensibility—*Baby baby baby where did our love go?*—the new world, submerged so long, invisible and now arising, slippy, shiny, electric—Super Scuba-man!—out of the vinyl deeps.

In a revealing passage in that introduction, Wolfe for the first time gave his explanation for why all these strange cultural phenomena had emerged in the Western world in the 1950s and 60s:

> The war created money. It made massive infusions of money into every level of society. Suddenly classes of people whose styles of life had been practically invisible had the money to build monuments to their own styles. Among teenagers this took the form of custom cars, the twist, the jerk, the monkey, the shake, rock music generally, stretch pants, decal eyes—and all these things, these teenage styles of life, like Inigo Jones's classicism, have started having an influence on the whole country.

Like *what?* Like *Inigo Jones's classicism?* What on earth is the man talking about? It is part of Wolfe's sleight-of-hand technique to rush the reader on at such a breathtaking pace that one does not always notice the "serious analysis" (usually by sweeping analogy) that he is trying to slip in along the way—and when it comes to deeper psychological or historical or sociological explanations, he certainly (like McLuhan) tries to pull some very fast ones.

Wolfe's basic thesis here (so often repeated since) is simply that money creates the opportunity for self-expression and always has—and that *all forms of expression are the same.* Take this sentence from the title essay of *The Kandy-Kolored etc.:*

> I don't mind observing that it is this same combination—money plus slavish devotion to form—that accounts for Versailles or St. Mark's Square.

Well, I suppose one can see what he is driving at—but if one is prepared to rest on the simple equation of any form of artistic or fashionable expression with any other, St. Mark's Square with the "custom car" or "the shake" or "decal eyes," then one is not running very deep in terms of analysis. Why not include Giotto's Arena Chapel frescoes, or Mozart's *Requiem* or Chartres Cathedral for good measure? The Rolling Stones equals Leonardo da Vinci. *Q.E.D.!* Indeed, whenever Wolfe ventures into these sweeping historical parallels (as in "The Me Decade"—John Wesley equals Germaine Greer) he is soon treading on very thin ice indeed, simply in terms of his own ignorance:

> I don't have to dwell on the point that cars mean more to these kids than architecture did in Europe's great formal century, say, 1750 to 1850 [*sic!*]. They are freedom, style, sex, power, motion, color—everything is right there!

It would be hard to conceive of a more utterly meaningless (and in the widest sense illiterate) string of words—and there in a nutshell is the very worst of Tom Wolfe.

Of course there is more to Wolfe than that. His real achievement (apart from providing a great deal of journalistic entertainment) has been to capture in words, and from the inside, some of the more bizarre cultural inanities of one of the most insane and fascinating decades in the history of the world. He has been able to see through "radical chic" and Hugh Hefner and the nonsense of the New York art world like nobody's business. But in the end, outside the world of the wonderful, exploding, self-expressing ego—however nightmarish and self-destructive and horrible that world can be—what is left? So let's just flow with it, baby! Wolfe's is a pretty bleak, harsh, loveless view of the world. He is like a man sitting on a fairground merry-go-round, feeling desperately sick, but seeing no way to jump off. Or like a soul doomed to wander for eternity through a particularly nasty modern version of Dante's Inferno, without the faintest hope of escaping into Purgatory, let alone Paradise. In the end, after rereading his collected works, I am afraid I just feel slightly sick myself. I don't think I shall want to read any more.

27

ARTHUR KOESTLER: SCI-FI SAGE

A review of *Janus: A Summing Up*, published November 1978.

One of the most remarkable events of our time has been the way in which, after several centuries of apparently brilliant progress, the whole post-Renaissance attempt to escape from metaphysics, and to explain the world rationally in terms of the physical sciences, has petered out in a series of baffling dead ends. In 1899, the German biologist Haeckel could confidently claim that of the "seven great riddles of the universe," six were now solved, while the seventh ("free will") was merely a subjective illusion anyway. Today, less than 80 years later, Haeckel's heirs on the frontiers of knowledge have not just been driven back into metaphysics (or what might often be more suitably described as simply a dogmatic irrationality); in fact their plight is infinitely worse than that of their medieval forbears; for at least the Christian world view of the Middle Ages gave its adherents the conviction that everything in the universe had both unity and meaning, whereas our postrational metaphysics of today can offer neither.

One man who has been quicker than most to catch a glimpse of some of the astonishing implications of what has happened is Arthur Koestler. Ever since a kind of agnostic mystical experience in a Spanish prison in 1936 helped him to see Marxist materialism as the God that failed, he has been on a long quest for some deeper and more satisfactory explanation of man's existence. And over the past 25 years, in a series of best-

215

sellers—*The Ghost in the Machine, The Roots of Coincidence*—
he has been reporting his findings.

No one has done more than Koestler to popularize an awareness of just what an extraordinary twilight world the physical
sciences have been moving into in our century. He has reported
at length, for instance, on how the biologists have staggered on
from one futile hypothesis to the next in their search for an
explanation of the mystery of evolution to the point where they
either join the former Professor of Evolution at the Sorbonne,
Grassé, in confessing that "confronted with these problems,
biology is helpless and must hand over to metaphysics"; or
more ominously, they take refuge like Monod or Simpson of
Harvard ("Man is the result of a purposeless and materialistic
process") in a kind of neo-occultism, elevating their faith in
"chance" into unshakeable dogma, without even bothering any
longer to provide a shred of evidence. Similarly the physicists
have stumbled into immaterialism, at both ends of their spectrum: in the world of subatomic particles, where an electron can
go through two holes simultaneously, where time itself seems to
"move backward," and where the universe appears ultimately
to be held together by something indefinable called "charm,"
matter, time, and space have all passed over into a kind of
dematerialized blur; while the astrophysicists, faced with such
a question as "what happens to matter when it is sucked into a
black hole?" can only reply "it may come out again in a 'white
hole' in some other universe, operating in a different dimension altogether." Then there are all those countless more mundane patterns of events which cannot be accounted for by any
apparent laws of cause and effect at all: why for instance does
the number of people bitten by dogs in the New York area
scarcely vary year by year (it is always around 72)? When the
atoms of a radioactive substance appear to disintegrate in a
totally random way, what force dictates that exactly half of
them will always collapse in an absolutely predictable period
(the half-life of Radium A, for instance, is always 3.825 days)? It
is one thing to say, with Jung and Pauli, that there appears to

be an "acausal connecting principle" at work in the universe which is just as significant as cause and effect (incidentally restating in Western terms one of the cardinal principles of Chinese philosophy)—but in doing so we are simply moving further from a rational, let alone material explanation than ever.

After years of exploring the fast-crumbling iceberg of post-Cartesian rationalism, Koestler has decided to summarize all his findings—and had *Janus: A Summing Up* merely been a recapitulation of the reportage in his previous books, it might have been a useful exercise. But, alas, Koestler cannot resist the temptation to stray from description into theorizing of his own—and here he exposes a contradiction so glaring as to call his whole world view into question.

Consider, for instance, his opening proposition. Faced with the possibility of man's nuclear extinction, Koestler asks: why, of all the species on earth, is *homo sapiens* uniquely self-destructive? The answer, he suggests, is that thanks to a trick of evolution, we have two brains, in uneasy coexistence. Firstly, we have inherited our "instinctive," or "animal brain." Super-imposed on this is our distinctively human "neo-cortical brain," which gives us the power to reason. The trouble is that our "reasoning brain" is unable to control our irrational, emotive "instinctive brain"—and we thus behave like animals, killing each other. But since, as Koestler has pointed out a few pages earlier, the whole point is that animals do *not* on the whole kill each other, then even in terms of his own highly questionable terminology, the cause of our uniquely self-destructive behavior cannot lie in our "animal" but in our "human brain."

Mr. Koestler's view of the human condition never recovers from this original crashing illogicality (perhaps his "animal brain" got out of control?). Indeed he is shortly afterward led to suggest that since it "stands to reason" that "a biological malfunction needs a biological corrective," then the answer to the problems caused by man's "split nature" must come from the "biological laboratories."

What is staggering about this is not so much its flavor of cheap, *Sunday Express* sci-fi sensationalism (of a kind one might have thought outmoded in the fifties), but that it comes from a man who is about to devote the second half of his book to a devastating critique of the whole reductionist, materialist position. What is shows, in fact, is that, far from being a wise old sage who has truly seen the limitations of the materialist view, Koestler is still absolutely trapped by it. He is a disillusioned fox, desperately longing to become a hedgehog—but he simply cannot get rid of that red, bushy tail. He recognizes, for instance, that everyone and everything in the universe is what he calls a "holon"—that is, both an autonomous whole and simultaneously a part of a greater whole; but, revealingly, although he can take up this progression from, let us say, the particle to the atom to the cell to the human individual to the group to the species, he nowhere seems to recognize that, by the law of infinite regress, he must eventually confront the question as to whether there is a whole so all-embracing that it can no longer be said to be a part of anything (i.e. the "One").

In short, no more than those he is criticizing can Koestler fundamentally change his perspective. As a civilization we have been hoping that reason *alone* will give us some ultimate illumination. Not only has it conspicuously failed to do so, but it ends up (like Koestler himself) by toppling over into howling unreason. Clearly, or so our reason *should* tell us, we may have been looking in the wrong place for the answer.

The most glaring omission from Koestler's chaotic jigsaw is any understanding of twentieth-century work on that very thing which lies at the heart of all our attempts to discern meaning in the universe—the human psyche. It is true that he includes an ill-digested sketch of Freud's Eros-Thanatos theory, for what it is worth. But of Jung, who wrote extensively and profoundly on so many of the problems which preoccupy Koestler, he appears to know virtually nothing. If he did, he might at least have been able to propound a somewhat more sophisticated account of the split which has so strongly emerged in the psyche of Western man since the Renaissance: between the "masculine," ordering, rational functions which have created modern science, and those "feminine," intuitive functions which have increasingly dominated art. In the almost total bankruptcy of both science and art, we today see the futility of all attempts to find meaning one-sidedly. The only road back to meaning lies through a reintegration of both halves of the psyche. The poignancy of Koestler is that, for all his awareness of the limitations of reason, he knows nothing else; he is all *yang* and no *yin*—as shows nowhere more painfully than in his pitiful chapters "analyzing" art and humor, full of such sentences as: " 'matrices' are mental holons . . . controlled by canonical rules, but guided by feedbacks from the outer and inner environment . . . ordered into 'vertical' abstractive hierarchies which interlace in 'horizontal' networks and cross references (cf. 'arborization' and 'reticulation.' " Here is a poor little fox, baying at the moon and talking pure gibberish.

28

JOHN BETJEMAN: THE LONELY TEDDY BEAR

Written on his seventieth birthday, August 28, 1977.

I have often wondered what English life would have been like over the past 30 years without the contribution of a very small group of remarkable men who were born within a few years of each other at the beginning of this century.

Perhaps to refer to such diverse figures as Evelyn Waugh, George Orwell, Malcolm Muggeridge, and Kenneth Clark (all born in 1903), Graham Greene (1904), John Betjeman (1906), W. H. Auden (1907) and Osbert Lancaster (1908) as in any way constituting a "group" may seem fanciful—although few would dispute how immeasurably the poorer we should all have been through the past few gloomy decades without them.

But two things I believe they have in common. The first is that (particularly as they grew older, which slightly excepts Orwell) they have all established in the public mind personalities so much larger than life as almost to verge on self-caricature. And secondly, they have all in their different ways betrayed an intense strain of melancholy, both about the world and about themselves.

Indeed one almost feels that the outer *personae* these men have developed over the years—Waugh's crusty old Catholic reactionary, the ice-cool urbanity of Clark's esthete, Muggeridge's world weariness ("As I grow older, dear boy, I more and more see the whole show as finished"), Osbert Lancaster's mustached White's Clubman—have been almost deliberately erected as shells against the outer world, to protect the unusually sensitive and vulnerable personalities within.

Only very occasionally (as in Waugh's Gilbert Pinfold) have any of them allowed the full tension between their outer and inner lives to show—with one major exception, and that ironically in the case of the man who seems to have grown into his own outward self-caricature more than any. I refer to the man whose seventieth birthday we are celebrating today, John Betjeman.

The newspaper tributes showered on Sir John this week have presented him almost entirely in the light of his caricature—the bumbling, cardiganed, decrepit old teddy bear, shuffling amiably through life with a "golly" and a "gosh" and an "isn't it fun?," interspersed with lovable mockery of the horrors of the modern world, and a few extracts from the better-known poems about property developers, the suburbs, and the brains of the senior civil servant like "sweetbreads on the road today."

Of course in a way it is understandable. I have had perhaps even more cause than most people to be grateful to the jolly, "outer" Betjeman—ever since the day 27 years ago when, as an 11-year-old school friend of his son Paul, I was first invited out for the day to the old rectory where the family then lived near Wantage.

Betjeman was a marvelous host to two small boys (I remember we always received, with complete impartiality, the princely sum of half-a-crown apiece when we returned to the Dragon School). We spent a memorable day visiting some people on a painted barge, and then William Morris's rather derelict house at Kelmscott by the Thames, while John bubbled with high spirits along the way (he had a phrase on the brain that afternoon about "caiffs and koisks the world over").

Since then I have always felt more cheerful at the prospect of seeing him, whether at some elegant country house, or walking down a scruffy street in Soho ("Look at that Novello building by Pearson, isn't it wonderful?"), right up to the most recent occasion a few months ago, when he was attending the christening of his latest grandchild, in a house which seemed to be full of large and distinguished red-faced racing men. He seemed somewhat out of place, and a little while later, as card playing began, we came across him sitting all alone in the lunch room, reading a copy of *The Well of Loneliness,* which he must have brought in some capacious pocket. "Isn't it a wonderful book?"

Like others, I have been endlessly grateful too over the years for the more public activities of the "outer" Betjeman—his "City and Suburban" column in the *Spectator* in the fifties, his masterly introduction to *The Parish Churches of England* (with its semisatirical account of what each succeeding century has given to the parish church), his television programs (of which the best of all, *Metroland,* was shown again last Tuesday), and above all perhaps, his role as the patron saint of the architectural conservation movement, dating back to that first forlorn struggle in 1956 to save Colcutt's Imperial Institute from the insatiable barbarism of London University.

But of course the one unmistakable thing about all the battles of the past 20 years against the final rape and desecration of Britain, despite the occasional seeming victory, has been just how forlorn they have all been. They have been Mrs. Partington-like battles against an insuperable tide, for an England already lost—as Betjeman himself seemed implicitly to recognize a year or two back, when he finally abandoned his little oasis at Cloth Fair, to leave the City to the curtain walls and the highways.

Turn then to the poems, still popularly supposed to be little more than jolly romps with Miss Hunter Dunn and amusingly outrageous invitations to lovely bombs to fall on Slough—and at last you are face to face with the real, inner Betjeman.

What hits you above all is what the late Lord Birkenhead, in his very perceptive preface to the *Collected Poems,* called "the abysmal depression," the absolutely shattering melancholy, the desperate sense of lost innocence, departed pleasures, dissolution, and decay.

Is there any poem in the English language more heartrending than the "Lament for Moira McCavendish?" Are there lines more bleak than the conclusion of "Norfolk"?

> The peace, before the dreadful daylight starts,
> Of unkept promises and broken hearts.

The truth is that, for all the fun and jokes and mannerisms John Betjeman has all along—later even than Hardy or Lawrence or Eliot—been the last poet of the last days of a civilization. He has lived his inward life in that twilight on the edge of the abyss, where it is hard for men to remember that they are part of anything larger or more lasting than themselves, and where they are therefore terribly alone.

The despair is overwhelming. And therefore, while we offer him conventional thanks for all the amusement along the way, one ends simply by wanting to send him some small sign of love across the dark gulf.

29

Thomas Hardy: Prophet to Our Rootlessness

Written on the fiftieth anniversary of the novelist's death, in 1978.

In the past ten years no English writer of the past has enjoyed such a dramatic return to favor as Thomas Hardy. Since the late sixties, when the lines first began forming for the film of *Far From The Madding Crowd,* we have been living in the age of the Great Hardy Boom. Scarcely a year has gone by when one of the novels has not been turned into a successful TV series. His paperbacks have sold in millions. Why is it that in the past decade Hardy has soared back into such popularity?

The obvious answer is simply that Hardy's wonderful evocations of life in the English countryside a century ago—before the arrival of motor cars, tractors, television, and all the raucous hubbub of the modern age—feed our seemingly almost inexhaustible appetite these days for nostalgia, for escape from the horrors of the present into a cosy, tranquil vision of the past. But it cannot be quite as simple as that. For a start, the very last thing one can say about Hardy's novels is that they are cosy. On the contrary, there are few stories so bleak in the English language: a sense of gathering gloom and despair hangs over the sequence of novels like a cloud. Yet in the reasons why Hardy himself was haunted by such increasing melancholy, I believe we may also find some clue as to why, at least unconsciously, they have struck such a chord in the imagination of our own time.

One of the things which may strike us most forcibly about Hardy's major novels is the extent to which the world they are describing is so sharply polarized. On the one hand, there is the timeless, instinctive, deeply rooted world of the Dorset country-side, the world into which Hardy himself had been born in 1840 and which can have changed only imperceptibly for centuries. Geographically, in the novels, this natural world is character-ized by the great waste of Egdon Heath, by the mysterious woods of the Hintocks. In human terms, it is personified by the "rustic chorus" of simple Dorset countryfolk, the kind of people among whom Hardy grew up—and above all perhaps by those three, virtually interchangeable characters, Gabriel Oak the shepherd, Diggory Venn the reddleman, and Giles Winterborne the woodman, each of them solid, loyal, and so close to his natural setting as to seem as much part of it as the furze or the trees themselves.

On the other hand, casting an ever longer shadow over the rustic simplicities of this rooted world is that persistent pres-ence in Hardy's novels which invariably proves as destructive in its impact as the railways and penny ballads which he saw beginning to destroy the ancient Dorset folk culture even in his youth. This dark presence is the outside world, represented by the "rootless ones," children of the restless future: Fitzpiers, the doctor, his head full of experimental science; Sergeant Troy, the freebooting, amoral philanderer; Eustacia Vye, longing to escape from the prison of life on the Heath to the fashionable vanities of Budmouth, out there in the great world beyond.

There is a third group in Hardy's novels, even more tragic than these: those characters who have got caught between the two great poles of Hardy's world, who have gone out into the great world, lost their roots, and then make hopelessly doomed attempts to return to put them down again—such characters as Clym Yeobright, Grace Melbury, and Mayor Henchard.

Another thing one cannot help noticing about Hardy's nov-els is the quite remarkable extent to which they are centered on their characters' desperate search for the other half who would make them whole. No other writer has ever been so obsessed with mismatches, with the hero or heroine whose whole life seems blighted through having been landed by a grim and malevolent fate with the wrong woman or man. But it was only recently, when I read the excellent new life of Hardy by Robert Gittings that all these things, for me at least, finally fell into place—and I began to see just why it was, I think, that Hardy speaks so eloquently to so many millions in our own time.

Gittings's biography has worked for our view of Hardy much the same miracle as a restorer who, by removing thick layers of varnish and overpainting, reveals to us an almost entirely new picture. No writer can ever have taken such trouble to conceal the truth about himself as the mournful old boy who died in Dorchester 50 years ago. The pedestrian, highly tendentious *Life* which he left to be published by his second wife after his death is now largely and deservedly forgotten. Since then our view of Hardy has been even more obscured both by the compilers of pious memoirs, and by the efforts of imaginative scandal mongers to invest his life with fictitious sexual drama. Now, at last, we have a portrait of Hardy which rings true, recognizably the author of some of the most melancholy stories and poems in the language. It is the picture of a deeply unhappy, insecure man who, for 50 years after being estranged from his own rustic roots and youthful faith, wandered through an inward world in an ever increasing confusion of bitterness and despair, seeking a security, an innocence and a sense of "wholeness" which would never come again. What Gittings has given us, in short, is virtually all the information we need to see how closely Hardy's major novels, written in only 20 years between 1872 and 1892, mirrored the unfolding of their author's own tragic inner life.

Hardy was born, in the third year of Queen Victoria's reign, in the little thatched cottage at Bockhampton which is today preserved much as it was—a perfect picture-postcard image of old rural England. His father, a humble stonemason, was known locally for his rustic fiddle playing, in church and at village weddings. Through his childhood and early teens, the simple people, scenes, and customs of this remote corner of Dorset were all the world that Hardy knew. But already he was marked out by his intelligence, his avid reading and his sense of separateness for a very different destiny. He began to study as an architect and even spent a short time in the distant great city of London. He showed his susceptibility to the opposite sex in a series of intense and unconsummated passions for various girls (Gittings shows how "mother-dominated" Hardy was, and how desperately ill-at-ease in sexual matters). He gravitated towards his career as a writer, he met and fell in love with Emma Gifford, the socially superior daughter of a Cornish clergyman, and in his early thirties he at last wrote his first really successful novel, *Under The Greenwood Tree* (1872). The happiest, most innocent of his books, this was like a charming retrospective snapshot of his own youthful state, while hopes still remained unblighted. It showed its young hero, Dick the tranter's son, obviously rather different in some way from all the villagers he had grown up with, falling in love with Fancy Day, the socially superior young schoolmistress, eventually winning her and presumably living happily ever after—a simple, wish-fulfillment fairy tale.

Two years later, the even more successful *Far From The Madding Crowd* (1874) was the last novel Hardy wrote in the cottage of his birth, still surrounded by his family and the rustic world of his childhood. Once again, his hero, Shepherd Oak, still wins through on almost the last page to the hand of the socially superior heroine, Bathsheba Everdene, but the happy ending is no longer achieved with the fairy tale ease of *Under The Greenwood Tree*—not least because of the intervention of the rootless, sinister Sergeant Troy, whose short-lived marriage to Bathsheba is Hardy's first serious mismatch. Even by the time the novel was published, in the year he finally married Emma, Hardy had already moved into the glamorous literary circle of his new editor Leslie Stephen in London. He was beginning to meet some highly intelligent, lively, liberated

young women, including Thackeray's daughter and his illus-
trator Helen Paterson, with whom Hardy was so taken that
even at the end of his life he was still wondering whether he
should have married her. He was already haunted, in fact, by
the possibility that he could have chosen better for himself
than poor Emma Lavinia. By his move to London Hardy
finally severed his social links with the world of his upbringing.
But for all the heady excitements of his new life, he was far from
finding anything in the great world to compensate for the
simple certainties of the world he had left behind—he had, for
instance, quite suddenly lost his old religious faith. And as
Robert Gittings acutely observes of Gabriel Oak's acceptance
by Bathsheba: "No Hardy hero from that time onward ever
comes to such an assured and happy ending. From this moment
on, the tragic and defeated hero arrives in Hardy's novels for
good."

In 1876, Hardy returned with Emma to Dorset—though not,
of course, to the simple life of a peasant, but to live in a new,
middle-class, red-brick villa in the little town of Sturminster
Newton. His return to his native county inspired him to write
The Return of the Native, describing how the wanderer Clym
Yeobright returns from the sophisticated world of Paris to recover his roots on Egdon Heath. But of course the attempt does
not work. The mold has been irreparably broken. The novel is
shot through with a darkness, often a quite literal darkness (as
in all the scenes which take place at night, or in twilight) which
is quite new in Hardy's work—culminating in the multiple
catastrophe in which Eustacia and Wildeve are swept one
stormy night to their deaths. Even the partial happy ending for
those two "rooted" characters, Diggory Venn and little Tamsin
Yeobright, was only included in the story's final draft, to please
the readers of the serialization.

Without getting too involved, I must just interpolate here a
quick word about the relations between heroes and heroines in
literature—and indeed about happy and unhappy endings in
general. When the hero and heroine are happily united at the

end of a story, it means basically something much more important than just a boy and a girl going off into the sunset. In fact, when we think about it, is it not remarkable just how many stories *do* end with a wedding or the prospect of a wedding? From ancient myths and folk tales to Shakespearian comedies, Mozart operas, and Jane Austen novels to twentieth-century musicals, it is the commonest ending to a story there is. And if we look carefully at some of the more subtly-worked out examples— *Jane Eyre, David Copperfield* to name but two—it is clear that the final union of the hero and heroine usually symbolizes something even deeper than just a marriage: it marks the point where they have each found out who they really are; in being united with their true "other half" they have become at last truly "whole," in a profoundly spiritual sense. In fact the heroine in stories stands, as it were, for the "inner feminine" in man, ultimately for his "soul." If trouble arises between the hero and the heroine, we can be pretty sure that something has gone wrong in his relations with his soul—and if that is true of the hero, the fictional character, it usually turns out to be just as true of what is going on in the inner life of the author whose unconscious has created that character. It was no accident, for instance, that shortly after Tolstoy had created that stupendous portrait of a woman throwing herself to self-destruction, *Anna Karenina,* he should have entered on the most agonizing spiritual crisis of his life, when the world seemed meaningless, he wished to do away with himself and he actually wrote that he felt he had "lost his soul."

As it happened, in the very years when Tolstoy was entering that crisis (around 1878-9), Thomas Hardy was entering on one not dissimilar. He went back to London, to spend some of the unhappiest years of his life. His outward relations with his immediate "other half" Emma were seriously worsening. He produced three, rather artificial and unsatisfactory novels—and then returned for the last time to Dorset, to the ugly house he had designed for himself on the outskirts of Dorchester, Max Gate. Once again, his return to his native county inspired a major novel—his bleakest so far—*The Mayor of Casterbridge* (1886). Again it was on the theme of the rootless wanderer vainly trying to put down new roots (quite specifically in Dorchester)—but even more important, of a man who has committed an offense against his feminine other half now so deep that it can never be expiated. Like Hardy, Major Henchard has known what it is to be successful in a worldly sense. But what about that more important world, so much less easy to subject to conquest, the world of his private, inner life? At the beginning of the book, Henchard actually sells his wife—and in doing so, as it eventually turns out, he has sold his soul. No matter what he does to make amends, he gets drawn into an ever deeper web of deception and self-deception. Step by inexorable step he is alienated from all he holds most dear, all he has ever hoped for, until finally, in a state of total self-abnegation, he wanders out into the wilderness to die.

In Hardy's next book, *The Woodlanders* (1887), he portrays the polarization between the rustic, rooted world and that of the restless outsiders who have lost their roots more starkly than ever. On the one hand, there is the world of the trees and the woodland folk who live among them, above all Giles Winterborne, the "man of the trees," and little Marty South; the other is that represented by the doctor Fitzpiers, by the rich and spoiled Mrs. Charmond who has taken on the big house without taking on any of its responsibilities, and also, alas, by Grace Melbury, the woodland village girl whose ambitious father has sent her off to school in the outside world and given her ideas above her station—or certainly above any notion that she should marry Giles Winterborne, who has loved her since childhood. Winterborne and Marty South are, of course, a replay of Diggory Venn and Tamsin Yeobright in *The Return of the Native*; but this time there can be no happy ending even for them, let alone for anyone else involved. The death of Winterborne, as the projection of Hardy's own lost rooted self, is a terrible moment; at least in the previous books it had been only the rootless ones who died. One of the most moving moments in the whole of Hardy is that where Grace Melbury realizes, only after Giles is dead, that all along it had been plain little Marty South who had been Giles's true mate: "You and he could speak in a tongue no one else knew . . . the tongue of the trees and fruits and flowers themselves." That and Marty's final farewell over Giles's grave ("no, no, my love, I can never forget 'ee; for you was a good man, and you did good things") are Hardy's elegy for the instinctive world he had lost for ever, where man is at one with nature, and faith is the expression of that fact.

Finally come the two most dreadful self-revelations of all. The first was *Tess of the D'Urbervilles* (1891), the story of the country girl from a poor and simple cottage home, who is bewitched by a story that she belongs to a great and ancient Dorset family. She goes out into the world in search of her destiny, becomes prey to the two men with whom she is, in different ways, mismatched, until finally, in an ever-growing nightmare of desperation, she kills one of them and is hanged. It is not surprising that Tess was Hardy's own favorite character, for she really was the deepest realization of all of his own "inner feminine"—and once we recognize that, how even more poignant the story becomes. There is Tess, Hardy's soul, torn from her roots, wandering blindly and distractedly across the face of an ever bleaker, more inhospitable Dorset countryside, looking for a home and resting place where she could be "whole," but eventually so tortured in her isolation that she kills and is killed. In Hardy's own, often-quoted phrase, "the President of the Immortals" had "ended his sport with Tess"—but of course the real power manipulating Tess from one improbable coincidence to the next, stacking up the odds against her to such deadly conclusion, was no one other than Hardy himself. In the three men of whom Tess was the victim—her father and Alex D'Urberville, both living in fantasy above their station, pretending to be descended from some great old family (as Hardy himself came increasingly to pretend *he* did), and on the other hand, Angel Clare, the high-minded, religiose progressive (just as Hardy had been in his own youth), we can only too easily see aspects of Hardy. Unconsciously, and more tragically than ever before, Hardy was revealing nothing less horrendous than the stifling of his own soul.

The last of the major novels was *Jude the Obscure* (1895), a fitting conclusion because it was little more than a spiritual autobiography, a summing up of Hardy's own inner life. It is the only one of the major novels to be set almost entirely away from Dorset—but in the eagerly self-improving young country boy, of firm religious faith, whom we meet at the beginning in the little village in Berkshire, it is not difficult to see the young Hardy of 30 years before. Jude's great ambition is to journey to the city of Christminster, shining on the distant horizon—the place where he will be able to realize himself to the full, among scholars and men of intellect and distinction—just as Hardy had once hoped to do when he set out from Bockhampton to London. On the way, Jude lands himself foolishly in marriage to a gross woman who is "unworthy" of him and in no way measures up to his spiritual aspirations, just as Emma Lavinia had failed to do in his own case. Jude meets his "soul" and "other half" in Sue Bridehead, clearly modeled on an idealized version of one of those liberated young girls he had met in London in the 1870s, when he was already committed to his future wife. And from then on the rest of the book is a story of growing agony and disillusionment, as Jude sees through the hypocrisy and shallowness of Christminster, seems first to win, then to lose, then to win again and finally to lose forever the love of his life, Sue, and having at last lost all faith and purpose, dies a lonely, miserable death amid the most alien surroundings imaginable.

By the time *Jude* was published, Hardy's outward estrangement from his roots, from the world of his upbringing, was so complete that when he bicycled through the village of Puddletown, where many of his family lived, he would simply stare stonily ahead when his relatives crowded to their cottage doors to wave to him, and ride on. The row over *Jude*'s reception in the British press (it was taken to be "atheistical," "nihilistic," and "immoral") precipitated Hardy's final estrangement from his increasingly Evangelical and strait-laced Emma (who signed letters to the press "An Old-Fashioned Englishwoman"). His only solace lay in an absurd series of infatuations with fashionable ladies up in London, would-be writers like Mrs. Henniker and Agnes Grove. The scene was set for the last 30 years of Hardy's life, dominated creatively by that great flood of poems of nostalgia and loss which reached its height after Emma's painful and miserable death in 1912, poems often devoted to her in which he sought to recapture that "inner feminine" which had always proved so elusive in life and whose presence never seemed so real to him as in death.

The second great task of Hardy's last years was the attempt to build up, through the biography he dictated to his second wife Florence, the wildly distorted picture of himself he wanted the world to remember. The exercise was, of course, futile— despite his efforts to falsify or destroy the evidence, so much has survived; partly because he had left such an unconsciously luminous record of the truth in his novels. But to devote so much time to such an enterprise was hardly the sign of a man at ease with himself or the world, of a man who had ever really understood or come to terms with himself. And ultimately there was no apter comment on Hardy's life than the gruesome fate of his poor, tortured old carcass when he died in 1928.

Hardy's body, burned to ashes, was buried amid the empty pomp of what amounted almost to a state funeral, in Westminster Abbey in London—while his heart was ripped out, to be taken back to Dorset to rest in the little churchyard of Stinsford near his birthplace. It was appallingly apt, because of course his heart had never really left that little corner of Dorset where he grew up—while his life out in the enticing great world symbolized by London had indeed turned to dust and ashes.

It is almost superfluous to underline why we find this story so haunting—and even more those novels which reflect it. The story Hardy was telling was not just his own. With the unconscious insight given to great artists, he was recording something that was happening all over Western civilization in his time, as the old unconscious ways of society, the close-knit web which had bound men so close to nature that they were really still almost part of it, gave way to the restless, progressive, mechanized world of the future. Made as he was, Hardy could do nothing else but go forth from the simple, enclosed world of his youth out into the great world beyond—but in doing so he more and more obviously lost touch with that elusive thing, his soul. Today we are all the children of that restless future and our sense of loss is acute, which is why we turn to the novels of Hardy in ever greater millions—because they are the record of a Fall from innocence of which we are all the heirs.

30

CHEKHOV:
MIRROR OF OUR MELANCHOLY

February 26, 1977

Last week Britain's theater critics scurried north to Manchester for yet another star-studded revival of *Uncle Vanya*. In London itself, over the past 12 months, "House Full" notices have gone up outside equally glittering productions of *The Seagull, Three Sisters* and *Ivanov*. How are we to explain this continuing modern intoxication with the plays of Chekhov, which seems if anything to grow in power year by year?

The simple, but curious answer to the question is that in some mysterious way these scenes of life among the Russian bourgeoisie 80 years ago strike us as instantly familiar and contemporary. The grocer's son from Taganrog still seems to be able to show us "life as it is" with a profundity equaled by no playwright since.

So what is this mysterious chord of recognition that Chekhov strikes in us? What sort of a world do we see in his five major plays?

First, of course, there is that peculiar, sweet Chekhovian melancholy which hangs about each of the plays (shot through with wonderful humor and beautiful drawing of the characters)—that quality which is summed up rather melodramatically on the cover of the Penguin Classics edition of the plays as "an overwhelming sense of the tedium and futility of everyday life."

It goes without saying that almost all of Chekhov's charac-

237

ters are frustrated, and deeply unhappy in some way or other.
There are no happily married couples. There is almost no one
who is not yearning for something that was, or something that
will be—the lost love, life, and youth of the once noble Ivanov
(who shoots himself), the three sisters rotting away in the
dreary little provincial town with their dream of one day getting back to Moscow, the feckless hopelessness of Liubov
Andreyevna eventually having to sell up her family home and
cherry orchard to the speculators, the aging actress Arkadina
clinging on to fond memories of her applause in Kharkhov, her
tortured, disregarded would-be writer son (whose parody "decadent play" in *The Seagull* is for my money the most haunting
fragment Chekhov ever wrote).

On the other hand, there are some characters who are
apparently "optimistic." In the words of the Penguin introduction: "each play contains one character who expresses Chekhov's hope for a brighter future." This may not be strictly true
(there are no such characters in *Ivanov* or *The Seagull*), but
nevertheless let us look at the nature of that optimism. At one
end there is the mere crude commercial "boosterism" of Lop-
hakin, the buyer of the cherry orchard, who cannot wait to get
his axe to the trees to build "a whole lot of new villas." "Our
children and great-grandchildren are going to see a new living-
world growing up here." At the other there is the vague, sentimental religiosity of Sonya at the end of *Uncle Vanya*: "We
shall patiently suffer the trial which Fate imposes on us ... we
shall hear the angels, we shall see all the heavens covered with
stars like diamonds ... we shall rest." And between the two
there are the various characters, ranging from Trofimov, the
"perpetual student" to Vershinin and Toozenbach in *Three
Sisters,* who look forward equally vaguely to a time, maybe in 30
years, maybe in 300, when Russia and the world will somehow
have been transformed, "Life will be different. It will be
happy," but "all the happiness will be reserved for our descendants, our remote descendants."

As we know, of course, this was the kind of vague, progressive
material optimism which Chekhov himself felt, when he looked

around sadly at his backward, primitive, sleeping Russia, where there were no proper doctors, no teachers, no energy for self-improvement. One day all this would be changed—meanwhile, as Gorky quotes Chekhov saying in his famous essay, "The Russian is a strange creature . . . in his youth he fills himself greedily with anything which he comes across, and after 30 years nothing remains but a kind of gray rubbish."

But still this does not account for the peculiar stifling, trapped air which surrounds every one of the people in Chekhov's plays.

Perhaps the real clue is this: that not one of them ever truly looks within himself to know and change himself, not one of them ever finds a spiritual center of new growth. Indeed there is no growth in the characters at all, except that of foolish dreams and decay. Not one of them ever changes course.

Almost all the great inspiring literature of the world, whether it be *Cinderella* or *The Divine Comedy,* is about transformation. Even great tragedy is about the working out of some terrible destructive force, through the elimination of which the world is purged and renewed.

In Chekhov there is none of this. No one in his plays even begins to embark on that voyage of internal discovery (like Tolstoy's Levin) which leads to transformation. We merely see static characters, creatures of circumstances, without self-knowledge, doomed to the eternal round of youthful energy and optimism pinned on false, external goals (Moscow, the wrong choice of marriage partner, literary reputation) slowly souring into non-comprehending exhaustion and futility. And in the end the only palliative for this is even more inchoate fantasies about distant future states, whether in this world or the next, where somehow "life will be different. It will be happy."

It is for our recognition of this melancholy, arid picture that I believe we have quietly elevated Chekhov into the supreme "serious" playwright of our age. For we see in him most clearly (and beguilingly) a mirror to ourselves—wraiths chasing shadows, hoping for the dawn which never comes. But we need not be so.

31

GERMAINE GREER: THE REAL FAILURE OF WOMEN'S LIB

In recent years, it has become almost a commonplace to say that the trouble with our civilization is that it has become overdominated by masculine values, has lost touch with and undervalued the feminine. Certainly it was scarcely surprising that, at the end of the "swinging sixties" in particular, there should have been something of a violent reaction to the "degradation" of women. For ten years, our machine-based culture had publicly debased the image of womanhood as never before in history. In millions of pornographic magazines, women had been portrayed as mere functions of onanistic male fantasies. Dressed up in mini-skirts and shiny PVC macs, given such impersonal names as "dolly birds," girls had been transformed into throwaway plastic objects. In books like *Last Exit to Brooklyn,* with its horrific mass rape, women had been treated with more violent contempt than in the fantasies of the Marquis de Sade. Even on the more "respectable" outer surface of our culture, in the TV commercials and color supplement ads, the bikini-clad girl had been used as the single most exploited stereotype to sell anything from drink to motor cars, deodorants to Spanish holidays—a mere marketing tool of the consumer boom. And then, at the end of the sixties, came Women's Lib—bra-burning, defacing the pornographic advertisements, and all the rest.

Was this, as claimed, the moment when women hit back on behalf of the values of their sex, the reassertion of the "feminine" in our culture? Or was it the manifestation of something

241

else, in its own way just as alarming as the degradation of the feminine which had set it off?

One of the most popular and articulate of all the books produced by the feminist movement was Germaine Greer's *The Female Eunuch*, first published in 1970. At the heart of Miss Greer's book was a savagely contemptuous attempt to contrast the public image of womanhood usually presented in our culture with what she saw as the reality of most women's lives. On the one hand, we have the Dream of the TV ads, the romantic novels, the *Sunday Times* women's page profiles of successful millionaire's wives, running smart dinner parties and being rewarded with all the jewels and expensive clothes they can wear; on the other hand, we have the Nightmare Reality— millions of bored, lonely, frustrated, exploited women, chained to screaming children, to "little boy" husbands whose only interests are sport, drink, and sex, driven to pills and alcoholism, ceaselessly mocked by the utter unreality of the Dream dancing over their TV screens. In fact, argued Miss Greer, "Women have very little idea how much men hate them." Even the best qualities of women are cruelly traded upon and exploited. Nurses, for instance, in an example she uses twice, kidded into "feeling good because they are relieving pain," underpaid and overworked, are almost invariably "tired, resentful, and harried." Women, in short, are "the only true proletariat left."

So what is the answer, where lies liberation? As one might expect when talk of the "proletariat" is flying around, Miss Greer's prescription was that women should rise up against their exploiters, should bring about a "revolution." But before we go on to the nature of that revolution, we might perhaps look a little more closely at the nature of that suppressed femininity in whose name the revolution was to be carried out.

One of the first things which strikes one about *The Female Eunuch* (even more perhaps, in the changed perspective of the past ten years, on rereading it) is Germaine Greer's anxiety to show how very similar women are, physically and psychologically, to the hated men. She begins by pointing out that the only difference in genetic make-up between the two sexes derives from one tiny chromosome out of 48. Later she compares the mental abilities of the two sexes, with such statements as: "Non-verbal cognitive abilities like counting, mathematical reasoning, spatial cognition, abstract reasoning, set-breaking and restructuring, perceptual speed, manual, mechanic and scientific skills have all been tested, and no significant pattern of difference has emerged, except this slight preeminence of the girls." Like many Women's Lib thinkers of the time, in heavily laboring the physical aspects of womanhood, she seemed to have a preoccupation with what is known as "the clitoral orgasm," i.e. that sexual gratification which is derived from the female's nearest vestige to a male sexual organ. And in one of the most poignant passages of the book, she lists some of the success stories of women who have made careers for themselves, including "Asha Radoti" who "is now Portfolio Manager for the Castle Britannia Unit Trust Group," "Miss Isabel Webster" who after "twelve years working as a depilator in the Tao Clinic" has "now patented her own formula for an aerosol depilator called 'Spray Away'" and a former housemaid from Camden Town who became "a director of Acme, Britain's largest firm of industrial cleaners."

In other words, the values by which Miss Greer measured the success, the capabilities, even the physical make-up of women, were as near as possible those by which men supposedly value themselves. Now, when we talk about "masculine" and "feminine" functions in the human psyche (those functions *all* of which have to be realized and brought into balance if any of us is to become truly "whole" and mature) what precisely do we mean? The chief "masculine" functions are physical power and sensation—those things which pertain to the body—and rationality, the organizing principle of the mind. The chief "feminine" functions, which are absolutely crucial to give the male functions balance, are sympathetic and protective feeling, and intuition, that enormously important function which, rooted in the unconscious, gives us a sense of the spiritual, of the hidden connections between things.

The one thing which hits one between the eyes about Miss

Greer's book is how completely lacking it is in appreciation of feminine functions, how astonishingly unbalanced it is in its reverence for the masculine. As for intuition, Miss Greer simply writes it off as "only a faculty for observing tiny insignificant aspects of behavior and forming an empirical conclusion which cannot be syllogistically examined." As for feeling, compassion, there is nothing so striking about the book as what an utterly bleak, loveless, tortured, hard view of the world and people it conjures up—it is almost totally lacking in real feeling throughout.

Now the question which arises is—why should Miss Greer have got into this state where she so undervalues the feminine in herself, in what seems almost like a parody of the masculine one-sidedness she is rebelling against? Like many of the leading figures in the Women's Lib movement, she makes no secret of the fact that she had a deeply unhappy childhood, "unspeakably dreary teens." She describes her domineering, unfeeling virago of a mother, constantly trying to emasculate her father, bullying the children, pouring contempt on their softer or finer feelings. To a psychologist, in short, Miss Greer presents an absolutely classic study of a girl who is the victim of the "Terrible Mother," without any proper model on which to develop her own femininity, her compassion, her intuition. The result, as in millions of other cases, is a girl who grows up, desperately overcompensating by her flight into masculine rational activity, but fundamentally hating the feminine, and unable to relate properly either to feminine or masculine—a girl, to use the jargon, possessed by her *animus,* that hard, masculine part of herself which is asserted against the world in a continual rant of often pyrotechnic mental brilliance, but almost completely without feminine softness or intuitive feel for the true "nature" of things.

It is scarcely surprising that Miss Greer came out of such a background with such a fierce, *animus*-ridden desire to avenge her own repressed feminine by proving that she, and her kind, could do just as well in a man's world as men—be successful, be intellectual, even enjoy "clitoral orgasms." She has hazy visions of a lost "Golden Age" when things might not have been so—a Calabrian village full of poor but happy extended families (though even here she cannot resist adding that the menfolk of the village were mainly away "working in Germany"—even this Utopia could basically do without men). She has an even hazier fantasy of her own personal Utopia—a kind of commune, again in Italy, where her own child need not know who her "womb-mother" was. But in general, collectively, the great revolution is to be achieved by a rising up of the "last proletariat"—of women like Abby Rockefeller who has a green belt in karate and the "Tufnell Park Liberation Workshop" with their magazine *Shrew*—who must assert themselves, not in the case of true femininity, but in the name of some shadow of precisely that unbalanced and therefore infantile masculinity they affect to despise.

Looking back after ten years, in other words, the real tragedy of Women's Lib was not that it expressed a reassertion of the feminine, so much, as the final victory of our culture's overdevelopment of the masculine (as the Women's Libbers unconsciously demonstrate, nowhere more clearly than in their passionate obsession with abortion—the ultimate denial of the feminine role). The catastrophic loss of the positive aspects of femininity in our culture is something which has been going on, not just for 20 years, but for centuries—certainly as far back as that overvaluation of the masculine reflected in the Reformation, and the hysterical hatred of the witch-burning new Puritans for everything that was symbolized by the Virgin Mary. The growing one-sided rationality of European culture, through the age of Descartes and Newton, reached a first peak in the obsession with order of the Age of Reason, then developed further into the love of technological power, the suffocating "masculine" respectability of the Victorian era. Meanwhile the loss of the feminine was unconsciously reflected with desperate poignancy in so many romantic stories of the nineteenth century—as we see in the consumptive heroines, the persecuted maidens, the "elusive *anima*-figures" who suffer or flit bewitchingly through so many operas, novels, and poems of that time. In the plight of the heroines of the age of romanticism—from Gretchen to Mimi, from La Belle Dame Sans Merci and the victims of de Sade to Tolstoy's Anna and Hardy's Tess—we see the most explicit record imaginable of a civilization which was literally "losing its soul." The real task which confronts us today is to do precisely what Women's Lib set out not to do—to rescue the "lost feminine" in all of us, men and women alike.

32

WATERSHIP DOWN: RABBITS AND REALITY

Arguably the most successful piece of fiction produced in the seventies (certainly by a Western author) was Richard Adams's mini-epic about the adventures of a group of rabbits in the Berkshire countryside, *Watership Down.* The story of the book's origins will probably be familiar—how it evolved from tales told to his two young daughters by a then obscure, middle-aged civil servant, working in the clean air and pollution section of the Department of the Environment, on their journeys up to Stratford-on-Avon. When the book was first published in 1972 it was given only a modest reception. The next year, after considerable trepidation and talk of extensive rewriting, Puffin put out a paperback edition. Within twelve months it had become one of the best sellers of the age. Its total sales to date, in the Puffin and Penguin editions alone, are around three million—and its world-wide sales are several times that.

Why should a fiction about rabbits, studded with somewhat portentous-looking chapter headings from Shakespeare, the Earl of Chesterfield, *Così Fan Tutte,* Xenophon, Yeats, Tennyson, Napoleon, and the South Sea Bubble company prospectus, have caught on in this way? The touching of what deep chord in the public imagination has led *Watership Down* to be accepted within such a brief space of time as one of those classics of children's literature which speak to readers of all ages, fit to be mentioned in the same breath as, say, *The Wind in the Willows, The Lord of the Rings,* or even *Gulliver's Travels?*

The story of *Watership Down* centers round that age-old

theme in the literature of the world, a Quest. It begins with a group of rabbits receiving the intuitive warning that some appalling fate is about to overtake their warren. Like so many fields on the outskirts of English villages in the early seventies, the rabbits' home has in fact been earmarked by a rapacious property company as the site for a "high-class" housing development. The little group of rabbits, who become the book's heroes, just manage to get away in time, before their *confrères* are hideously gassed and bulldozed to death. The rest of the story tells how they make their way, through all sorts of perils, across the countryside to Watership Down, where they eventually manage to establish a flourishing new warren.

In all of these respects, the story is remarkably similar in outline to other, more celebrated Quest stories, such as the *Aeneid,* describing how Aeneas and his friends leave the burning city of Troy to found their new city in distant Italy, that of the Children of Israel escaping from bondage and threatened destruction in Egypt to set up a new home in the Promised Land, or Christian in *Pilgrim's Progress* leaving the "city of destruction" (which he has a premonition is about to be engulfed by fire) to set off on his perilous journey to the distant Celestial City.

In fact the parallels between *Watership Down* and other stories formed by the Quest archetype run even deeper. It is a misconception, for instance, that the essence of Quest stories is that they simply describe a long journey toward a distant goal. In almost all the best-known stories of this type, the journey itself only accounts for a part of the tale. The worst ordeals of all await the hero and his companions when they have already come within sight of the goal, and face the obstacles which still stand in their way of winning it and securing it for the future. The whole of the second half of the *Aeneid* is taken up with Aeneas's battle to secure his new home in Italy against the tribes who already live there. The same is true of the Jewish Exodus (the Battle of Jericho, etc). Jason's fiercest tests await him when he has already arrived in the neighborhood of the

Golden Fleece in Colchis, just as Odysseus's arrival in Ithaca before the final great battle with the suitors occurs exactly half way through the *Odyssey*. And it is here that we can see, in almost every instance, what is the real nature of the goal of the Quest story. What matters is not mere arrival at a goal, the winning of a treasure, or whatever, so much as the securing or establishing of a Kingdom, and usually, simultaneously, the winning of a Princess into the bargain.

In this respect, *Watership Down* is absolutely true to its underlying archetype—to an extent which I suspect even Richard Adams, for all his background in Jungian analysis, was not fully aware of. The journey across country to the new home takes up only a comparatively small amount of the story. The rest describes the great struggle which faces the little group of male rabbits when they get there, first to win a group of rabbit "Princesses" from the hostile warren of Efrafa and then to make their new kingdom secure against the avenging depredations of the "monster" General Woundwort. Only then, after their final victory, is the future of the new kingdom secured, and can "King" Hazel die in peace, knowing that the union of "masculine" and "feminine" has assured future generations of little rabbits to carry the kingdom on into the future.

But at this point, having moved in the lofty realms of comparison between a children's book of our own time and some of the greatest stories in the history of the world, we come down to earth with a bump. It is all very well to descry these heady similarities with the *Odyssey* or the *Aeneid,* but the fact remains that *Watership Down* is not about great mythic heroes, cosmic enlargements of our own human nature. It is about bunny rabbits—and in the very nature of the somewhat sentimental association that conjures up, not to mention the diminution rather than magnification of scale it implies, I believe we have a further very important indication as to the reasons for *Watership Down*'s success.

One of the book's most appealing qualities is the way it transforms a stretch of our own familiar, Home Counties countryside into a vast, seemingly mythic, realm. Just a few miles of fields, woods, and downland have been magnified into an almost boundless kingdom. The English Channel, as visited by the black-headed gull Kehaar, seems unimaginably far away. Crossing a railway line or a tiny stream becomes for the rabbits a gigantic ordeal, comparable with Odysseus evading the clutches of Scylla and Charybdis. Now, as we all know, the trouble with the modern world as seen on a human scale, or through human eyes, is that it is no longer like that. There are virtually no more "boundless, unknown realms" left. The world has shrunk to a tiny, overpopulated, overexplored, overmechanized backyard. It takes a great feat of the imagination to transmogrify the contemporary English countryside, with its broiler farms, barbed wire fences, highways and housing projects, back into a "faery realm" of romance and high adventure. But by diminishing his heroes to mere rabbit size, it is that which Adams has achieved—thus creating the most successful "pseudomythic" landscape since the imaginary world conjured up by Tolkien.

Similarly—and ironically—one of the great advantages of having animals as your heroes, rather than human beings, is that you can invest them with purely *human* qualities, as opposed to all those dehumanizing distortions of human qualities which are unavoidable when you set an adventure story in our modern world of motor cars, airplanes, space rockets, telephones and all the rest of the gadgetry. With James Bond, *Star Wars,* and the rest, the dehumanizing of the epic hero, by placing him perpetually in the shadow of machinery and technology, has gone just about as far as it can. With the rabbits of *Watership Down,* however, we are firmly back in a premechanical world, where the hero and his friends can only survive by their direct exercise of a balance of our primary, innate functions—physical strength, intuition, a courageous heart, and all the rest.

And herein, I believe, lies the real clue to *Watership Down.* The very fact that in order to conjure up a fully human story, according to the age-old pattern of the Quest, the author has had in effect to escape from our modern technological world altogether is the most revealing comment of all on the nature of the book's appeal. It is no accident that men, with their cars, trains, bulldozers, traps, and gassing devices, are by and large seen in the book as enemies, as the greatest "monster" of all in the natural world of the bunnies. Equally it is no accident that the rabbits' adventure is set in motion in the first place as an attempt to escape from that supreme symbol of the steady advance of an alien, dehumanizing future, a development scheme—nor at a deeper level still that the whole book should be about an attempt to escape from these manmade horrors into some place of distant, happy, innocent security.

As may be apparent, I have great admiration for Adams's book. I find it gripping, moving, and in many ways profound. But let us not at the same time overlook the horrific message which is implicit in the book's success. At the deepest level, it is yet another of those countless fantasies of escape thrown up by the unconscious of modern man—escape from the unspeakable, inhuman world we are creating for ourselves by technology, shot through with every kind of premonition of some ultimate disaster. It is all very well to dream of getting back to a simpler, more natural world where we might once again become fully human. But in the conscious, outward world, the truth is that we are still doing almost everything we can to ensure that we are traveling self-destructively in the opposite direction. On that level, alas, *Watership Down* must be seen as nothing more than a charming piece of nostalgic wishful thinking—as was demonstrated for me by nothing more clearly than a copy of the local Newbury paper which I saw a year or two after *Watership Down* had raced to the top of the best-seller list. The front-page headline announced that there was such a "plague of rabbits" on the nearby Berkshire Downs (the very place where Watership Down is situated) that £20,000 was to be spent on a "massive extermination program." It is one thing to dream of that purer, simpler world, where we are once again at one with nature and with our own nature. But if, in the tiniest respect, such dreams conflict with our drive to subject nature to our own use and comfort, it becomes a different matter altogether. Then is our sentimentality as a species shown up in its true colors as nothing more than the most appalling double think—if not as the expression of our potentially quite catastrophic self-deception.

Part Five

CULTURAL COLLAPSE

INTRODUCTION

Of all the views expressed in this book, none is likely to meet with more resistance than the suggestion that, in the past ten years, our culture in the widest sense—architectural, artistic, scientific, philosophical—has reached the most dramatic dead end in the entire history of mankind. Like the real estate agent who assures you that the old house he is trying to sell you is "in absolutely sound condition—needs nothing more than a lick of paint and it will stand for another three hundred years" (when in fact it is so riddled with dry rot that it would collapse into a pile of dust at the press of a finger), the professional boosters of our culture—TV impresarios, saleroom directors, the publishers of coffee table books, newspaper critics—will tell us that it has never been in a more thriving state. They will point to expensive television series bringing artistic riches and philosophical debate to a wider audience than ever before in history; to lavish art exhibitions; to the feast of music available on the airwaves and in our concert halls, the almost unprecedentedly high standard of performance; the world-wide ferment of scientific research; the record flow of books from the presses. Thanks to the omnipresence of our modern image-conveying apparatus, we have been able to blur all the world's "culture" together and to keep it constantly before our eyes and minds in such a way that we scarcely notice how much we are simply feeding on the stored-up vitality of the past. By an ingenious sleight of mind, we are able to convince ourselves, through the frenzy of cultural activity that constantly surrounds us, that we are still adding to that store. And if anyone dares for a moment to question such a comforting notion, no one will come down on him more like a ton of bricks than those diehard Old Believers who are still conditioned by the ideology of the Modern Movement to believe that the less something is liked and understood today, the more certainly will its genius be recognized tomorrow—without noticing the fact that, in the past decade, the Modern Movement itself has finally disintegrated.

In fact the whole of post-Renaissance Western culture has suddenly become nothing more than a vast, fascinating museum piece—a huge, rickety memorial to a civilization which simply lost its way. Of course along that way there were many brilliant achievements. The artists, scientists, and philosophers of the past few hundred years have made astonishing advances, carried human experience and observation into realms undreamed of. But suddenly, standing at the end of that great adventure, we can see with appalling clarity where it was all leading—to the eventual complete loss of *meaning*. First in the aftermath of the Renaissance, even more since the simultaneous rise of Industrialism and Romanticism 200 years ago, a great split has opened up in the Western psyche: on the one hand, the scientists have accumulated more and more facts and "knowledge," the philosophers have subjected language to ever more minute and rigorous examination; on the other, artists have more and more pursued effects, sensations, illusion; and as that gap has opened ever wider, so, almost without our noticing it, has meaning gently been sliding further and further out of view—to the point where, confronted with the gaping void, the cosmic despair which lies at the heart of our contemporary culture in all directions (except where we can paper it over by rushing back for consolation into those embodiments of meaning which survive from the past), we do not even recognize the fact.

But part of the extraordinary importance of the past ten years has been the fact that, despite all the whistling in the dark, the din of self-congratulatory reassurance from the media, the bankruptcy of our culture has intruded more inescapably and prominently than ever before. This section in fact continues in more

general vein the theme of the last, "Nostalgia and Self-deception"—and it opens with two essays on the deeper significance of
our sudden astonishing passion for conserving the past in architecture. The first consists of thoughts inspired by the campaign
in 1977 to preserve Mentmore House in Hertfordshire, complete
with its bizarre collection of *objets d'art* (the campaign was, of
course, unsuccessful, the art objects were sold off in an undigni-
fied scramble, and the shell of the house rather suitably became a
center for that vacuous vestige of man's search for spirituality,
the Transcendental Meditation movement, run by the old meg-
alomaniac whom *Private Eye* once nicknamed the Veririshi Lots-
amoney). The second essay, "Something Old, Something New,"
takes a somewhat deeper and broader view of the growing conservation craze of the past hundred years, showing how the final
collapse of architectural self-confidence in the seventies marked
the end of a cycle that had begun at the time of the Renaissance.

A third essay examines that other phenomenon of our times,
the great craze for nature. The two which follow examine aspects
of the way we have more and more desperately and confusedly
tried to sustain our faith in science as the way to truth and a
better life. The pieces on the collapse of the Modern Movement
and on latter-day philosophy are, I fear, little more than jottings
on subjects worthy of deeper and more detailed consideration
elsewhere. There are notes on the psychology of modern architecture and society's obsession with abortion. Finally, in rather
different vein, there is an analysis of the various attitudes com-
monly held today toward the possibility that our civilization may
be facing some ultimate catastrophe.

33

MAD FOR CONSERVATION

Written during the controversy over the future of Mentmore,
February 12, 1977.

In the past few days the press has been filled with news of yet
another "conservation battle"—one which I believe casts particular light on one of the most profoundly revealing dilemmas
facing our late-twentieth-century civilization. I am referring to
the debate over the future of Mentmore Towers, the great mysterious Rothschild treasure house which stands in Jacobean
splendor in the English countryside near Luton. Years ago,
reading Robert Rhodes James's *Life of Lord Rosebery,* I was
haunted by the photographs of the Liberal Prime Minister's
four houses: Barnbougle, a bleak little Scottish baronial box
standing by the Firth of Forth; Dalmeny, a huge, almost
equally bleak four-square Scottish mansion; the Durdans, a
cosy, low, ivy-covered Victorian house near Epsom; and finally,
by far the most impressive, the misty towers and pinnacles of
Mentmore (which came to Rosebery as a result of his marriage
to Hannah de Rothschild).

The little-known story of this fabulous Aladdin's Cave of a
house, built by Joseph Paxton for the Baron Meyer Amschel de
Rothschild between 1851 and 1854, has been so superbly set out
by that admirable organization SAVE in their new pamphlet
"Save Mentmore for the Nation" that I cannot but recommend
anyone who is remotely interested to send for a copy. With the
aid of an astonishing set of hitherto unpublished photographs,

Marcus Binney of *Country Life* and a small team of experts have for the first time in this century brought to light one of the most extraordinary houses in Europe. Inside, Mentmore is a cross between the "Italian Palazzo" style of Barry's Reform Club (the great Hall and Staircase), and a series of "French Versailles' rooms—crammed with one of the greatest treasure troves ever amassed in private hands. For page after page, Binney and his colleagues lovingly unveil one glittering assemblage after another—Gobelin and Flemish tapestries, gilt lanterns from the Venetian state barge, the *Bucintoro,* curtains of Genoese velvet and others worked on by Marie Antoinette, a mass of magnificent clocks, the great chimneypiece designed by Rubens for his house in Antwerp, an untold wealth of furniture, ranging from loot from the Doge's Palace to a vast rococo cabinet made for Augustus III of Poland in the 1750s, Sèvres porcelain, jewels, and *objets de vertu,* paintings by Titian, Rembrandt, Greuze, Boucher, a unique sporting scene by Gainsborough, two fine Turners—it is a haul of "world importance."

Even in the crudest economic terms, the SAVE team's case that Mentmore should be bought for the nation is unanswerable. The house and its entire contents have been offered to the government for a laughable £2 million (in lieu of death duties which would be payable anyway on the 6th Earl of Rosebery's estate). If the contents of the house go to auction in May, as seems likely, Sotheby's alone may well make more than half that sum, just in commission fees. As Marcus Binney suggests, it would be quite absurd of the government not to accept the offer, at least for two years, while a "permanent solution" to the endowment of the house can be explored—at the end of which time, if the search is unsuccessful, the entire £2 million investment could be recouped just by selling off half a dozen or so of the chief treasures.

It was only when the SAVE team goes on to outline what a "permanent solution" for Mentmore might be that certain deeper questions begin to intrude themselves. Undoubtedly, they argue, such a house standing just half an hour up the M1 from London could become a major national tourist attraction. Even if it drew only 100,000 visitors a year, spending £1 a head on tickets, souvenirs, postcards and ice creams, that would yield the greater part of the £100,000 needed annually to run it. While the house's grounds and other amenities would lend themselves admirably to such other profitable uses as a "national equestrian centre," complete with three-day events, Princess Anne falling off her horse, and all the rest.

Faced with this prospect of Mentmore transformed into a kind of "cultural Longleat," the Scenicruisers nose to tail in the new asphalt car parks, the aimless mass of tourists wandering like bewildered sheep through those great, dead rooms, does not a terrible weariness of the soul set in? In some ways, the spectacle of any great house transformed into a museum is always depressing. Similarly, one of the most extraordinary cultural phenomena of our time is the spectacle of tens of thousands of tourists wheeling endlessly through any stately home (or art gallery, or museum) somehow seeking a sense of significance from mere contact with the artefacts of the past that, even when there is a guide to tell them the exact value of each item and the dates of the artist, they simply do not know how to find.

If this is true of a house which was once for centuries a home, how much truer would it be of Mentmore, which was actually built as a museum (or *kunstkammer*) and was therefore in a sense never truly alive in the first place. One of the more curious claims made on Mentmore's behalf in recent days was that of James Lees-Milne in a letter to *The Times* that it "in the eyes of discriminating people, constitutes one of the glories of Britain's peak of greatness." The only "British" thing (and indeed the only remotely "creative" thing) about Mentmore is the house itself, designed by a Derbyshire gardener who was undoubtedly one of the most remarkable and gifted Englishmen of the nineteenth century. But even Paxton's design was unashamedly an imitation of other models. The house is a magnificent pastiche, a masterpiece of that eclecticism which was in itself so telling a clue to the underlying spiritual nullity of the Victorian age. As for Mentmore's contents—what are they but simply the accumulation by a rich Jewish banker, of Austrian stock, of a great magpie jumble of pretty things, pillaged with discriminating indiscrimination from three centuries of the culture of post-Renaissance Europe? In a way nothing has reflected the spiritual decline of Europe more surely over the past five centuries than the different stages whereby supremely rich and powerful men have in succeeding centuries managed to build up these great treasure hordes—the Dukes of Mantua, the Hapsburgs, Charles I, the "Grand Tour" collectors of the eighteenth century, Beckford and George IV, then the nineteenth-century commercial and industrial magnates, from the Rothschilds to the Vanderbilts, finally shading off in our own time into the ultimate absurdities of the Citizen Kanes, the clients of Duveen, Hitler, and Goering. At every stage the distance between the collector and the spiritual roots of the art and craftsmanship that was the object of his desire has yawned ever wider (at least the Gonzagas patronized Mantegna, Charles V befriended Titian, Charles I employed Rubens and Van Dyck). While today we see the final *reductio ad absurdum* in the pillaging of Western culture for trinkets and toys by the oil sheiks of Arabia, or Impressionist-hungry Japanese transistor billionaires. The severing of cultural roots is complete.

That is why, while I applaud the SAVE campaign for Mentmore (*sic et non*) the prospect also fills me with a great melancholy—at the thought of that great, dead house as yet another tombstone to our rootless, disintegrated civilization. We should wander round it (if it were saved), not with the joy of new life in our souls, but with little more than an increasingly oppressive sense of looking back to a life that has gone. This raises questions about the whole cultural significance of the great mania for conservation presently sweeping the world to which I would like to return.

34

SOMETHING OLD, SOMETHING NEW

February 19, 1977

In the first program of his *Civilisation* series, Kenneth Clark quoted Ruskin as saying, "Great nations write their autobiographies in three manuscripts. The book of their deeds, the book of their words and the book of their art . . . of the three, the only trustworthy one is the last." Clark went on to add, "If I had to say which was telling the truth about society, a speech by the Minister of Housing, or the actual buildings put up in his time, I should believe the buildings." But what are we to make of a society like our own, which, for the first time in history, has virtually lost faith in its ability to put up new buildings at all?

To see this extraordinary fact in its proper perspective, let us begin by taking a historical excursion through one of the most fascinating cultural pendulum swings of the past 500 years.

In the autumn of 1503, the dashing and cultured Cardinal Giuliano della Rovere became Pope Julius II. As the supreme embodiment of High Renaissance self-confidence, one of Julius's first actions was to plan for himself a magnificent tomb. The work was to be carried out, of course, by the most distinguished sculptor of the day, Michelangelo. But the more Julius considered his monument, the more ambitious he became that it should be seen to the very best advantage. It was thus there came into his head what Lord Clark has described as "a project so audacious, so extravagant, that the thought of it to this day makes me slightly jumpy."

For more than a thousand years, the vast basilica of St. Peter's, begun by the Emperor Constantine in 326, had been the largest and most venerable building in Christendom. Julius's plan was simple as it was breathtaking. St. Peter's must be swept away—and replaced with a new building, by the most distinguished architect of the day, Bramante, which would without question be even larger and more magnificent. By 1506 so much of the ancient cathedral had already been razed to the ground that Bramante became known as "the ruinous architect."

In a sense, to appreciate the full measure of Julius's incredible audacity has been reserved for us who live at the end of the twentieth century. For even though his particular act of daring remained the supreme example of its kind (it is, for instance, a remarkable fact that, apart from fires, not one of Europe's great Gothic cathedrals was pulled down during three centuries when their style of architecture was largely scorned as barbarous and "mean in spirit"), men all over the West continued until well into the nineteenth century to demolish and replace ancient buildings simply as need arose. In the eighteenth century, fine Elizabethan and Jacobean houses were destroyed by the score, to make way for more sumptuous mansions in the modern style. In the nineteenth century, of course, the havoc wrought to medieval churches in the name of "restoration" was untold. But from Wyatt to Scott, it never for a moment crossed the minds of the architects (or their clients) that what they were doing was anything other than by way of that great keyword of Victorian culture, an "improvement." What was old might be good. But what was new was still without question better.

The first portents of a great shift in cultural attitudes came quite suddenly, in the seventh and eighth decades of the nineteenth century. In 1865, the Metropolitan Board of Works conceived a plan to drive through a new road from Trafalgar Square to Bazalgette's new Victorian Embankment. The scheme would require the demolition of Northumberland House, the large Jacobean palace standing on the southeast corner of the square. But when plans for the compulsory purchase of the house became known, it was not only the Duke of Northumberland who was enraged. There was also a howl of protest against the pulling down of this fine old building from the public at large.

It was a profoundly significant moment. In fact, after a fire in 1868, the scheme for the new Northumberland Avenue did eventually go through, and the house was demolished in 1875. But in the same year, the destruction of the Oxford Arms, a galleried sixteenth-century coaching inn near St. Paul's prompted the foundation of a Society for the Photographing of Old Buildings. In 1877, alarmed by the rate at which old churches were giving way under the onslaught of Victorian "restoration," William Morris founded the Society for the Protection of Ancient Buildings. Sir John Lubbock began his annual attempts to bring in an Act for the preservation of ancient monuments which, when it was finally approved in 1882, laid the foundation for the whole of our elaborate structure for the legal protection of "listed" buildings today. For the first time in history, in short, men were beginning to feel such an affection for old buildings, for their own sake, that they were actually prepared to battle to save them.

Even so, for nearly a century longer, despite the ever-growing nostalgia for old buildings, the conviction still remained that on the whole to pull buildings down to replace them with something better was still quite natural and desirable. In the 1920s, Nash's Regent Street, one of the finest of nineteenth-century townscapes, was swept away almost without a thought. In the 1930s, only the coming of war prevented the similar destruction by Sir Reginald Blomfield of the Nash Terraces in the Mall. To today's reader, one of the most startling things about that celebrated book *The Face of London* by Harold Clunn (published in the 1930s) is the relentless way in which any large development of those times (the "splendid" new Shell-Mex building, the "magnificent" new ICI block on Millbank) was still automatically looked on as a mark of ever-onward, ever-upward progress.

In fact this underlying sense of confidence survived until

remarkably lately. Certainly through the first two decades after World War II, despite the steady growth in legislative protection of outstanding gems, despite the odd public furor over an Imperial Institute or a Euston Arch, we embarked on the greatest transformation our cities had ever known, with high-rise buildings and "comprehensive redevelopment schemes" and the new technological style in architecture, with a confident abandon that would almost have done justice to Julius II himself.

Then suddenly, in the 1970s, came the collapse. Within just a few years, the great conservation movement mushroomed into one of the most powerful social forces of the age. For the first time we had seen the future, and it did not work. Our architectural and cultural self-confidence disintegrated with quite astonishing speed. From Michelangelo's Rome to Britain in the late 1970s, the pendulum has finally swung its full arc.

And so we arrive at the extraordinary dilemma we are in today. Firstly, far from believing that anything new is better, we are now (generally) convinced of almost exactly the reverse—that anything new is worse, and that almost any old building should be preserved at all costs. So total is our lack of confidence in our ability to design, to plan, even to build properly, that we are now prepared to revere almost any building from "the past"—not just masterpieces, or Georgian terraces, but grim Victorian warehouses, factories, back-to-back jerry-built Victorian slums, even the serried ranks of suburban semis of the 1920s and 1930s.

But secondly, and here is the rub, as our society continues to change with great speed old buildings still continue to outlive their original uses. Churches, railway stations, warehouses, town halls, country houses continue to become redundant, or uneconomical in ever greater numbers. But just as we can no longer bear to think of anything old being pulled down, so we desperately switch all our architectural skills, our resources, and our cultural ingenuity to adapting these old structures to new uses. Churches become concert halls, warehouses become

World Trade Centers, country houses become museums (or "garden centers" or "equestrian centers"), Cotswold tithe barns become trendy restaurants. Yet, in some mysterious way, almost every time the trick is performed, something of the essential spirit of the old building vanishes. As one wanders around the beautifully restored fragments of what survives of St. Katharine Dock, the eighteenth-century timber-framed warehouse transformed into a trendy pub, across the twee little "authentic" cobblestones, one is no longer in a grim survival of nineteenth-century commerce, but a sub-Williamsburg fantasy world. Even some of our great cathedrals which in the past 20 years have been lovingly restored and cleaned and floodlit, have (for my taste at least) been transformed into little more than beautiful soulless film sets.

We are, in short, finally stuck, trapped in our wonderful, comfortable, late-twentieth-century material prison. We can neither build anew with faith in the future nor can we preserve the past that we love by artificial means and yet preserve that intangible thing about it which we feel our civilization has mysteriously lost. But here I believe we are confronted with the heart of the cultural crisis which in the past few years has finally crept up on our civilization without our being fully aware of it—and it is something which runs much deeper and wider than mere considerations of architecture.

35

BACK TO NATURE?

July 1, 1978

What are we to make of the great nature craze presently sweeping our civilization? Thirty years ago, when I first began looking at birds and butterfles, the botanist or entomologist, roaming the countryside with his butterfly net and specimen box, was still generally considered a pretty odd sort of cove. Today, when natural history has been transformed into environmental studies, scarcely a middle-class British family does not have its copy of Keble Martin on the back seat of the car. Not a month goes by without some new Guide to Fungi or Complete Book of Waterplants racing up the best-seller charts (in the past ten years, more new nature books must have been published than in the whole of the previous five centuries since Gutenberg). Even for those whose interest is more casual, the television screens pump out an almost nightly diet of films on "the vanishing Broads," the corncrakes of the Hebrides, the voles of Cumbria. For media exposure, the birds and the bees leave the World Cup nowhere.

It might seem a trifle ironic that this obsession with Wonderful Nature should coincide with the very moment in history when *homo sapiens* seems generally bent on the destruction of nature more ruthlessly and efficiently than ever before. But of course the two phenomena are hardly unconnected. It is true that, in a sense, the whole story of mankind has been written in our attempts to separate and emancipate ourselves from nature, to transform the world into a safe, tame, hygienic place, in which we can live out our lives in the maximum of material comfort. Nevertheless, the more we have managed to insulate ourselves from nature, the more do we seem to feel that something important is missing. Living in our cosy little technological prison, the more do we seem to be afflicted by a terrible yearning for that lost sense of wholeness with the rest of creation of which we are still, like it or not, a part; the more desperately do we seek our lost souls in that very thing from which we have become so estranged—the free, untamed world of birds, flowers, animals, and the few remaining uncontaminated places of the earth.

In short, we are utterly bewildered by our attitude toward nature. We are unable to make up our minds whether it is simply an object, to be probed, taxonomized, despoiled, polluted, and generally put to our egocentric use; or the last relic of a beautiful, free, instinctive world which mirrors our own lost harmony. But it would be a mistake to think that this ambivalence is a new thing. Take for instance, what is perhaps the most famous nature book ever written, Gilbert White's *Natural History of Selborne*. In the late twentieth century, the earthly paradise conjured up by the obscure Hampshire curate is usually presented to us as the very picture of lost innocence. Nothing could seem further, we think, from that other more terrible world which was coming to birth elsewhere in England in precisely the years White was writing (1767-88)—the age of steam and iron and rampant technology, whose bemused heirs we are today.

Reread White more carefully, however, and we may recognize that the difference was not so great. The exact observation which led White to become the first man to distinguish scientifically between a chiff-chaff and a willow warbler sprang from that same restless, inquiring eighteenth-century mind which was contemporaneously producing Watt's steam engine, or Abraham Darby's iron bridge in Coalbrookdale. White's measure of value for all his industrious botanizing was not just that it might induce "his readers to pay a more ready attention to the wonders of the Creation," but utility ("he would be the best commonwealth's man that could occasion the growth of 'two blades of grass where one alone had grown before'"). Although we think of White as inspired by a deep love and sympathy for the creatures he described, we may note that, if he wished to examine a bird more closely (particularly if it was rare), he never hesitated to shoot it. In fact it was only because White and his eighteenth-century contemporaries, such as Linnaeus, were becoming even *more* separated from nature than their predecessors—as a man's self-consciousness increased and the duality between observer and observed opened up in such spectacular post-Cartesian manner—that they were able to describe and catalogue the natural world so memorably.

One consequence of the fact that it was European civilization which led the way in this estrangement from nature was that it was in Europe before anywhere else that men first reached that point of eleventh-hour shock which has led them to take measures to prevent the actual disappearance of fellow species threatened by human aggrandizement. Not the least of the many fascinating facts in Jeremy Mallinson's efficient memoir of 33 species of European mammal currently faced with extinction is that, of the 36 species which have already disappeared from the face of the earth since 1600, only one was native to Europe (the aurochs, which died out around 1627). Populations of such once-widespread species as the wolf, lynx, and brown bear may have been reduced to only tiny, isolated fractions in the wilder parts of Europe—but in recent decades, conservation measures have resulted in small but significant increases. The European bison was actually exterminated in its wild state, when the 737 animals living in the Bialowieza Forest in Poland were killed during World War I—but thanks to the fact that 66 bison from Bialowieza survived in captivity, enough could be released back into the wild over the next 40 years for the total population (wild and captive) to have risen by 1973 to 1,514 animals.

In a sense, in fact, the title of Mr. Mallinson's excellent little book, *The Shadow of Extinction,* is misleading, in that quite a number of the species he describes (with, in each case, a profile of the animal's characteristics, distribution, and prospects for survival) seem not only to be surviving fairly well, but even to be multiplying quite rapidly (e.g. the wild cat, the European beaver, the pine marten). The species which seem to be most seriously under threat tend to be those which are too small and elusive to command dramatic national conservation programs, such as the poor little Pyrenean Desman, a furry creature of mountain streamsides, which is threatened by hydro-electric schemes; or of the Greater Horseshoe Bat, whose numbers have declined in England by an estimated 90 per cent in the past 30 years, due to a variety of factors ranging from insecticides (responsible for a general catastrophic collapse in European bat populations) to "the trade in cave-dwelling bats for museums, schools, and research."

Such discrimination might confirm the suspicion that we really today have less of a true kinship than ever with the millions of species with whom we share the earth. Whenever they stand in the way of our comfort, or our imagined quest for "knowledge" (e.g. those wretched, vivisected bats), we still have remarkably little compunction in consigning them to destruction. I shall always recall a few years ago meeting a group of schoolboys on the Berkshire Downs, each clutching a jam jar packed with dead and dying butterflies. The insects were all of the same species—Meadow Browns and Small Whites. I asked them what they were up to and they said that they were on an "environment project." Their biology master had told them to go out to collect as many butterfles as they could find. Of course this is only a microcosm of the way in which, finally separated from nature as we are, our civilization is in effect waging ruthless war on the rest of creation in almost everything it sets its hand to—usually quite unconsciously (for every feathered victim of the *Amoco Cadiz* oil pollution disaster depicted struggling in its death throes on "News at Ten," millions die unremarked so that we can go on driving our motor cars). Perhaps the sickest thing of all, as we engage in this ubiquitous, round-the-clock carnage, is the way we finally turn around to sentimentalize that which we are destroying—congratulating ourselves, as we go off to gawp at our victims in those unspeakable safari parks and dolphinariums, or flip over "shock" color supplement articles about "the doomed forests of Amazonia," that we are actually doing something to help "nature survive."

36

FAUST WITHOUT THE HELLFIRE

There is usually no more sure-fire contributor to the silly season than the annual proceedings of the British Association for the Advancement of Science.

There was, for instance, the year not long ago when an American biologist described how he had injected an unfortunate rabbit with meat tenderizer, only to find that its ears "flopped like those of a spaniel."

In another paper, a psychiatrist solemnly reported his finding that "in general fat people do not go to university." Best of all, a professor of geology announced his discovery that rocks brought back from the moon showed certain properties which are only to be found on earth in Cheddar and Emmenthaler cheese.

These farragos of improbable pseudery, reminiscent of Swift's projectors who sought to extract the sunlight from cucumbers, tend to be prefaced by an enormously portentous address from whatever *savant* happens to be President of the Association, in which he invariably states that science is morally neutral and that it is time the rest of the human race caught up with the scientists, by developing the ethical framework whereby science can be used to benefit mankind rather than destroy it.

This year's presidential address, delivered in Guildford Cathedral on Wednesday night by Sir Bernard Lovell, was no exception. "SCIENCE NEEDS ETHICAL BASIS" was one headline. "Science itself" proclaimed the proprietor of the Great Dish, "is neither a magic wand nor a poisoned arrow"—but unless we find that dear old "ethical basis and moral purpose" soon, man might not "long survive the consequences" of the scientists' probings.

Decked out with impressive quotations from Carlyle, about man being a fumbling midget at the "center of mysterious immensities," Sir Bernard seemed to be particularly worried about the consequences of the search for life on other planets— although it wasn't quite clear whether the mysterious dangers he spoke of would come from invasions of Quatermass-like cacti from Jupiter, Venusian plagues, or just that we might soon find the universe so incomprehensible that we should all simply go off our heads.

Isn't it really time that this ludicrous argument over the "moral neutrality" of science was knocked on the head for once and for all? The truth is that our one-sided Western attitude to science carries with it the very deepest moral implications— and has done ever since the rise of the philosophy of experimental science with Bacon and Descartes in the seventeenth century.

Implicit in the great Western "scientific experiment" of the past 300 years have been two assumptions. The first is that the purpose of scientific technology is to ensure for the human race an ever greater degree of material comfort by controlling and dominating the rest of nature. The second is that by the mere accumulation of scientifically observed facts we shall eventually come to some kind of superior illumination about the nature of the universe and of ourselves.

It is now abundantly clear that the pursuit of each of these two assumptions has produced a host of unforeseen and unpleasing consequences. The more we attempt to subdue the rest of creation to our own immediate advantage, the more we become separated from nature, and the more we store up for ourselves a host of appalling side effects—ranging from overpopulation and pollution to the prospect of the exhaustion of natural resources, and nuclear destruction. Similarly the more we seek to replace our old mythical frame for existence with an infinite series of apparently unconnected material facts, the more we become disoriented, rootless and confused.

All these things are precisely implicit in the Mephistophelean bargain.

There is almost no belief more firmly rooted in the mythology of the human race than that which holds that man is part of the natural order which he can only interfere with at his peril. It was the ancient Chinese view. It was the Greek view, expressed through the legends of Prometheus and Icarus. It was what Horace touched on when he wrote that if you chuck out nature with a pitchfork, it will come back some other way. It was an awareness of the terrible dangers implicit in the pursuit of science which led Pythagoras and his followers to designate philosophy as a "sacred mystery," only to be divulged to those who had undergone the proper moral initiation. It was a desire for "new experience of the uninhabited world behind the sun" which, in the *Divine Comedy,* led Ulysses to self-destruction.

And as for the spiritual and mental confusion which follows from the scientific exploration of the universe, when Sir Bernard Lovell spoke on Wednesday of "the mind of man" being "adrift," he had advanced not one jot from Donne's tragic version in the heyday of Bacon, Descartes, Kepler and Galileo:

> The sun is lost and the earth and no man's wit
> Can well direct him where to look for it.
> And freely men confesse that this world's spent
> When in the Planets and the Firmament
> They seek so many anew; then see that this
> Is crumbled out again to his Atomies.

In fact all that Sir Bernard and Lord Todd and all the others mean when they say that we must develop the "ethical base" to allow us to control the destructive power of science is that they want the human race to enjoy the benefits of scientific advance without its inevitable consequences—an ever uglier, more dangerous, more sterile world, leading to spiritual death and probably physical destruction into the bargain. They want the fruits of the Faustian pact, without having to pay the price—as did Faust himself.

It really is time that, as the heirs of Pythagoras, they began to take a more truly "scientific" view.

37

ROUND IN SCIENTIFIC CIRCLES

November 9, 1978

Two of my favorite minor characters in the surreal Commedia dell'Arte of our times are that Tweedledum and Tweedledee-like pair, David Wilson and Peter Fairley, whose job it is to come on the BBC and ITN television screens to tell us about the latest exciting scientific breakthroughs.

We usually see these comfortably rotund men, with strained concerned looks on their faces, standing in white coats by models of satellite solar panels, or machines for getting energy out of waves—and their essential role is to reassure us, as a great black wall of evidence to the contrary mounts up on all sides, that everything is going to be all right.

Don't worry. The good old scientists are still there, working away at breakthroughs for mankind—test-tube babies, energy from winds, two grains of rice growing where one grew before. Technological man is still in control of his destiny.

A rather grander version of Dum and Dee is someone called John Maddox, who first hit the headlines a few years ago, during a particularly nasty outbreak of "eco-panic," when he was editor of the scientific magazine *Nature*. Maddox would have none of this talk about exhaustion of energy sources, or pollution, or fears of overpopulation. This wild scaremongering was simply a passing phase, as mankind headed upward into an ever brighter future, where there was no problem which could not be solved by our inexhaustible scientific ingenuity.

277

Now the important thing about all these men—Maddox, Dum, Dee, and Co.—is that they are not really connected with science at all. They are in a more literal than strict sense of the word the soothsayers of our time, soothing our fears with constant promises of unlimited energy, health, and scientifically produced happiness which is always just round the corner in the future. In order to understand their role properly, it is necessary to look below the surface at the very simple message they are constantly repeating—and at what it indicates as to their view of man.

A good example of what I am talking about came on Wednesday night when, on Radio Three, John Maddox was again addressing himself to one of his favorite themes—the belief that has grown up in recent years, among certain doctors, that mental illness, and in particular that series of conditions generally described under the heading of schizophrenia, may have purely physical or chemical causes. What these doctors have discovered is that, in the brains of schizophrenic patients, there appear to be deficiencies or oversupplies of certain chemical substances which transmit messages from one brain cell to another. If this is the case (and the evidence appears to be strong that it is so) then what more tempting, you might think, than to argue that these chemical malfunctions are in themselves the *causes* of schizophrenia. Because of course the corollary is that if mental illness has purely physical causes, then we can envisage that it may have a purely physical *cure*.

This is such an enticing vision that it is tempting to overlook altogether the possibility that the chemical changes might be merely by-products of psychic malfunctioning which stems from altogether deeper, more complex and therefore less tractable causes. As man has become increasingly bewildered by his inability to understand or to cope with the problems that are caused by his own advancing consciousness, few dreams have haunted him more than this one—that somehow, one day, a magic pill might be discovered that would put an end to all the mental and spiritual ills our flesh is heir to. Never mind that

Aldous Huxley viciously satirized this dream in his zombie-like *Brave New World,* dependent on the "happiness drug" soma, or that the LSD-generation of the sixties pursued their hallucinatory visions of "oneness," only to find that in many cases it led to an even greater psychic confusion than before. The dream dies hard—and earlier this year even Arthur Koestler (one of the poshest of all the Dums and Dees) was peddling in his book *Janus* the idea that somehow, in the chemical laboratories, might lie the answer to wars, crimes, and all the other psychic disorders which appear to be so uniquely endemic to mankind.

Now the most important thing of all is to recognize the view of man which underlies all these fantasies and wishful thoughts. We often hear it said that we live in a materialistic civilization—and the image this usually conjures up is of supermarkets and color television sets and everyone wanting to go on strike all the time for more money. But the real sense in which our civilization has become materialistic goes so much deeper that it is almost impossible for us any longer to "stand outside ourselves" and see what it does mean. It means that by imperceptible stages, over eons of time, our whole level of consciousness about the world and our existence within it has changed, to the point where we see just one part of ourselves as infinitely important—and that part is our bodies. Of course we still talk blithely about other "bits" of ourselves—our hearts, our minds, even on sentimental occasions of something called our "souls." But most people have simply no conception just what an astonishing change has come over us in the extent to which we now see the highest end of life and civilization as being to achieve physical comfort for our bodies, and to prolong the life of those bodies for as long as possible. The other "bits" have become mere appendages, to be soothed, stimulated, suppressed, or stilled.

What is existence? The very term itself has come to mean mere *physical* existence, and that is why there is such a deep yearning in our collapsing, spiritually and mentally bankrupt, nightmarish civilization to cling on to any last, vain hope that somehow this attempt wholly to re-interpret ourselves and the universe in purely physical terms is going to work.

It is not—and it is one of the saddest commentaries of all on the pitiful state our Western science has reached that, in its closing stages, it has become so totally *unscientific*. The truly scientific, "whole" view would be based on trying to appreciate *all* the evidence—and that means seeing physical explanations for phenomena in their true perspective as part of a whole hierarchy of other relationships.

The true lesson is that once men lose their sense of the whole, and concentrate their view on one part of the picture, they always end up trying to put together a jigsaw that simply does not fit any more. And inevitably, as an iron law of the human psyche, they collapse into nothing more than vapid and fundamentally ego-centered wishful thinking.

38

THE COLLAPSE OF "THE MODERN MOVEMENT"

May 24, 1977

My eye was recently caught by a phrase in a new book by the journalist Paul Johnson, in which he referred to Harold Pinter as "a major tragic writer in the tradition of Ibsen."

The odd thing was how ludicrously hollow this claim for Pinter now seemed. At a debate at the Cambridge Union, a month or two ago, I heard a visiting speaker completely dismissing Pinter and Beckett as having absolutely nothing of importance or interest to say. The fascinating thing is that there was not even the slightest murmur of dissent from the audience—the remark was simply accepted, in a way which even five years ago would have been unthinkable.

Lying behind this shift of opinion is, I believe, one of the most important things to have happened in our culture in the past decade. I refer to the sudden and almost complete collapse of what has so far been the most important artistic force in twentieth-century Western civilization—what may be called, in the broadest sense, "The Modern Movement."

Just consider how many of the artistic giants of our century have died in the past ten or 15 years. In painting, the modern movement was symbolized above all by those twin geniuses of post-Cubism, Braque (died 1963) and Picasso (died 1973). In architecture the giants were Le Corbusier (died 1965), Gropius (died 1969) and Mies van der Rohe (died 1969). In poetry, there were Eliot (died 1965), Pound (died 1972), and possibly Auden

281

(died 1973). In music, Stravinsky (died 1971), Shostakovich (died 1975), and possibly Britten (died 1976) and Kodaly (died 1967). With the exception perhaps of Solzhenitsyn and Beckett (both of whom I shall refer to later) and of one or two curiosities like Salvador Dali, most of those international stars who remain, Stockhausen, Pinter, Henze, Hockney, are pretty thin stuff by comparison.

Lying behind the physical departure of these towering figures, however, has been something even more revealing in recent years—and that is an increasingly general sense that most of the ideas which lay behind that great explosion of creativity that was the Modern Movement have reached a point of almost complete exhaustion.

On all sides these days one can see signs large and small of a great reaction to what the Modern Movement stood for. One of the most glaring examples is the revolt against "modern architecture"—the complete reaction against high-rise buildings and all the forces which made such a nightmare wilderness of our cities in the fifties and sixties. In painting there is the remarkable resurgence of interest in the United States and elsewhere in the sort of academic painters of the nineteenth century for decades laughed to scorn—who are now back in vogue simply because people can "understand" them. In music, after 60 years of modernism, the popularity of composers of almost any century but our own has never been higher.

What was the Modern Movement about? Clearly it produced many artists of astonishing talent. But what did they use their talent to express? For a start they were in revolt against the past—they were seeking liberation from all the old forms and conventions. In poetry this led to free verse, in painting to abstrationism, in music to atonality, in architecture to a kind of individualism run riot so that every building had to be conceived anew and from "first principles."

For the first 20 or 30 years of this century, while they wre still in the first flush of revolt, and being derided and misunderstood by conventional society, the modernists gloried in being an avant-garde minority. By the fifties and sixties, modernism had swept into triumphant acceptance as the orthodoxy of the age. No longer would anyone deny that Picasso or Le Corbusier were towering artists, fit to rank with the greatest names of the past. But built into the whole modernist adventure was a kind of self-destruct. At the end of every line of liberation there appeared to be a black hole of meaninglessness. The painters reached the blank canvas, the composers reached random, uncontrolled noise, the writers pushed through the final frontiers of meaning to the point where, like Beckett, they claimed that they had nothing left to say except that there was nothing left to say.

That is the point we have reached today. And suddenly we can look back over the Western art of the past five centuries and see with dazzling clarity that what has been laid out before us is a perfect model of the psyche of man, and a beautiful demonstration of what art is all about. We can see that what has happened is that Western man has progressively lost touch with the very center of his being, the sense of union with the divine. The more he has explored the bypaths of his material consciousness, the more the artist has come to see himself as an isolated figure expressing his own individuality—rather than drawing that strength from the sense of belonging to some infinite, spiritual "whole" which gives him universality. Of course along the path of the past 500 years there have been many great artists who (against the general trend) have still managed to make that return to the "center"—Titian and Rembrandt, Bach and Beethoven, Dostoevski and Tolstoy, and many others. Even in our own disintegrated times, many of the leading artists (Eliot, Britten, Stravinsky, Auden) have burned with a "low blue flame," as Edmund Wilson called it, of that religious sense which must lie at the heart of all true creativity. And today it is no accident that one of the few remaining artists with a claim to universality and real meaning is Solzhenitsyn, who through the purging away of all material irrelevance in the horrors of totalitarian Russia, has been brought back into contact with spiritual reality.

But the final lesson of the story is that it is only in recognizing our divine center that we can in fact be fully human and flow with the creative stream of the universe, what Dante called "the love that moves the sun and other stars." Once leave that, and inevitably at the end of the day you will end up with the blank canvas, the play that is just a despairing silence and the inhuman moonscapes of modern architecture. If we are to regain our sense of meaning and life, we simply have to learn and accept once again who we truly are—divine sparks, floating in a beautifully ordered, living universe. Then, and only then, will the wellsprings of art once again put forth living water.

39

THE DEATH OF PHILOSOPHY

January 28, 1978

There was something deeply melancholy last week about the sight of Sir Isaiah Berlin and Byran Magee sitting on a large green club sofa in a television studio, opening BBC-2's monster series of 15 discussions which will give the intelligent layman some idea of the state of modern philosophy.

Magee could scarcely have done better than to introduce his series with Sir Isaiah, who is not only one of the most intelligent men in Britain, but also beats George Steiner and A. J. P. Taylor by a short head as the best academic music hall turn in the Western world.

Yet even this first episode seemed somehow pervaded by an air of weariness. Sir Isaiah once again rehearsed the familiar distinction between the two kinds of statement which philosophers will allow as possible to settle—statements which are empirically verifiable, and those, like the propositions of mathematics, which relate to a set of formal rules.

But between them, as the proper province of philosophy, lie all those other questions to which inquiring men have sought answers since time immemorial—what is the purpose of my life, what is good, what is God?—and upon which modern philosophers find it almost impossible any longer to pronounce.

Although it is early days yet—Magee promises a grand tour through almost every conceivable byway of modern philosophy, from Marx to Marcuse and Wittgenstein to Chomsky—I think one can safely make two predictions about this series.

The first is that it will attract a surprisingly large audience. The second, I suspect, is that at the end of the series, many of those viewers who last the course will feel somehow profoundly cheated and let down.

For more than 50 years it has seemed that the history of Western philosophy was rather like a man climbing up a tree. He begins with the solid trunk (as philosophy began with the central mysteries of human existence); as he climbs higher and higher, the branches get thinner and thinner, until finally he is perched on a tiny twig at the top of the tree. He then prepares to saw it off.

In fact the evolution of philosophy conjures up an inescapable parallel with that of modern art. Every new development has seemed in retrospect a logical progression from the last. Yet, at the end of the day, there is nothing left but a hubbub of chattering voices, trying by their babbling to cover up a desperate void of meaning.

It was as long ago as 1922 that, at the end of the *Tractatus,* Wittgenstein wrote what is probably the only widely familiar utterance of any modern philosopher—"of those things of which he cannot speak, man must remain silent" (in other words, more or less all those questions which older philosophers took as their starting point). It is only lately that the artists have consciously arrived at the same position, as in Samuel Beckett's statement, "I have nothing to say, and I can only say to what extent I have nothing to say."

It is a general rule of human affairs that, when the end of one road of development has been reached, the next great source of life and spirit-renewing inspiration will come from some quite unexpected quarter, which for a long time is not recognized by orthodox opinion.

My own view is that the one really promising road toward an entirely new philosophical perspective on human existence has in fact been opening up now for some 50 years—since almost the exact moment when, in those closing lines of the *Tractatus,*

Wittgenstein in effect sawed off the last twig on which rationalist philosophy rested.

I believe that, over the next 50 years (if mankind survives), the most startling philosophic development will be the move right into the center of philosophic concern of the workings of that very instrument from which all philosophy stems in the first place—the human psyche.

I believe that the reason why the philosophers have apparently led themselves up a mental cul-de-sac is that, by pursuing the rationalistic road to its logical conclusion, they have lost their overall perspective on the different functions of the psyche.

The depth psychology pioneered by Jung is still only in its infancy as a scientific discipline—but in a curious way, Jung began his researches into the way we actually look at the world at precisely the point where the Wittgenstein of the *Tractatus* left off.

Just when the philosophers were saying, "we cannot say anything meaningful about ideas such as God," the depth psychologists were saying "quite right—of course we cannot say anything meaningful about these things in themselves. But what we can observe are the ways in which the human psyche seems at its deepest levels to work naturally around precisely the forms and patterns which have given rise to these ideas. The patterns whereby we find a sense of meaning and purpose in life seem to be imprinted in us, in almost exactly the way that an acorn is imprinted with the coding which will transform it into a mighty oak tree. This is what we should be looking at—and it is this which we ignore at our peril."

I am more convinced than I am of anything that this is the way through which (without for one moment veering off into leaps of faith, or onto paths which contradict reason), science will one day lead us back to an entirely new dimension of self-understanding and to that proper preoccupation of philosophy which is wisdom. Then one day we shall perhaps be able

to look back on the terrible sterility of twentieth-century philosophy as simply part of "a long dark night of the soul"
through which humanity had to pass in order to reintegrate its
view of itself, and once again to find the spiritual meaning
which lies behind the extraordinary mystery of our existence.

40

COLLECTIVISM BY DESIGN

February 24, 1979

A good many *Daily Telegraph* readers may have sat up to watch at least part of *City of Towers,* my mammoth television documentary on the destruction and rebuilding of our cities in the past 20 years, last Monday night. The film had to be as long as it was because the purpose of my exercise was not, as a number of feather-brained critics seem to have thought, just to pass a few random prejudiced opinions on modern architecture.

I was trying to tell, for the first time, the full story of a certain image of the city. I tried to show how that image, of collossal buildings and restless traffic, first came to haunt a number of science-fiction writers and architects more than 50 years ago—and how eventually their ideas became the orthodoxy which hovered over the wholesale reconstruction of many of Britain's cities in the sixties and early seventies.

It is indisputable that, in the great revolt against high-rise buildings, "concrete jungles," and comprehensive redevelopment, those dreams have in recent years ended up the most bitter disillusionment.

But one of the more predictable criticisms made of my film is that, in the course of this gigantic story, I was "unfair" to modern architecture. I failed to put the case for all the *good* buildings put up in Britain in the past 30 years.

Such critics need only have waited a few days for Patrick Nuttgen's film *Architecture for Everyman* and they would

289

have seen just what they were waiting for—a sympathetic account of the brighter side of the great modern architectural experiment, an anthology of some of the new buildings we really can admire, ranging from the Festival Hall to the Regent's Park bird cage, from an office block in Ipswich to the Byker housing estate in Newcastle.

My overall reaction to Mr. Nuttgen's film was that he had made just about as neat a job of defending modern British architecture as anyone could want. The kernel of his case was that the best modern architecture uses technology to create spacious, uncluttered, "free-flowing" environments, full of light and air—as his title implied, a truly "democratic" architecture in which "Everyman" and "Everywoman" can wander expansively through halls of metal and reflecting glass, in which all conventional distinctions are broken down (even those between the outside and inside of the building).

Yet it was precisely here, as I watched, that I began to see forming yet again the deepest reservation of all I have about modern architecture—which is that it cannot allow anyone to have an *individual* identity.

No one in his right mind would deny that modern architecture has created many visually stunning buildings, admirably fitted to serve the needs of a technologically based mass society. But its overriding message (and all architecture *has* a message) is that you can only join in this fantasy world of happy consumers, or office workers, or airline travelers, so long as you submerge your individual identity in the collective.

When I say that all architecture has a message, I mean that all architecture, whether it be a medieval cathedral, a thatched cottage, or a 30-story building, makes an implicit statement about the nature of man and his relations to himself and the universe.

Architecture is ultimately about human identity—it is one of the most important external things which help to tell us who we are. There is no clearer book in which to read the changes in the prevailing view of who we are and what is most important to us than in the kinds of building which our civilization has raised over the past 800 years.

In the soaring verticals of the great Gothic cathedrals we see the reflection of a society ultimately centered on its sense of the transcendent. In the harmoniously proportioned horizontals of the Renaissance or the eighteenth-century terraces of Bath, we see a society becoming more materialistic and "man-centered," but for which the highest values were still esthetic and intellectual.

In the hideous sprawl of the nineteenth-century factories, railways, and slums, we see a society for which the highest value was becoming man's material power to transform nature. In the suburban semis of the first half of the twentieth century, we see the true architecture of democracy, everyone an individual in his own individual (though almost identical) box.

Finally, in the neogargantuan architecture of the past 30 years, the great office buildings and housing projects, shopping centers and multistory car parks, we see the full visible reflection of a society whose highest values are material comfort for the greatest number and the resubmergence of the individual in a new kind of collectivism, based on subservience to a form of political Utopianism and to the all-providing machine.

What really worries me about almost all modern architecture, both good and bad, is its extraordinary ambivalence, the ease with which it seems to pass from "dream" to "nightmare."

Almost the entire theme of my film on Monday was the contrast between the architect's vision, the dreamworld, and the hideous, dehumanizing nightmare which has so often succeeded it.

Mr. Nuttgen, not unnaturally, was at pains only to show the dream—the vision of "Everyman" strolling happily through his technologically-shaped fantasy world. But even here the dark underside of the dream of man liberated rather than trapped by his technology could not help showing through.

One of the more haunting images in his film was of a West Indian steel band playing for the swimmers in a municipal "leisure pool." Compare the dead, sad expressions on their faces with the gaiety of almost any group of folk musicians in the pretechnological world, and you have the whole story in a nutshell.

Human beings do not find their inmost identity, that thing which tells them who they truly are, in any submergence in the collective, however lavishly and agreeably it is packaged. The dreamworld created and held out by modern technology is one of the most beguiling men have ever created for themselves—forget who you are, runs the message, surrender to your material appetites and to these free-flowing fantasies, and you will be happy, liberated, a child of the future.

It does not work for the simple reason that such illusions contradict the very structure of our human nature. There is always a terrible price to be paid for such dreams, and if it is not just some of the grimmer of the concrete wildernesses and anthills I showed on Monday, it may well be lurking in the missile silos of Nebraska and the Urals.

If we insist on turning mankind into an infinite mass of dehumanized, despiritualized children, we may unconsciously be led to doing away with ourselves precisely because we shall have finally lost sight of that which not only tells us who we are, but which alone tells us why life is really worth living.

41

WHY ARE WE SO KEEN ON ABORTION?

February 16, 1980. Although this essay was written just after the end of the seventies, it discusses a theme which preoccupied us throughout the decade.

What are we to make of those strange scenes in London last week, when groups of women with strained faces paraded around the street chanting slogans and howled like cats from the gallery of the House of Commons? What they were nominally protesting about, of course, was the latest attempt to revise Britain's laws on abortion, presently going through Parliament. But what came through their demands for "a woman's right to choose" was something much more cosmic altogether, nothing less than a collective cry of rebellion against the whole condition of womanhood since time began. What do such deeper undertones of the present abortion debate say about the state of our culture? Are they truly the harbingers of some new springtime in the human condition, the prelude to some great moment of unprecedented liberation, a matter for joy? If so, one cannot help musing, why are the proclamations of the coming age of freedom couched in such accents of negativity and pain?

It is no accident that abortion has cast such a shadow over so many Western societies in the past 15 years. It is one of countless symptoms (though one of the most deeply symbolic) that we have arrived at a very late stage in a process which has been unfolding for tens of thousands of years. In a sense, the whole history of human civilization has been written in our attempts to emancipate ourselves from unthinking dependence upon and identification with nature. Step by tiny, painful step we have won an ever-greater degree of conscious control over our lives and our surroundings, from our former state of brute, instinctive unconsciousness. And in our own century, of course, building on all that came before, the degree and scope of our conscious decision taking has enlarged by geometric progression, to the point where there is almost no corner of the natural kingdom where we think we cannot intervene at will, to reorder its processes to our own convenience.

It is hardly surprising that, placing such a high valuation on our powers of conscious control, we should have chosen more than ever before to intervene in such a centrally important aspect of our dependence on nature as the reproduction of our own species. We have sought to "plan" the patterns of our reproduction much as we have sought to "plan" the previously haphazard and "organic" development of our towns and cities. And when the main "planning control" of contraception has failed to produce the desired results (as "planning controls" have unfortunately so often failed to do in the evolution of our cities), we have more and more found it acceptable to bring up the second line of defense by simply aborting the child which has been conceived, in accordance with the best calculations of our conscious power to weigh advantage. If the child is likely to be born mentally or physically deformed, if it is unlikely to receive a proper, balanced upbringing, if it is simply "not wanted," then consciousness dictates that the child should not be born. Q.E.D.

The trouble is that, in our advance toward seemingly ever greater consciousness, we have not simply left behind our old instinctive nature. The more we try to ignore or repress it, the more it remains to dog us from the shadows—and the more an absolutely fundamental gulf opens up in our society between those who see consciousness as everything and those who are still in touch with, or pay reverence (even sometimes, it must be admitted, a merely sentimental reverence) to the deeper, more instinctive, more unconscious levels of being. From the conscious, rational point of view, a baby exists only when it is born. It is therefore ultimately the mother's "right" to decide whether that baby should be born or not. From the instinctive view, the picture could not look more different. The new life exists from the moment of conception, the mother is then merely participating in some great, mysterious, transpersonal process of nature, and to intervene in that process from the limited little point of view of ego-consciousness is a denial of life itself.

It is because there cannot possibly be any meeting ground between these two fundamentally different psychological points of view that the political debate over abortion has such a ragged, thin, unsatisfactory air. Responding to all the pressures of our psychically confused age, the politicians pathetically try to scrabble around for some compromise—fixing the legal term first at the 28th week of pregnancy, then trying to push it down to 20, then suggesting that maybe 24 weeks would be about right. This process of deciding when a baby shall be legally considered a living human being has reached its *reductio ad absurdum* in the present mass of amendments before the House of Commons, of which there appears to be at least one for every week between 20 and 28.

Of course one can see why all these confusing pressures should have arisen. The fact is that the overvaluation of consciousness, split off from instinct, has produced mounting chaos in our time wherever it has manifested itself—whether in the planning of our cities, the application of science and technology to nature, or just in the way we lead our everyday lives. One of the great characteristics of our time has been the desire to separate actions from their consequences—because I wish something to be true, because it suits my convenience, because it gives me pleasure, then hang the consequences—it shall be so. The triumph of ego-consciousness is in fact the final subjective delusion because it depends on ruthlessly stuffing away into the unconscious everything which truly connects us with the living reality of the world around us. It ends up by producing the dead moonscapes of the modern housing project, the bleak poisoned deserts of our modern countryside, the mountains of corpses of Pol Pot's Cambodia.

In our attempts to escape from unconsciousness, from nature, and ultimately from our own nature, we have tried in recent times to reorder the world and reality to suit our own convenience on an unprecedented scale. With every step we take, the consequences become more horrific, the more we are removed from direct contact with that thing we claim to prize more than anything—life itself. And few groups in our contemporary society bear more poignant witness to the appalling tragedy which is overtaking mankind than those haggard-faced flocks of women, possessed by their *animus,* who have lately become obsessed by the "right" to destroy unborn life to the exclusion of almost all else. For thousands of years, as our civilization has inched its way upward from the state of nature, women have been the supreme guardians of that most precious thing we possessed—the link with our deeper instinctive selves. As our destructive, Luciferian consciousness drove us ever upward, even onward, it was the feminine alone which kept us in touch with the inner reality of the earth. And now, so beguiling is the deadly power of ego-consciousness, that even the women have been sucked up into it, pouring such contempt on their instinctive, unconscious selves that they deny such things ever existed. Like the very worst of men through history, they no longer wish to give life but only to fantasize about destroying it. As Shakespeare put it in *King Lear:*

> She that herself will sliver and disbranch
> From her material sap, perforce must
>   wither
> And come to deadly use.

Let us hope that it will not come to serve as a final epitaph on mankind.

42

Facing the Catastrophe?

June 1977

I recently reviewed a book by Mr. Paul Johnson, called *Enemies of Society*. I am afraid that, like one or two other reviewers, I was not very friendly to the book. Considering Mr. Johnson's continued public declarations of total devotion to Socialism, the book's most remarkable characteristic seemed to be the fact that on almost all the most important issues of the day—political, social, moral, artistic, philosophical—Mr. Johnson has arrived at a view indistinguishable from that taken for the past 40 years by the *Sunday Express*.* Perhaps he draws comfort from Scott Fitzgerald's remark in *The Crack-Up* that "the test of a first-rate intelligence is the ability to hold two opposed ideas in the mind at the same time and still continue to function."

Nevertheless Mr. Johnson was not pleased that anyone should venture to oppose his thesis. And two weeks ago, readers of the *Daily Telegraph* must have been somewhat startled when he devoted a whole column to an explosion of rage against all those, such as myself, who dared to disagree with him.

The particular point on which Johnson was infuriated was the response to just one chapter in his book, which he called

---

*The most right-wing newspaper in Britain and also the most petty bourgeois in social attitudes.

"Ecological Panic." He pours infinite scorn on those people who in recent years have expressed concern that our civilization might be facing a grave crisis, from such things as overpopulation, the exhaustion of natural resources, pollution, or the H-bomb. Protesting his own total devotion to reason, and calm pursuit of the truth, Johnson describes all such doom talk as insane alarmism, the creation of an "eco-lobby" of members of the middle classes, who mostly live in "pleasant rural suburbia." The kindest thing he can say about these people is that they are "the respectable end of a spectrum of middle-class cranks which embraces such sects as the Christian Scientists, the antivivisectionists and those who campaign fanatically against the fluoridation of water supplies." Otherwise they are "trendy," "irrational," and "hysterical." In reaction to his book they rarely speak in tones other than "snarls and shrieks of rage." (I fear that I myself am "a modern flat-earther" who would "like us all to return to living in caves," living off "marinated seaweed.")

The destructive power of these cranks knows almost no bounds. "The eco-lobby's most impressive triumph so far" has been the great world oil crisis since 1973, "a disaster of the first magnitude for our civilization." This was almost entirely brought about by the effect of the propaganda of the eco-lobby on the "less sophisticated governments" of the OPEC countries (the Arab-Israeli War was "merely a pretext" for the quadrupling of oil prices). "The precise economic effects, in terms of misery and death, of the eco-lobby's coup will never be known." In the West, by enforcing cuts in public spending on such things as education, hospitals, and pensions, disaster has fallen on "the innocent heads of the urban poor." In the poorer countries of the world the catastrophe has been immeasurable. "In spring 1976 more than 500 million people were near starvation level in the Third World." In Africa, the "economic climate" produced by the crisis pushed country after country near to totalitarianism. "In Asia it brought down the world's largest democracy, India, which in 1975 abandoned free speech and the rule of law." "The only gainer was the archetype [*sic*] totalitarian state, the Soviet Union." Quite an achievement for a handful of middle-class cranks in their comfortable "rural suburbia" (who presumably want everybody to live off seaweed).

Why have I devoted so much space to Mr. Johnson's views? Because I think that unconsciously he has here raised an extremely important point about this whole debate over whether our civilization is heading for eco-catastrophe or not. Mr. Johnson, as I say, attaches great importance to the use of "reason," to working "from the facts to opinions" and not vice versa. But in the end, I do not believe that "examination of the evidence" or the pursuit of reason, however rigorous, can in themselves lead us to any firm conclusion as to whether mankind is facing an unprecedented crisis today or not. Whether one takes population curves, estimates of natural resources, or any of the other possible statistical measures, there are simply too many variables and unpredictable factors to be fed into any equation, for the evidence to provide anything other than a rather shaky support for the case one has already chosen to put for quite other reasons.

Of course this does not mean that we should be anything other than extremely careful in our use of that evidence, when we do use it. There is no question that "facts" and statistics are very often flung about by almost all parties to the argument as if they were nothing more than mud pies. No one can doubt that there has been a laughable degree of inconsistency among the eco-lobbyists (some, for instance, saying that we are all going to drown because the heating up of the atmosphere by carbon monoxide will melt the ice caps, others saying that we are all going to freeze to death because a new ice age is going to cover the earth). Equally there has been a widely irrational optimism among the "growth lobby" that at whatever speed we continue to use natural resources, we shall always somehow find more, and that man is ultimately a rational creature who will manage to control his self-destructive urges.

Nevertheless, in the end, the evidence one chooses to look at

and to believe is that which broadly supports one's preconceived position. Some years ago when I took part in a television
discussion on this issue with three other people, it struck me
that there are four possible general attitudes to the "eco-crisis,"
each of which was represented by one of the speakers on the
program.

The first view (represented today by Paul Johnson) argues
that everything is fundamentally fine and that the eco-
lobbyists are just irresponsible neurotics. There will always be
enough energy (if we run out of existing sources we shall find
new ones). Forecasts of the exhaustion of other natural resources are ludicrously exaggerated. Population curves will
flatten out. We have absolutely nothing to worry about.

The second view (perhaps represented today by Jimmy Carter) says—yes, there is a crisis. We have to accept that resources
may be finite, that civilization cannot expect indefinite material growth for ever. We shall have to make certain sacrifices,
certain changes in our way of life. But man is rational, and he
will not destroy himself. Ultimately, by ingenuity, self-
discipline and a little adjustment, we shall survive.

The third view is that we are facing a really major, unprecedented crisis, which can only be faced up to by taking unprecedented and drastic steps. In 50 years time, if we are to survive at
all, we shall all (particularly in the West) be having to live a
very different kind of life. We shall have to use natural resources at a much lower rate. We may have to accept compulsory birth control. We can make it, but only at a terrible price,
which may involve serious disorders on the way.

The fourth view is entirely black: that we are bent on a course
of self-destruction, that man is ultimately an irrational, greedy,
aggressive creature who will find it impossible to make the
sacrifices and changes which would be necessary to save him
(in any physical sense), and that sooner or later we shall face a
holocaust of destruction, from which something may survive or
nothing—certainly nothing remotely recognizable in our present highly sophisticated, growth-bent materialistic civilization.

I now believe that there is also a fifth view, which draws perhaps on a wider base altogether. This says that man is certainly heading for catastrophe, the way he is going, but that there is infinitely more to the great mystery of existence than just the material survival of one little civilization (or even, in the end, that of man himself). If there is to be a holocaust, it will merely be part of the endless cycle of death and rebirth. Something will survive, whether it is a new kind of man with a wider consciousness of himself and his place in creation, or just that spirit which Dante calls "the love that moves the sun and other stars," which is in all of us and imperishable.

Such a view would clearly strike most people as so irrational as to be verging on the insane. But the fact remains that *whichever* view one takes is beyond the power of reason to decide. It is an entirely metaphysical question, reflecting the metaphysical view of each person who adopts an attitude toward it. If, at one end of the spectrum, one believes that man is essentially a good and rational creature, and that his material well-being is his highest good (as Paul Johnson does), then he will take the view that civilization can survive on its present course without much problem. If at the other end of the spectrum one believes that what is important about man is that he is merely a material expression of the spirit which moves in all creation, then one is likely to accept firstly that our present civilization is rooted in a denial of that truth and will probably destroy itself— but secondly that in doing so the world will in some sense be renewed, and whether man himself survives is in the most important sense irrelevant. As I say, which of the five positions along this spectrum that a man chooses says a great deal about the man who chooses it, and really nothing about what is actually going to happen. And certainly reason alone (while it must not be denied its proper place and use) will not tell us which of these positions should be ours.

Part Six

REAPPRAISALS

INTRODUCTION

In the year before the seventies began, 1969, two quite disparate happenings each cast fascinating light on the curious position mankind has reached in the late twentieth century. The first, as I have already described, was Kenneth Clark's enormously popular *Civilisation* series—on the face of it, a triumphant celebration of our civilization's most glorious achievements, yet underneath giving such an extraordinarily despondent picture of just where we have all got to in the 500 years since the Renaissance.

The second event, in the same year, was America's first manned landing on the moon—in a sense the symbolic culminatory moment in the whole of man's post-Renaissance exploration and "conquest" of the external world. Again, on the fact of it, this should have been a moment of unadulterated triumph—the supreme justification for that road mankind has set out to travel when the first late-medieval explorers had set out from Europe to subdue the vast unknown realms of the earth beyond the sea. Yet in fact, as I analyze in the opening essay of this section, the whole event left us feeling, once the superficial excitement had died away, strangely baffled and flat.

In the ten years since those two strangely ambivalent events there has been abundant evidence that the glorious age created by post-Renaissance civilization, from the late fifteenth century to the present day, may be nearing some fundamental turning point. Behind the roar and clatter of collapsing old ideologies, beliefs, and illusions, amid mounting pessimism, disillusionment, and despair, we cannot possibly see with clarity what the future holds. But on the other side of the great darkness which appears to be gathering over the human race, it may well be that some entirely new era awaits the world—and that we are already living in the seed time of that future epoch. Certainly in the seventies there were already countless embryonic signs of a great change beginning to come over our human perspective on ourselves and our place in the universe—and in this section I refer to some of them.

One of the most interesting things to have happened in the past decade or so has been the emergence of the so-called "ecology" movement. By the end of the seventies, scarcely a week went by without reference to some new campaign to save seals, whales, eagles, or other species from extinction at the hands of man. Undoubtedly there was in this eleventh-hour uprushing of compassion a considerable element of sentimental confusion and double-think (as when oil companies engaged in the wholesale unconscious extermination of wildlife through pollution ostentatiously contributed funds to the "saving of the tiger"). But beyond the sentimental veneer, there was beginning to dawn, all over the world, a new attitude to nature—an awareness that man is inextricably part of some great Whole, that he disturbs the balance of the Whole at his peril, and that somehow he must find the way to restore the harmony between himself and nature.

This attitude expressed itself in the seventies in countless ways, large and small: through the growing revulsion against modern technological farming methods, and the cult of "organically" grown foods; through the increasing recognition by more thoughtful scientists of the inbuilt limitations of technology and the "scientific method" itself; through the growing interest in Eastern philosophies and religions, centered on a more "holistic" attitude to man in nature than the Judeo-Christian tradition, which has only too easily been used to underpin man's illusion that he could and should somehow become the "master" of nature.

It would of course be foolish to overestimate the importance of these signs and portents. The prevailing momentum of our civilization in the seventies remained overwhelmingly, seemingly unstoppably, committed to the "conquest" of nature, to technological "progress" and to all that legacy of beliefs and assumptions which had grown up in the great era of "scientific method" since the seventeenth century. But never before had the foundations of that mighty edifice seemed so shaky. Even many of those who still inhabited it, such as the philosopher Stuart Hampshire, whose lecture on "The Future of Knowledge" makes the basis for my last two essays, were beginning to get an alarmed glimmering of just how worm-eaten the whole, rickety structure had become (though they could not as yet think their way outside it). Even here change was inescapably on the way.

43

REACHING FOR THE MOON

Written on the tenth anniversary of the first moon landing, July 21, 1979.

President Nixon called it "the greatest week since the creation of the world." Norman Mailer, in *Of a Fire on the Moon,* was a little more modest, describing it only as "the greatest week since Christ was born." But the fact remains that, even when these hubristic claims were first uttered, they had a hollow ring. Despite the astonishing wave of world-wide excitement engendered by the event, the actual response of most of the human race to the news that on July 21, 1969 two of their kind had set foot on the Moon was, deep down, one of strange bafflement.

We watched the two figures in their diving suits slowly blundering about on the Moon desert. We listened to their euphoric clichés. We knew it was all terribly important, the greatest thing ever to happen, the greatest triumph of man's ingenuity since... well, since ever... and somehow, at that secret level deep within ourselves, we simply did not know how to relate to it at all. As some joker pointed out, and there was more truth in the jest than might have appeared, we actually had no evidence that the whole thing was not taking place in some television studio somewhere, was not an elaborate hoax. The problem with the Apollo Moon landing was that it was literally outside our frame of reference.

On the face of it, this might have seemed curious. After all, men had been dreaming of this moment for centuries. The literary history of men's imaginary journeys to the Moon long predated Jules Verne—stretching right back *via* Cyrano de Bergerac, Kepler, a seventeenth-century Bishop of Hereford and Ariosto's *Orlando Furioso* to the very dawn of the Renaissance. It was the symbolic culmination of the whole of that great adventure which the men of Western Europe had embarked on in the late Middle Ages when, in an entirely new way, they had begun to seek ultimate significance in the external world outside themselves.

They had discovered America and that the earth was not flat. They had been through the colossal psychological upheaval of discovering that the earth was not even the center of the universe. They had invented steam trains capable of traveling at 80 miles an hour, internal combustion engines which might actually lift them up above the surface of the earth, rockets which could soar up into the stratosphere. Step by step, over 600 years, they had totally readjusted their way of relating to the natural frame which had given them birth—as they subdued distance, calculation, and everything else to their vaulting ambition, with radio, television, computers, and all the rest. Finally all this mountain of knowledge and hardware had carried man up to the height where he was ready to make the most symbolic leap of all out of his original natural frame—actually to leave the earth behind, to set foot on another solar body, that "pale Sister of the Night" which for tens of thousands of years had exercised a symbolic hold over the psyche of man second only to that of the life-giving Sun itself. It was the ultimate act of man's self-liberation, the moment when Apollo, the god of the Sun, and human consciousness, was finally, once and for all, to ravish Diana, the goddess of unconscious night. And yet when this glorious act of emancipation took place, what happened?

We saw two men stumbling out of a metal prison, cocooned in plastic, still connected by umbilical cords with every single thing—even air—that was necessary to keep them alive. There was nothing they had not had to bring with them from the distant world they had supposedly left behind. They arrived on a completely dead lump of matter, more inconceivably dead than any square inch of the earth. And apart from dust and rock and an unearthly light, the only thing they could see which they could not have seen back on Earth, was the Earth itself floating unimaginably beautiful above them, the only home they knew, the only center to the universe which really mattered.

It should hardly have been surprising that no one at that moment of shock could make sense of what had really happened because almost everyone on earth had been so seduced into the point of view which gave rise to the experiment in the first place that almost no one at the time realized that it might be looked at from a totally different psychological perspective altogether.

It was some months before there was even the glimmering of an attempt to give what had happened some kind of deeper perspective, in Norman Mailer's book *Of a Fire on the Moon*—a journalistic *tour de force* which at least tried to set that first Moon journey back in some kind of metaphysical dimension. As, with enormous skill, Mailer reconstructed the whole awe-inspiring episode, right down to the technicalities of the nuts and bolts (for which he had been surprisingly well equipped by his early training as an aeronautical engineer), seeing it as the ultimate triumph of "WASP culture," his constant theme was the question—"Was God or the Devil at the helm?"

Looking again at Mailer's book nearly ten years later, I regret to have to report that it nevertheless now seems pretty thin stuff—strained, naive, sentimental—because ultimately, for all that he tried, even Mailer himself was still so awed by man's achievement that he could not escape the pull of that view which did see the Apollo mission as a divine act—and, for all his outsider's scepticism toward "WASP culture," there was no doubt in Mailer's mind as to whom the responsible divinity was—*homo sapiens* himself.

But over the past ten years, almost without our being aware

of it, perhaps we have been just beginning to change our perspective a little. As we look back on that astonishing episode, we can see that it certainly *was* a supreme symbolic moment in the history of mankind. By the most titanic concentration of effort, in developing just one part of himself, man *had* managed to "break free" from nature as never before. It *was* the supreme achievement of his wonderful, separating consciousness, centered as all consciousness must be on the *ego*.

But the whole point of the way our minds, our psyches are ineradicably constructed is that, try as we might, we cannot find ultimate *meaning* by traveling such a road. As Romantics of every hue and permutation have endlessly demonstrated in the past two centuries, we may find every kind of thrill and sensation—even the tantalizing promise (*à la* Faust) of fathomless meaning. But we cannot find that sense of engagement with some "ultimate reality" that alone brings real meaning into human existence because that can only be found not in *separation* from nature but in rediscovering that other hidden center of the psyche, the Self—that which alone gives us a sense of our participation in the totality of existence. The patterns made through the *ego* alone can never be ultimately resolved.

As we look back over the past ten years, it is hard not to be struck by what has happened to America, after working up through the sixties to that concentration of energy (contemporaneous with America's rather more obviously "dark" concentration of technological energy in Vietnam). After those climactic efforts of the sixties, America has more and more come to seem like an exhausted giant—the collapse in Vietnam, Watergate, the resignation of Nixon, the presidency of Jimmy Carter, and now the energy crisis itself.

Indeed, in the wake of the Moon shot, a strange new exhaustion has come over the whole of mankind's great post-Renaissance adventure. The "mastering" of nature, the finding of new frontiers to cross, has all suddenly seemed to become much harder work. We may sometimes try to recapture the old thrills, as we acclaim the "first balloon crossing of the Atlantic" or "the first man-powered flight over the Channel"—but in fact the whole "new frontiers" show is over, and deep down we know it.

When the ancient myths spoke of a Quest to some distant, immeasurably valuable goal they were ultimately speaking not of an outward journey to some material treasure, but of an inner journey—that journey which the hero must make in order to realize himself, to become fully a man, to discover who he really is. For 600 years, men have externalized that deep inner drive in what seemed like the greatest series of quests of all—those to explore, to "conquer" the external world around us, the South Pole, Everest, the cures for diseases, and all the rest. The Moon was the greatest example of all of such an external projection of the Questing drive. And when the goal was realized, we just could not perceive the true lesson which the whole experience should have taught us with beautiful, profound clarity. But there it was, as Armstrong and Aldrin stumbled about on that dead surface, looking back toward the infinitely beautiful, soft, blue planet 240,000 miles behind them. Their presence, as our representatives on that dead satellite, had made of the Moon nothing more than a symbol of man's dead *ego,* when separated from the lost life-giving totality of the Self. At that moment, if we had been heedful, we should have realized that the real goal of our Quest was not there at all. It was not out in the immeasurable, dead, silent emptiness of space that we should have been seeking our lost identity. That could only be found right here at home, where it had been all the time.

44

LUMEN DE LUMINE

Written on the centenary of the birth of Einstein, March 1979.

It was perhaps inevitable that the prevailing tenor of the recent Einstein centenary celebrations should simply have been one of bemused awe. No one has become more symbolic than Einstein of the mental labyrinth into which the advance of science has led twentieth-century man. Few of us are equipped to follow him in detail around the twists and turns of that labyrinth, through which his unique genius wandered for 50 years. But all of us feel in some sense heirs to the terrifyingly remote impersonality of the view of the universe which he opened up. More than any other human being he helped to shatter forever the last vestiges of that original, cosy frame of reference with which man emerged from the darkness of nature, and self-consciously began to assess the "true" nature of the world. It has been a "Fall into consciousness" of tragic dimensions—and it is a measure of the perspective Ronald Clark has managed to draw on the subject of his admirable biography—*Einstein: The Life and Times*—that he should not hesitate in his foreword to describe Einstein as "one of the great tragic figures of our time."

To see Einstein in his proper context, it is necessary to look back to the situation of Western man at the beginning of the twentieth century. For 300 years, ever since the Renaissance had blown the medieval world view into pieces, men had sought to rest their need for understanding and security on a new world view. Maybe, as Copernicus, Columbus, and others had shown, the world was by no means as straightforward as it appears to "common sense," to that "natural" frame of reference which decrees that the earth is flat and that the sun goes around it. But thanks to Descartes, Newton, and others we could come to a new understanding that the universe was still a harmonious, ordered place, operating under strict, observable laws of cause and effect, within the absolute coordinates of space and time. It was a wonderful classical construct, portended by the rise of perspective in painting, and reflected by the age of tonal harmony in music. But as the Age of Reason passed, and the nineteenth century became increasingly carried away on the torrent of progress, shadowed by the growing irresolutions of Romanticism in the arts, the sands beneath the construct began to shift. In science, as elsewhere, thanks to the experiments of Maxwell, Michelson, Morley, and others, the harmonious classical structure became shot through with cracks and contradictions.

Then suddenly, as technological progress carried us into the twentieth century with the first airplanes, motor cars and wireless telegraphy, the foundations began to give way with a roar. Freud and Jung began to show how relative is our conscious view of the world—merely an island floating on the dark sea of unconsciousness. With Picasso, Schoenberg, and Joyce, such guidelines as perspective, tonality, and narrative collapsed into a new kind of artistic "relativity." And by the greatest series of intuitive leaps in the history of science, a young German Jew from Ulm (parallelling Freud) perceived that Newton's universe was merely a little "convenient fiction" produced by man's limited consciousness, resting on a sea of infinitely greater mystery beyond.

Perhaps the greatest irony of the recent Peter Ustinov television spectacular on Einstein was the sight of hundreds of millions of dollars worth of machinery—radio telescopes, cyclotrons, space rockets—being used simply to demonstrate that the conclusions about the structure of the universe arrived at 70 years ago by a young patent clerk, working alone in his room in Bern, with no more complicated equipment than a fountain pen, were correct. Just how it was that this young man, turned down for a job at the Zurich polytechnic where he had been given his formal scientific grounding because his abilities did not seem to outweigh his rebelliousness, came purely by intuition (backed up by a formidable rational apparatus) to see through the whole existing fabric of physical science poses some of the most interesting questions about the human mind one can possibly ask.

At the age of 26, in 1905, Einstein staked his claim to the attention of the scientific world by three papers in a Leipzig technical journal, the *Annalen der Physik*. One, an explanation of why microscopic particles in liquid move as they do, provided "the first visible proof of the molecular constitution of matter." A second resolved a contradiction about the supposed nature of light which had become one of the "scandals" of physics— light, Einstein showed, must consist of both waves *and* particles (or "quanta") simultaneously (this was to win him the Nobel Prize in 1921). The third paper, "On the Electrodynamics of Moving Bodies," exploded the bombshell. Space and time were not, as Newton and almost every other human being except Leibniz had supposed, absolutes. There was only one constant in the entire universe—and that was the speed of light. As you near the speed of light, space and time both shrink—in other words, they are entirely relative.

Throughout his thinking life, Einstein was obsessed by two things. The first was the conviction that, if only we can know enough, we should find one simple, elegant theory which would embrace all the laws governing the physical universe. The "Old One," God, has so constructed the world that it was only our own imperfections which stood in the way of our perceiving that unifying law. His second obsession was with the nature of the one great constant, about which everything else revolved and to which everything else was relative—light.

The ten years which followed his *annus mirabilis,* 1905 (the year in which, almost as an afterthought, he had thrown off a fourth paper showing, in the most elegant of all his equations, $E = mc^2$, that mass is simply "congealed energy") were what one might call the "dream stage" of Einstein's life. He rocketed to the forefront of European physicists, was given professorial posts in Prague, Zurich, and Berlin, and meanwhile worked on the extension of the theory of "Special Relativity" that was to bring gravity into the equation of space, time, and light. This General Theory of Relativity, published in 1916, followed up by a further paper on its cosmological implications, and described by Max Born as "the greatest feat of human thinking about Nature" ever known, was the theory which finally turned the classical Newtonian universe into a kind of funfair Crazy House, with its non-Euclidian geometry of "space which curves back on itself" (allowing the universe to be both finite and unbounded at the same time). It also, by the simple British experiment in 1919 which bore out the General Theory's implication that the gravity of the sun can "bend" light, made the 40-year-old Einstein overnight world-famous, the supreme symbolic figure of twentieth-century science. But from that moment on, the shadows almost imperceptibly began to gather.

He began what he hoped might be the last stages of his great quest for the "unified field theory"—the final theory-to-end-all-theories which might embrace all physical laws and forces, from those holding together the atom to those governing the universe. And always at the heart of his thinking was the ultimate mystery—what *is* light? "I want to spend the rest of my life thinking about light quanta," he often remarked. In the mid-twenties, however, came the shattering moment when the greatest physicist in the world suddenly became isolated from his fellow physicists. By the notion made famous as Heisenberg's Uncertainty Principle, they concluded almost to a man that there were certain phenomena, such as electrons, which simply could not be subjected to uniform observable rules. One could measure the position of a particle, or its speed, but not both at the same time. One could only predict by statistical probability when, for instance, an electron might jump from one orbit into another. Einstein, cheerfully unshaken in his faith that "the most incomprehensible thing about the universe is that it is comprehensible," replied, "I cannot believe God plays dice," or "God is subtle, but he is not malicious." But the tide of physics began to move on without him. Suddenly Einstein himself, with his "old-fashioned" belief in cause and effect, began to seem almost Newtonian.

He was also being drawn into the even more unpredictable, "relativistic" maelstrom of politics. As the most famous Jew in the world, he had been persuaded to lend enthusiastic support to Zionism—but only as "an absolute pacifist" who believed that "the murder of men is disgusting" and that the Jewish State should be built on complete cooperation with the Arabs. In 1933, with the advent of Hitler and his own exile to America, he began to relativize his pacifism. In 1939 he lent his name to the letter advising Roosevelt to consider the military possibilities of nuclear fission. By 1944, as a technical adviser to the U.S. Navy, he was approving new bombing techniques as "very ingenious." By 1948, the man who had once described murder as "disgusting" was helping to raise funds for Haganah, the Zionist nationalist group which supported acts of terrorism. And by 1950, expressing his horror and alarm at America's decision to make the H-Bomb, he foresaw "the annihilation of all life on earth"—"a weird aspect of this development lies in its apparently inexorable character."

In other words, as the white-haired "wise old man" of his last years, he viewed the world which twentieth century technology had brought into being with the utmost horror and foreboding. He had played no direct part in any of it. Like a detached observer, he had described in his $E = mc^2$ equation the principle underlying the nuclear bombs, long before they seemed remotely feasible technically (just as his 1905 paper on "photons" had described the principle on which television would one day be based). But he was not an "inventor." He was merely a "pure" scientist who had given his life to the hope that one day he might find the ultimate, beautiful, simple theory which could make sense of the universe.

Einstein never found his Holy Grail. Even when he died in 1955, the paper beside his bed was covered with spidery equations, as he vainly sought his "unified field theory" to the last. Yet as one contemplates the melancholy failure of this noble lifelong quest to make perfect sense of the outward world through intellect alone, it is perhaps hard not to see in it a tragedy that was not just Einstein's alone.

The story of Einstein reflects the tragedy of our species—which once, long ago, when it still lived like all other animals in a state of unconscious identification with nature, *did* see the world as subject to one great unified law, because it could see nothing else. But then came that unique two-edged gift of our human consciousness. As step by step man moved out of his natural frame of reference, he gradually lost touch with that sense of one great unifying power binding the whole together—simply because his conscious mind could no longer hold together in balance and proportion all the components of a picture which he had once held unconsciously, instinctively within him. His restless, questing conscious mind became split off from the deeper, instinctive layers of his psyche. He began to seek the sense of ultimate meaning which he still craved not in the harmony between his inmost being and the natural world around him ("Two things fill me with awe," as Kant put it, "the starry heavens above and the moral law within")—but in the external world alone.

The most haunting thing of all about Einstein was his lifelong obsession with light—which, as in "the light of lights," "the light of the world," or even the very word *deus* itself (from the Sanskrit *dyaus* or "day") has always been a synonym for God. "I saw Eternity the other night," as Vaughan wrote, "like a great Ring of Pure and Endless Light." But perhaps the mysterious frame of our existence is so constituted that if man looks for the meaning of that light outwardly, in the physical world (as, even in the most "pure" and spiritual-seeming way,

Einstein did), he must ultimately be doomed to frustration. Physical light, unlike the light of the spirit, the light within, must always cast a shadow. And part of the shadow of that light which beckoned Einstein on is the infinitesimal nucleus of matter, the disintegration of which—by fearful symmetry and by a law which Einstein was the first to perceive—may yet destroy us all

45

THE ARROGANCE OF HUMANISM

May 26, 1979

As the seventies come to an end, what is the most important thing happening in the world? The Middle East "peace process?" The political reorientation of China? The gathering prospect of a world oil shortage? The development of the neutron bomb? I believe there is one thing which runs much deeper than any of these. As yet it is only in such early stages that most people are scarcely aware of it. But what I am referring to amounts to the dawning of one of the most profound shifts in human self-awareness that has ever taken place—and this book, *The Arrogance of Humanism,* by David Ehrenfeld, is just one of its growing multitude of symptoms.

Its author is the Professor of Biology at Rutgers University. In recent years, like more people than he is aware of, he has found himself beginning to look at the whole great "experiment" on which Western man has been engaged in recent centuries from an entirely new perspective. He perceives that the driving force of that experiment has been what he calls "the religion of humanism" (something far transcending mere political ideologies, like Communism or Capitalism)—a psychological perspective which has led men to believe that they can understand the world by reason alone and that they can thus take control of their destinies in a way which to our ancestors would have seemed inconceivable. The essence of this humanism, as Professor Ehrenfeld puts it, is that for rational mankind "all problems are soluble." By the use of technology and applied science, it is within our grasp to produce a perfectly ordered, problem-free, materially comfortable world. We may seem at present still to be faced by serious problems, but, "When the chips are down, we shall apply ourselves, and work for a solution before it is too late." "Human civilization will survive."

What is interesting about Professor Ehrenfeld is not that he has lost his faith in these incantations—so, to a greater or lesser extent, have many people. It is the manner in which he has done so. He begins, conventionally enough, with a chapter entitled "Myth," in which he details a whole range of the boasts and achievements which might underpin an optimistically "humanist" view of the world, such as our astonishing advances in conquering diseases like cancer, in learning to monitor human behavior through such statistical devices as "castastrophe theory," in obtaining an unprecedentedly accurate view of the historical past through the science of "cliometrics." He describes schemes to bring deserts into flower through damming rivers, our hopes of obtaining "clean," unlimited power through nuclear fusion, our plans to build whole new artificial "worlds," fit for human occupation, in space. There is almost nothing we think we cannot do, from devising machines to pick the tender shoots of asparagus to saving the windows of Chartres Cathedral by coating them in plastic.

In the succeeding chapter, "Reality," Professor Ehrenfeld examines each of these boasts again, in the light either of how they have already proved empty or how they are based on so inadequate an appraisal of evidence and probabilities that they amount to pure wishful thinking. For every acclaimed "advance" in curing cancer, the "fundamental breakthrough" remains as elusive as ever, while the figures of deaths continue to rise. Mathematical attempts to "monitor" human behavior are shown to be based on so pitiful a choice of variables as to be meaningless. The "cliometric" approach to history is exposed as so selective in its choice of evidence as to be mere charlatanry. The damming of the Nile, far from solving Egypt's problems, brings such a host of unforeseen ecological disasters in its wake that it might have been better if the Aswan Dam had never been built. Calculations of the benefits to be derived from the still unrealized dream of "clean" power from nuclear fusion demonstrably fail to take into account a further enormous range of ecologically catastrophic consequences which would inevitably follow simply from the use of that power. Almost wherever we look, wherever man is seeking to use his reason and his technology to give him greater mastery over the mysterious world of nature (including his own nature), the story is the same. Even the asparagus-plucking machine proves to be so much useless metal because it cannot distinguish between shoots that are ready to pick and those which are still immature—while a coating of Viacryl has already irreparably destroyed the sombre luminosity of three of the thirteenth-century windows of Chartres, by turning them into mere tinted glass.

It is at this point that Professor Ehrenfeld comes to the crux of his argument. Human rationality, he argues, however sophisticated it becomes, is simply not equipped to match up to the literally unimaginable complexities of nature. There will *always* be something that we have not foreseen. In words he quotes from the meteorologist Eric Kraus: "All science involves simplifications. There is an inevitable discrepancy between our scientific models and the much more richly textured world of everyday experience . . . this means that the model does not contain all the information which would be needed to simulate the process as it occurs."

Now the importance of this realization—which is beginning to dawn these days on a wide variety of people, including a number of more thoughtful scientists in many different disciplines—can scarcely be overestimated. For what it means is that what we have been trying to do in the past 400 years may, in essence, simply be something which cannot ultimately be done. With our conscious, rational minds we can only construct models, theories, approximations to the reality of nature which are inevitably oversimplifications, telling us only a fraction of the real story. And when, at the instigation of our collective ego-drive to reshape the world to our own better material advantage, we carry those oversimplifications out into the infinitely complex world of nature by means of technology, we are faced with those now all-too-familiar chains of "unforeseen consequences" which ultimately bring disaster, in seemingly direct ratio to the degree to which we sought to interfere with the patterns of nature in the first place. What is truly radical and revolutionary about the kind of attitude which Professor Ehrenfeld and his like represent is that they are saying the time has come when we have to start accepting these limitations on human reason and human capability as part of the unshakable constitution of the universe. This does not mean to say that we should have avoided traveling the route we have come—the roots of our one-sided love affair with reason go back so far into human development that it is simply a fact. Nor does it mean, as the human race seems hellbent on turning the world into a technological wilderness, that we can necessarily do anything practical to avert the major catastrophe or series of catastrophes which are probably the only way in which our "humanist" adventure can be checked.

What it does mean, however, is that at least individually (and preferably, of course, on as wide a scale as possible) we have to find an entirely new (ultimately spiritual) perspective on who we are and just how we relate to the nature which has given birth to us and of which we are still inextricably a part. I say "new" perspective advisedly because, for the first time in human experience, we have actually traveled right through the tunnel of rationality—and we are at last beginning to discover its limitations by the very method which is its own supreme value, by empirical verification.

Again and again while following Professor Ehrenfeld's argument I found myself thinking of another, very different, book, Fritjof Capra's *The Tao of Physics*. As a physicist, Capra showed the quite remarkable correspondences between the view of the world opened up by post-Heisenbergian physics and that underlying Chinese mystical philosophy—a world in which all the "oppositions" and the rigid logic of cause-and-effect which lie at the heart of Western rationalism are seen for the very partial kinds of explanation of "reality" they are. Capra concludes that "the world-view implied by modern physics" is simply and utterly inconsistent with our present conventional thinking and forms of society, which do not "reflect the harmonious inter-relatedness which we observe in nature." He believes that the survival of our civilization depends ultimately on "our ability to adopt some of the *yin* attitudes of Eastern civilization; to experience the wholeness of nature and the art of living with it in harmony." As another scientist, Professor Ehrenfeld would agree. Perhaps the ultimate cosmic profundity of human existence we have to face up to, however, is that we could only be brought to the final "scientific" realization of that truth by traveling the very path which has so separated us from the rest of nature that it has brought us to the brink of extinction.

46

THE NEW RELIGIONS

April 13, 1977

This week I had a fascinating experience. I spent an afternoon at Olympia wandering around the so-called "Festival of Mind and Body," a "celebration of the New Age."

The temptation to poke cynical fun at this strange assemblage of "freaks and weirdos" under the unlikely setting of Olympia's vast Victorian cast-iron canopy is one which a number of journalists have found irresistible. The *Times* diarist, for instance, almost fell over himself with excitement when he was able to light upon "the bio-activity translator which allows plants to talk to you," or the stall offering to "photograph your aura for £1," or the "pleasant young woman munching some nutty confection" with whom he fell into conversation at the (strictly vegetarian) snack bar.

The stands fall into four main groups. Firstly there are the health-food enthusiasts. Then there are the eccentrics of an ageless nature, such as Mr. J. Rutherford of 31 Station Road, Harpenden, who advertises his "theory that the passages and chambers of the Great Pyramid depict in stone God's plan for mankind through the ages." Thirdly, there are the commercial stands, showing everything from frisbees to karate equipment (most incongruous of all is the stall which consists merely of a rather melancholy-looking character standing by a shiny kidney machine bristling with dials). Lastly, there is the mass of stands occupied by more or less serious representatives of what,

327

if you were being rude, you might call the "New Religions"—taking forms which are sometimes Christian, sometimes Eastern (several gurus are on offer, via their smiling bearded photographs) and sometimes not particularly either.

One cannot escape the fact that the emergence of this new "spiritual wave" across the West, in all its myriad manifestations, has been one of the most surprising and interesting developments of the past decade. Indeed, we forget just how unexpected it was when it began to break the surface (at the time the sixties pop-culture madness was at its height, in 1966 and 1967). At that time, many of its more obvious, headline-worthy forms were so blatantly dubious or shallow—the great LSD craze, the instant mysticism of the Beatles and the dear old Maharishi, flower power and hippy bells—that it might have been easy to dismiss as just another passing fad. But behind the craze for "whole food" and the smoke of a million joss sticks, I believe that this sense of what many of its adherents describe as "the dawning of the age of Aquarius" constitutes part of the most remarkable shift in Western consciousness for several hundred years.

What do the more impressive of the adherents of these new movements have in common? Firstly, a tremendous sense of liberation from the sterile deadweight of our collectivist, technological, materialist, rational culture (it can no longer lay claim to the title of "civilization"). Secondly, they share a belief that we all of us initially (and particularly under the influence of the dominant orthodoxies of the age) tend to look at the world through a limited "ego-consciousness"—but that if we learn to travel within ourselves, we become aware of a second, much deeper self within us which in some mysterious way is not only much more individual to us than our little ego-self, but universal. Thirdly, they have refound in everyday life a sense of the sacred, of the kind which has long since departed from our trivial, neurotic, rationalist society (not to mention from most established Churches).

Now all this has an uncanny bearing on the model of man's psyche discovered over 50 years of observation by the great

Swiss psychologist Jung. In any attempt to survey the re-emergence of this view of man in the twentieth-century West, Jung must obviously have a very important place—and I say "re-emergence" because of course, in its broad outlines, this is a view of man which has been held many times before in history—by the neo-Platonists of the Renaissance, by many of the Ancient Greek philosophers, by the Eastern religions, by Christian mystics. Indeed, before the institutionalization of Christianity, it was the very essence of Christ's own message—which was always directed to individuals, that they should find "the kingdom of Heaven within." But as Jung in his role as twentieth-century scientist continually emphasized, the battle to discover that "deeper self" within us is no easy, instant thing. It means becoming aware of all those hidden parts of ourselves (what Jung called our "shadow") which, so long as we remain unconscious of them, remain to leap out and dominate our behavior without our even being aware they are doing so.

The fact that this is so difficult means of course that many of the more modish, group-centered cults of recent years (all those instantly mystical pop singers, for instance) are really doing nothing more, in Jung's words, than show "a positively morbid avidity to practice Indian yoga, observe a strict regimen of diet, learn theosophy by heart or mechanically repeat mystic texts from the literature of the whole world" simply because they dare not face themselves.

To be frank, in fact, it is here that I think we should be most worried by the "New Religions," or rather by all those groups operating on the frontier between religion and psychology which have sprung up in recent years (many of them originating in California). Unlike many more cynical critics, I do not doubt that such groups, and their often charismatic leaders, are playing with something real in the human psyche. That is why introduction to these groups has such a dramatic and profound affect on so many people, and only someone with a very limited knowledge of human psychology or of himself would fail to understand this fact.

Nevertheless the operative word is "playing." The fact that

something has psychic reality (and therefore can have the power to move us deeply, give us a sense of inner liberation, radically alter our lives) does not mean that such an aspect of ourselves cannot be played upon and manipulated in ways which fall far short of satisfying our real psychic needs. That is after all why Marxism has had such an appeal to the young people of our time—because it too plays with the hunger for a great, transpersonal cause, it too offers a total explanation for the world and a promise of unimaginable future liberation.

The real danger of so many of these "New Religious" groups lies in their essentially collectivist nature, made all the more dangerous and deceptive by the fact that they seem to be promising the very opposite—namely individual liberation, the chance for each disciple to discover his or her own absolutely unique "inner self." In fact, as is only too often obvious, the "inner self" these people discover is remarkably similar in every case. The happy converts, fluting their newfound joy in the prescribed, homogenized jargon, have not discovered their "true selves" at all; they have been brainwashed into a kind of group stereotype, laid down by the charismatic leader who himself, as it eventually turns out, was unconsciously after little more than personal power and glory all the time.

At their darkest, of course, these cults can turn really nasty— into tight little exclusive sects, projecting all their collective "shadow" onto the wicked, unseeing outside world in a thick paranoiac fog, feeding the inflated *ego* of their leader or guru until it is fit to bursting, and probably leaving a trail of psychic wrecks, broken families, even suicides in their wake.

For all these reservations, however, I would not dismiss the profound significance of this wave of cults and sects and re- awakened spirituality which is sweeping through the Western world. As we approach that great turn in history which has long been foreshadowed for the end of second millennium of the Christian era, something of the greatest importance is struggling to get through in the psyche of Western man. The fact that so many of its more obvious manifestations are trivial, misguided, and inadequate may be only a tribute to the appalling deadweight of anthropocentric materialism our culture has been accumulating for so long. When a cripple who has relied on crutches all his life begins to show signs of a return to health, it usually takes some time before he can fling them away altogether and run free.

47

KNOWLEDGE AND ILLUSION

April 9, 1977

There is a strange mood abroad in Western civilization at the moment—a general sense that, after the frenzied forward rush of the sixties, we have suddenly come—politically, artistically, morally, scientifically—up against something of a blank wall. All the great collective twentieth-century adventures—the myriad forms of political and social Utopianism, the modern movement in the arts, the great "leap forward" of personal liberation and emancipation ("Self-Fulfilment the Freudian Way")—have lost their steam, and petered out in exhaustion. The ever-rising escalator of technological progress and eternal growth has faltered, if not stopped. Around the corner, we see the distant sky looking very black: overshadowed by overpopulation, nuclear holocaust, totalitarianism, all sorts of unimaginable horrors. But for the time being, the foreground is still reasonably sunlit. There is no extreme sense of urgency. We dimly sense that we have reached the end of all kinds of roads, but no one wants to admit it too loudly for fear that we might actually be forced to start thinking about it all.

One man who has given these deeply important questions some thought, however, is Stuart Hampshire, in his recent lecture called "The Future of Knowledge." Professor Hampshire's thoughts are a fine starting point for considering where we have to go to, and where we might be going, if only because, as one might expect from such a distinguished philosopher, he gives such eloquent voice to what might be called the conventional wisdom on these matters.

He begins by claiming inspiration from his seventeenth-century predecessor as Warden of Wadham, John Wilkins, founder and first secretary of the Royal Society in 1662. Hampshire sees Wilkins's enthusiasm for the "new science" as a symbolic landmark: "Three hundred years of accelerating understanding of nature as a rational system had begun."

But today we are at another such turning point. In the past decade there has been "more authoritative questioning of technology and even of the future of natural science than ever before in the last three hundred years." Here the Professor adduces two examples, in rather strange juxtaposition: the first is that "after two centuries we still have not come anywhere near to an exact understanding of human behavior and of social change"; the second is that, by "scientific calculation," we still cannot "design a new town, or even a housing development . . . as a center of pleasure in living, or as a fully human environment." Some might say that a truly scientific attempt to understand human nature might well begin from an attempt to grasp precisely why it is that we cannot create "fully human environments" by "scientific calculation," but let that pass.

Professor Hampshire goes on to talk about the way in which, in the past 300 years, scientific knowledge has become so fragmented. All very natural, he admits, but we cannot afford to let this go on indefinitely: "The time to provide for the survival of the nation and of the species is too short." We must learn how to resynthesize. Could we perhaps set up a "Supreme Academy to oversee inquiry?" Oh beautiful Enlightenment thought—an Academy of Lagado, a Super-Pugwash, to ensure that all future research should be coordinated for the good of mankind! One of the first aims of such an Academy would be to study human nature. It would (of course) accept that "mathematics is the language of the intellect," which, coupled with recent advances in linguistics (in search for some common basis for the study of man) should give up "the beginnings of a new self-understanding which could have an extensive feedback effect."

But even Professor Hampshire realizes that this is scarcely the Panacea he is searching for. What about the social sciences, which have let us down so badly? Alas, psychology is not much good. "If you want to understand states of mind and their causes ... you cannot expect to make them the subject of an exact, experimental science unless you find their physical equivalents." He flirts with the idea that all mental processes are "ultimately to be explained in terms of physics and chemistry." If only it were true. Just a few more experiments, a little more money on research, and bingo! We should understand Man, the Physical and Chemical Being! We might even be able at last to design the Ideal Housing Estate for him to live in!

So where is the Panacea? Of course "the Academy will encourage economics." Why? Because "when it has confined itself to carefully abstracted aspects of human behavior, economics has avoided the uncertainties and vagueness of psychological explanation." Economics, the exact social science! No messy, unpredictable human psychology around there!

Then there is history. This is important because ... why is history important? Because, in our "bored," trivial, "modern advanced industrial civilization," cut off from the rhythms of the seasons (and from the "beliefs, principally religious, associated with such rhythms"), we need an identity, which we derive from "the consciousness of a long history." "Every time a street or building that incorporates a considerable history is destroyed ... some future happiness is destroyed along with it." So we must all become conservationists, to preserve our sense of identity.

But we must also find a way forward, "some pride in the monuments of the present age," not just in architecture, but in all the arts. And here at last, Professor Hampshire leads us, almost before we notice it, into his Panacea. What has gone wrong with our culture? It has become one-sided, too rational, too technocratic. We have missed out something vital. "Adult reason, employed in administration and technology" must be counterbalanced. And with what? Creativity! The wonderful arts, summed up in the most revealing sentence of Hampshire's entire lecture, as "opportunity for free imagination, for fiction, deceit, illusion, showmanship, irresponsibility." Oh, Ed Berman, with your street theaters, you have not lived in vain!

To revive our culture we must revive our arts. That is the Professor's final prescription. And how? "By a great central push." "A change of attitude is needed, both in the taxpayers and in the government, toward supporting the arts as a source of glory and as a necessity of continuing life." The English language, finest jewel of our heritage, is sustained by those who extend its resources and refine it by their inventions, "the poets, dramatists, and novelists of our time." Stand up Harold Pinter, Samuel Beckett, Brigid Brophy! You are the saviors of our culture, and Professor Hampshire thinks you should all get a huge increase in subsidies so that you can keep us all (and our little language) refined, extended, and alive.

It would be hard to conceive of a more eloquent parody of the utter bankruptcy of our present conventional wisdom, than this mishmash of rationalism, materialism, utilitarianism, and finally crazy Utopianism. Professor Hampshire's lecture is indeed the very last gasp of the Enlightenment as it subsides into total exhaustion. Such men (for Hampshire is by no means alone, but has merely said out loud what most distinguished minds in our culture would say if they dared to think about it) know that "the smile of reason" has led us to a sense of spiritual bankruptcy and intellectual disillusionment unique in the history of the human race—but they cannot see that it is precisely their faith in "reason" (as they would define it) which has led us there. They see the "creative" part of man (as opposed to the physics and chemistry which may still "explain" human nature) as simply a desire for "fiction, deceit, illusion"—and not as stemming from those very forces in his psyche which, cruelly repressed and distorted as they have been for so long, may yet lead him back to a sense of wholeness, integration, meaning, and all the things which the rationalists know they have lost without knowing why. They cannot see that the ultimate "illusion" is precisely the kind of rationalism to which they themselves so desperately cling and yet which has led humanity up such a dreadful cul-de-sac that we even face the possibility of destroying life itself.

48

Beyond the Riddle

April 16, 1977

There is a view, so common that it must be regarded as the implicit orthodoxy of our time (admirably reflected in Stuart Hampshire's recent lecture on "The Future of Knowledge") which sees the present plight of mankind as a great riddle.

On the one hand, says the conventional wisdom, we stand here in the late twentieth century as heirs to the greatest adventure of the "human spirit" ever known: 500 years of ever-advancing scientific knowledge about ourselves, the world and the universe. By the consequent advance in our technological skills, we have won an incredible mastery over our environment, annihilating almost all our enemies, from disease to discomfort, and emancipating us, to a wonderful degree, from our previous nasty, poor, and brutish "dependence on nature."

Similarly we stand as heirs to 500 years of social and political advance, liberating us from age-old subjection to ancient hierarchies and feudal monopolies of power. We stand as heirs to a great, remorseless artistic advance so that from the time of, say, Giotto or Josquin des Prés, each generation in turn has built on and extended the achievements of its predecessors in an almost logical progression—each step in turn giving a new sense of liberation and understanding. We stand as heirs to 500 years of spiritual advance so that we have been gradually liberated (via the Reformation, Deism, Secularism, and Couldn't-Care-Less-ism) from our ancient subjection to superstititon and belief in a supernatural order.

339

All in all, these 500 years of the increasing "light of reason" have given us (deny it if you will) the sense that we stand at the top of a long climb out of darkness and that it is somehow open to us to "fulfil ourselves as individuals" and to order things better to our advantage than any generation which has ever gone before.

And yet somehow (*vide* Professor Hampshire's lecture) we are left deeply baffled by the upshot of this wonderful advance. Instead of feeling like gods, in total, self-assured control of our environment, we have to fight off, repress or otherwise ignore a growing sense of hopelessness, which in the past ten years has begun to attack us with unprecedented force.

Our great advance in perception of the physical universe has certainly brought within our collective grasp a fantastic accumulation of physically undeniable facts. But at the same time it has not brought us any glorious new synthetic illumination, but merely a helpless sense of fragmentation—so that we feel we know everything, and also nothing.

Our "conquest of nature" by technology has assuredly brought us health, comfort, and power of a kind which to our medieval forefathers would have seemed positively magical— but at the same time it has mysteriously made our world progressively uglier, noisier, and more dangerous, brought us face to face with the immeasurable perils of the population explosion and the strong possibility of nuclear extinction, and at the very least, by the rate at which it exhausts natural resources, has ensured that our present state of industrial civilization cannot be more than a very short-lived phase in the history of mankind.

Our political and social advances in the name of equality and toleration have left us with the knowledge not that the countries of the world are now free and properly ordered for the first time in history, but at best that they are socially confused and potentially chaotic, and at worst that more of them now languish under totalitarian tyrannies than at any time before. Our great artistic "advance," while bringing many miracles along the way, has left us with the uneasy sense not just that we are now facing such a final and total disintegration of forms that there is no freedom left to win, but that our poor artists have really nothing of profound interest left to say. While finally our spiritual "liberation" from the forms and content of a fundamentally religious view of the world and ourselves has left us not exhilarated and triumphant, but only with a dull sense of shallowness, lack of meaning and our own insignificance.

Such is the nature of the twentieth-century riddle. We have dreamed a dream and created a nightmare, and we cannot see any connection between the two. Like poor Mr. Stephen Gardiner, whose letter to last week's *Spectator* could see no connection between the visions of Le Corbusier in the 1920s and the hell that was made of our cities in the 1960s, or like those sentimentalists of revolution who can see no connection between the paradise promised by Lenin and Marx and the hell of postrevolutionary Russia, we have in our century shown no more consistent and profound intellectual characteristic than our quite literally schizophrenic desire to separate human actions and ideas from their inevitable consequences.

The "solution" to the twentieth-century riddle is in fact very simple. It merely requires a complete shift of our center of intellectual and spiritual gravity—to recognize that the great "emancipation of man" over the past 500 years and its consequences, the dream and the nightmare, are in fact inextricably intertwined. We are in fact living under a set of rules, which Pythagoras and the philosophers of the ancient world perceived very clearly, but which the modern world has tried completely to ignore. If one looks at the modern world through the framework of those rules, instead of seeing just an insoluble riddle, everything that has happened to mankind in the past 500 years makes perfect sense.

The essence of that ancient view of man was that he is part of a beautifully harmonious whole, a sense of which is imprinted deep in his psyche. But in some unique way he is "separated" from that whole—and he can either spend his life in search of re-establishing the sense of wholeness, or he can be determined to become just a part, separate from and somehow "against" the rest. If he does this, as the ancient Greeks would have said, he is guilty of *hubris,* and sooner or later an inevitable nemesis will fall upon him, re-establishing the whole by the extinction of the "rebellious" part.

In recent years there have been many signs that modern man is beginning to recapture a dim sense of that ancient perception (although to accept it entirely involves such a blow to the ego of poor little modern man, and involves such a large-scale junking of all the paraphernalia of the conventional wisdom that it is going to be a long haul). Nevertheless it is only by beginning from such an acceptance that one can hope to make any "sense" of what is happening to us all today. It is only thus, for instance, that we can see how it is not just malign chance that our great technological conquest of nature (oh, hideous *hubris*) should have produced not only color television and DDT and oil-fired central heating, but also pollution, ugliness, and enough nuclear weapons to kill us all a thousand times over. And it is only thus that we can see how, in his one-sided pursuit of more physical knowledge and material comfort (which are ultimately what the great modern adventure is all about), that man has himself become so disintegrated and so out of touch with literally vital parts of his psyche that we have reached that ultimate point of bankruptcy where Professor Hampshire can talk of "creativity" in man as being merely an adjunct to an otherwise full materialistic life (what the Professor calls the need for "fiction, deceit, illusion, showmanship, irresponsibility").

Would Rembrandt, or Dante, or Beethoven, or Shakespeare (or any of the men whose "creativity" makes any artist of today seem like a poor stunted victim of mental disorder) have viewed "creativity" as the need for "fiction, deceit, and illusion?" Of course not. They would have seen "creativity" as the fundamental drive in man to establish his relationship with what, when he finds it, he knows and feels beyond any argument to be "reality"; the reality both of his own nature and of the entire universe that is both outside us and inside us. Of course distinguished philosophers have long since defined and logic-chopped any such absurd notions out of existence. Of course they have! For a crucial part of that "sense of reality" is a perception of the true relationship between *all* the parts of man's psyche (reason, sensation, feeling, intuition—or, if you prefer, mind, body, heart, and soul) and that he who aspires to perceive the universe through only one window (such as "reason") is doomed to a sense of ultimate meaninglessness and death.

If our upholders of the conventional unwisdom, be they Professor Hampshire or whoever, persist in their desire to differentiate, they will continue to see our plight as an insoluble riddle to the end of our civilization (which may not be very far away). "Who sees the variety and not the unity must wander on from death to death," as the old sages used to say. Fair enough. It's a free country, as we say. But let us no longer make the mistake of considering the one-sided, arrogant, limited little rationalistic view of man and the universe that has increasingly dominated our culture for the past 500 years as having anything to do with the *true* light of reason—which can only shine as part of a much wider apprehension altogether.

Part Seven

Epilogue: Act Five, Scene One

There is a curious moment just before the end of several of Shakespeare's tragedies. In *Hamlet,* the most obvious example, it is occupied by the graveyard scene in Act V, Scene 1, when—in a long passage often omitted from stage versions—Hamlet and Horatio muse on the emptiness and futility of worldly striving, before falling to badinage with the gravedigger. In *King Lear,* the same moment is marked by the great reconciliation between Lear and Cordelia at the end of Act IV. The whole gigantic mechanism of the tragedy has long since been set inexorably in motion. Nothing awaits but the final catastrophe, in which the hero is to be engulfed by nemesis and the stage is to be left strewn with corpses. But just before that final climactic scene there is a pause: a moment for philosophical reflection, for humor, for the reassertion of love, above all for some understanding of just why it is the story has to end, however horribly, the way it must.

Such a moment is that I believe we may be living through in the history of our civilization.

Many people reading this book (if indeed they have got this far) will have found the cumulative picture I have painted of our times quite absurdly gloomy. As one chapter has succeeded another, portraying our culture as sick, shallow, disintegrated, full of immature children chasing self-destructive fantasies and illusions, they may have thought: this is carrying the fashionable pessimism of our times altogether too far. Things cannot be as bad as that. How could anyone take so unutterably jaundiced a view of the world?

There will be a few, however, who will recognize that, beneath the surface, I have not been painting an entirely black view of human nature, nor even of our plight—because they will recognize that all I have been doing, again and again, in countless different keys, is to sound out and to reflect upon just one aspect of human nature: that near-mortal sickness which lies so heavy over humanity, over the world, over each one of us, that we scarcely recognize any longer that there is anything else to our existence.

In fact what has gone wrong with the human race today is something quite simple. We have lost touch with our roots. We have been carried away so fast and so far by the incredible changes which have come over our world in the past few generations that we have simply forgotten, in the most basic human terms, who we are. When men get carried away from their roots, and from their own deeper selves, the symptoms are always the same: they become egocentric, swept up into all kinds of limited, one-sided, fantasy-based views of existence—and for a while all may seem to go well. But eventually, precisely because they have forgotten who they are and have lost touch with the springs of their true identity as complete human beings, they begin to lose their way. They find life mysteriously puzzling, trivial, and meaningless. In their desperate search for identity and meaning, they may take refuge in that most damaging of all the forms of illusion to which humanity is prey, the collectivist cause which is only a blown-up aggregation of individual egotisms writ large, which ruthlessly projects its "shadow" outward onto other groups, other ideologies, even onto nature itself—and which is always a denial of life. Almost all the things I have been describing are only manifestations of these truths, which remain truths even though every word I have written will be dismissed as mere sentimental rhetoric.

There are various ways in which I could conclude these reflections on the nature of the seventies. On the one hand, I could attempt some prognostications of the future, along the lines of all those already forgotten (and probably already disproven) newspaper forecasts—"Whither Mankind in the Eighties?"—printed at the turn of the decade. I could essay such a suggestion as that the most obvious immediate dangers confronting mankind would seem to spring from the jockeying already taking place to get a stranglehold on the world's diminishing sources of energy. But why should my predictions be of any more interest or value than anyone else's?

On the other hand, I could attempt a rather more rigorous analysis than this book has so far contained of just where and how I believe Western man has gone psychologically adrift in the past few hundred years: how certain functions of his psyche, the "masculine" functions relating to power and rationality, have got out of balance in our culture, so that we have lost touch with those "feminine" functions of feeling and intuition which alone can preserve a living relationship with nature and give us a true perspective on who we are and how the world actually works. But to do that in any systematic way would involve such an extensive look at the foundations of human psychology as to require a book in itself—and is anyway rather beyond the province of a survey of the seventies, however circumambulatory.

A third possibility, the one I have in fact chosen, is to conclude this book with something much more specific—a look at two outstanding figures of the seventies, neither of whom have yet had any mention in these pages. I have reserved them for this place, partly because they only seriously began to impinge on our attention in the closing months of the decade, but even more because between them, I think, they could not embody better the two aspects of the most important single dilemma which confronts us.

It might seem strange in our sophisticated age that, in the last twelve months of the seventies, the two new figures on the world stage who most obviously caught the imagination of mankind should both have been religious leaders. Both men exercised considerable powers of personal magnetism. But beyond that, it could scarcely seem possible for two human beings to have had less in common. I am referring, of course, to Pope John Paul II and the Ayatollah Khomeini.

Why, in the 18 months after he was so unexpectedly elected Pope in 1978, did Karol Woityla make such a *personal* impact on us all? It was not just the charisma of his office which surrounded his visits to Poland, to Ireland, and to the United States with such a remarkable atmosphere. It was the man himself—and as the commentators at the time were not slow to point out, one of the more obvious qualities of the new Pope was how, as a man, he seemed to dwarf our present generation of political leaders—the Carters, Kennedys, Reagans *et al.* He seemed to tower above them because, in comparison, he seemed so solid, so authoritative, so mature.

The real significance of John Paul, in the way he was presented to us at that time, was that, in an age when we seem to have lost the art of fully growing up, he called us back to some recollection of what it means to be a proper, mature human being. The Pope was, in fact, the most "complete" man who had occupied a position of world prominence for a long time. And the reason why he seemed so complete, why he shone forth at the center of those vast crowds, in Cracow, in Drogheda, in Dublin, in Boston, was that he showed us what stature a man may rise to when he develops all the main parts of a human personality.

As I have observed on several occasions in this book, in psychological terms, regardless of our sex, we all have four chief psychic components or functions, two which may be called "masculine" and two "feminine." On the "male" side of the psyche, the first is that which relates us to our bodies, to the physical world—that which, when fully developed, gives physical power and authority. The second "masculine" function has to do with the mind and rationality, that which can give intellectual authority. The "feminine" functions, on the other hand, are, firstly, sympathetic and compassionate feeling—the heart; and, secondly, that vastly underrated but vitally important function, our intuition, that which gives us an awareness of things which are hidden from the senses.

It is one of the most important things we have lost sight of in our time that, in any fully-developed human personality, *all* these functions have to be developed and brought into balance, or we remain, without being aware of it, in some way lop-sided, incomplete, immature, and egocentric. It is only when all the functions are developed and in play together that a man or woman emerges as, in Jungian terms, living in harmony with the Self, transcending the limitations of the ego.

The point about Karol Woityla, as he emerged to our Western eyes from his courageous obscurity as Bishop of Cracow, was that he was so transparently a man in whom all these functions—body, mind, heart, and soul, as one might put it—were in balance. He had an easy and powerful relationship with the physical—in his skiing and mountaineering, his healthy appetite, his sheer physical presence. He had a first-class rational mind—trained in philosophy, a voracious reader, a true intellectual. While on the "feminine" side, he had equally well-developed those two gentler functions which are necessary to make the "male" side of the psyche life-giving—i.e. his real, in no way sentimental sense of compassion and that intuitive "inner eye" which ultimately gives an awareness of the spiritual, the transcendent dimension of all existence.

That, I believe, is why we found the spectacle of the new Pope so hugely impressive. Of course no human being is perfect. No doubt in the years to come we shall hear much criticism of Pope John Paul (as we already have done in respect of his conservatism on doctrinal and moral matters). Nevertheless, it was not on this level that the Pope made such an extraordinary impact during his first year in office. Just as when he returned in the summer of 1979 to his native Poland, the Pope had been transformed into a symbol—the most powerful symbol known to man. Like Christ his master, he came among us as a symbol of the fully developed human Self—what each of us may strive to become, which is why he himself continually exhorted each of us to become "kings" in our own inner kingdom.

The contract between all this and the image presented to the world by the Ayatollah Khomeini could not have been more marked. Nothing seemed more clearly to exemplify the strange nature of the "revolutionary regime" set up in Iran by this grim and vengeful old patriarch in the early months of 1979 than the reaction of him and his followers toward the end of the year (just before the occupatin of the U.S. Embassy in Teheran) to the news that the overthrown and exiled Shah lay dangerously ill in a hospital in the United States. The Ayatollah himself was reported to have expressed the hope that it was "correct that the Shah has got cancer." One of his judges was reported to have quite solemnly sent out the order to "all students and Moslems" in the United States that they should drag the sick Shah "out of hospital and dismember him."

There were essentially two ways in which, by seeming to cut across our normally preconceived categories, the Ayatollah's regime puzzled the world. The first was purely political. According to our usual preconceptions, the former government of Iran under the Shah was what we would call a "right-wing regime"— a repressive, militaristic monarchy—while the "popular revolution" led by the Ayatollah seemed to have many of the characteristics of a typical "left-wing" reaction. But in many ways, of course, despite attacking landowners, the middle classes, and such familiar left-wing targets, the Ayatollah proceeded to behave like a much more extreme right-wing leader than the man he replaced. His calling on traditional religious values, the suppression of women and, in general, his attempts to abolish the wicked twentieth century, made the Shah's Iran seem in retrospect like a hotbed of progressive liberalism.

The second way the Ayatollah puzzled many people in the West was that he should have set up so heartless a dictatorship in the name of religion. Despite Calvinism, the Inquisition, and the ages of persecution, we still in the West have a vestigial notion that religion is associated with kindness and compassion—and therefore the spectacle of men behaving in the name of religion just as ruthlessly and inhumanly as if they were mere political ideologists was still somehow rather disturbing. But a clue to unraveling these apparent riddles may be found in the peculiar nature of the religion to which the Ayatollah subscribed.

Islam is based wholly on the Koran, the recorded visions and revelations of just one man, the Prophet Mohammad. And for anyone brought up at all on the Christian tradition, there is an enormous shock in store when the pages of the Koran are opened. Despite the fact that each of its 114 chapters is prefaced with the words "In the name of Allah, the Merciful, the Compassionate," it is a book from which all those softer, gentler qualities we normally associate with religion are almost wholly absent. Chapter after chapter goes on about the Last Judgment, righteousness, the wicked being punished, the need to declare holy war against the unbeliever, and so forth. It is like a replay of the very darkest, most chauvinistic passages of the Old Testament. Nowhere in the book does there seem to be anything about the creative power or necessity of love.

In other words, Islam (which means "submission") is a religion which concentrates almost wholly on the tough, hard, moralistic "masculine" side of human nature. The softer, more compassionate, more "feminine" qualities have no more place in its scriptures or its rigid framework of religion (prayer five times a day, rigid dietary laws, obligatory pilgrimage to Mecca) than do women in traditional Islamic societies, where they are treated as little more than semidisposable chattels who should not only not be heard, but should scarcely even be seen.

The other salient feature of Islam (despite its later mystical tradition) is the extent to which it is so uniquely a collectivist religion. All religions have their collectivistic side (and the more it is developed, the more dangerous do they become). But in none is this aspect so fully developed as in Islam. The emphasis is not on its believers discovering the "kingdom of heaven within," or growing internally as individuals, so much as on their becoming good little indistinguishable units in the great collectivized mass of other believers. And it was this aspect of Islam which was most forcibly impressed upon us in 1979, when the television screens of the Western world were nightly filled with the howling mobs of Teheran as, acting like men possessed (which of course they were), they paraded up and down swearing death and vengeance to all "unbelievers," "imperialists," and anyone who dared stand in the way of their dark collectivist vision.

The revival of militant Islam came upon the world in the late seventies, in fact, like a shadow or caricature of all those other forms of collectivism which have swept mankind in our time. Like Communism, it proclaimed "Power to the People." Like the myriad forms of terrorism, it was an expression of psychopathology, transforming its adherents into "collective psychopaths" in whom all normal human feelings and morality were suspended, prepared to commit any crime for the cause. And, like Western consumer capitalism itself, the new force in Islam was sustained by and identified with that most soulless, heartless expression of technology triumphant, the pouring of precious oil out of the desert sands simply to fuel man's greed and restlessness in his ever more frenzied drive to escape from his roots.

Of all this dark new destructive force unleashed on the world in the seventies (introducing heaven knows what deadly new factor into the already fragile equation of world peace), the Ayatollah stood as a suitably representative symbol. In purely human terms, what was most disturbing about him was that he came across psychologically as so strikingly one-sided. He reflected what may happen to any man, or any culture, if man evolves only on the "masculine" side of the psyche—when the legalistic, ordering function of the mind, coupled with brute physical power, develop without that vital, life-giving "feminine" balance which comes from feeling and intuition.

When we think of an old man who is still vigorous, we can see him essentially in terms of three images. The first is that figure, running through the literature and dreams of mankind, whom Jung called "the wise old man"; a man who is essentially the mature mixture of both masculine and feminine qualities, who, without relinquishing his physical and mental strength, is at the same time kindly, merciful, and sees with the inner eye of the spirit.

Then there is the old man in whom the masculine has never

been properly developed at all—who remains effeminate, self centered, and self-pitiful.

Finally there is that other type of old man who is not wise because he has never developed his "inner feminine," the figure whom Jung called *Senex;* the grim, patriarchal tyrant who is determined to hang onto his power, administer the law with total severity, and has not an ounce of human kindness in him.

Such a monster, familiar from stories and judicial benches down the ages, was the Ayatollah. In our own culture these days, outwardly so dominated by "masculine" values but inwardly so prone to an effeminate, weak infantilism, we are no longer very familiar with such grimly one-sided old men. Our own "senior citizens" these days, pursuing the vision of eternal youth around the fairways in their electric caddy cars, are much more likely to fall into the second category. But even so, in contemplating the Ayatollah, we perceived not a riddle: merely one of the absolutely stereotyped ways in which any human being may end up, so long as he (or she) does not learn the true secret of what we are all here to do—to set out on the development of all those parts of ourselves which alone can make any of us truly human.

In this context, it was no accident that Karol Woityla (like that not wholly dissimilar figure Solzhenitsyn) should have worked toward his impressive degree of self-realization through his long ordeals under a totalitarian regime. For what we are seeing in the world at the moment is a polarization, not of political systems, but of the two extreme states to which human beings may aspire.

On the one hand there is that state of true human fullness and maturity, which can only come from the realization by each individual of his or her own unique human potential. On the other hand, there are all those ideologies which offer precisely the opposite: those collectivizations of the ego which keep men frozen in a state of incompleteness and immaturity, make it impossible for them to grow to their full stature, and fill them with all that is negative—not with warmth and openness but with greed and envy, not with honesty and truth but with self-deception and hypocrisy, not with love but with hatred.

That is why the images of Pope John Paul and the Ayatollah Khomeini have presented us with such a contrast—because they have shown us in such striking terms the two roles in the psychic drama of mankind each of us must choose to play (and for the Ayatollah, I might easily substitute terrorists, British trade union leaders, or even, ironically enough, the evangelists for that collectivist form of decadent self-indulgence known as consumer capitalism). We can either become true "kings" in the sense John Paul implied—or we must remain miserable slaves, dreaming false dreams of a "liberation" (through power or sex or material abundance) which can only be achieved at the price of untold suffering. Ultimately, of course, this is not a matter of politics, whether of Left or Right or Center. It is how we each of us dispose ourselves toward that kingdom which is within us. From that alone, everything else follows.